U.S. LATINOS AND EDUCATION POLICY

With the American dream progressively elusive for and exclusive of Latinos, there is an urgent need for empirically and conceptually based macro-level policy solutions for Latino education. Going beyond just exposing educational inequalities, this volume provides intelligent and pragmatic research-based policy directions and tools for change for U.S. Latino education and other multicultural contexts.

U.S. Latinos and Education Policy is organized round three themes: education as both product and process of social and historical events and practices; the experiences of young immigrants in schools in both U.S. and international settings and policy approaches to address their needs; and situated perspectives on learning among immigrant students across school, home, and community.

With contributions from leading scholars, including Luis Moll, Eugene E. García, Richard P. Durán, Sonia Nieto, Angela Valenzuela, Alejandro Portes, and Barbara Flores, this volume enhances existing discussions by showcasing how researchers working both within and in collaboration with Latino communities have employed multiple analytic frameworks; illustrating how current scholarship and culturally oriented theory can serve equity-oriented practice; and focusing attention on ethnicity in context and in relation to the interaction of developmental and cultural factors. The theoretical and methodological perspectives integrate praxis research from multiple disciplines and apply this research directly to policy.

Pedro R. Portes is The Goizueta Foundation Distinguished Chair in Latino Teacher Education and Executive Director of the Center for Latino Achievement and Success in Education (CLASE), University of Georgia, USA.

Spencer Salas is Associate Professor, University of North Carolina at Charlotte, USA.

Patricia Baquedano-López is Associate Professor, University of California, Berkeley, USA.

Paula J. Mellom is Assistant Research Scientist, University of Georgia, USA.

Sociocultural, Political, and Historical Studies in Education
Joel Spring, Editor

Portes/Salas/Baquedano-López/Mellom, Eds. • *U.S. Latinos and Education Policy: Research-Based Directions for Change*

Wolfmeyer • *Math Education for America? Policy Networks, Educational Business, and Pedagogy Wars*

Spring • *Political Agendas for Education: From Race to the Top to Saving the Planet, Fifth Edition*

Picciano/Spring • *The Great American Education-Industrial Complex: Ideology, Technology, and Profit*

Spring • *Education Networks: Power, Wealth, Cyberspace and the Digital Mind*

Hemmings • *Urban High Schools: Foundations and Possibilities*

Martusewicz/Edmundson/Lupinacci • *EcoJustice Education: Toward Diverse, Democratic, and Sustainable Communities*

Spring • *The Politics of American Education*

Smith/Sobel • *Place- and Community-Based Education in Schools*

Spring • *Political Agendas for Education: From Change We Can Believe In to Putting America First, Fourth Edition*

Sandlin/McLaren, Eds. • *Critical Pedagogies of Consumption: Living and Learning in the Shadow of the "Shopocalypse"*

Shapiro, Ed. • *Education and Hope in Troubled Times: Visions of Change for Our Children's World*

Spring • *Globalization of Education: An Introduction*

Benham, Ed. • *Indigenous Educational Models for Contemporary Practice: In Our Mother's Voice, Second Edition*

Shaker/Heilbrun • *Reclaiming Education for Democracy: Thinking Beyond No Child Left Behind*

Ogbu, Ed. • *Minority Status, Oppositional Culture, and Schooling*

Spring • *Wheels in the Head: Educational Philosophies of Authority, Freedom, and Culture from Confucianism to Human Rights, Third Edition*

Spring • *The Intersection of Cultures: Global Multicultural Education, Fourth Edition*

Gabbard, Ed. • *Knowledge and Power in the Global Economy: The Effects of School Reform in a Neoliberal/Neoconservative Age, Second Edition*

Spring • *A New Paradigm for Global School Systems: Education for a Long and Happy Life*

Books, Ed. • *Invisible Children in the Society and Its Schools, Third Edition*

Spring • *Pedagogies of Globalization: The Rise of the Educational Security State*

Sidhu • *Universities and Globalization: To Market, to Market*

Bowers/Apffel-Marglin, Eds. • *Rethinking Freire: Globalization and the Environmental Crisis*

Reagan • *Non-Western Educational Traditions: Indigenous Approaches to Educational Thought and Practice, Third Edition*

Books • *Poverty and Schooling in the U.S.: Contexts and Consequences*

Shapiro/Purpel, Eds. • *Critical Social Issues in American Education: Democracy and Meaning in a Globalizing World, Third Edition*

Spring • *How Educational Ideologies are Shaping Global Society: Intergovernmental Organizations, NGOs, and the Decline of the Nation-State*

Lakes/Carter, Eds. • *Global Education for Work: Comparative Perspectives on Gender and the New Economy*

Heck • *Studying Educational and Social Policy: Theoretical Concepts and Research Methods*

Peshkin • *Places of Memory: Whiteman's Schools and Native American Communities*

Hemmings • *Coming of Age in U.S. High Schools: Economic, Kinship, Religious, and Political Crosscurrents*

Spring • *Educating the Consumer-Citizen: A History of the Marriage of Schools, Advertising, and Media*

Ogbu • *Black American Students in an Affluent Suburb: A Study of Academic Disengagement*

Benham/Stein, Eds. • *The Renaissance of American Indian Higher Education: Capturing the Dream*

Hones, Ed. • *American Dreams, Global Visions: Dialogic Teacher Research with Refugee and Immigrant Families*

McCarty • *A Place to Be Navajo: Rough Rock and the Struggle for Self-Determination in Indigenous Schooling*

Spring • *Globalization and Educational Rights: An Intercivilizational Analysis*

Grant/Lei, Eds. • *Global Constructions of Multicultural Education: Theories and Realities*

Luke • *Globalization and Women in Academics: North/West–South/East*

Meyer/Boyd, Eds. • *Education Between State, Markets, and Civil Society: Comparative Perspectives*

Roberts • *Remaining and Becoming: Cultural Crosscurrents in an Hispano School*

Borman/Stringfield/Slavin, Eds. • *Title I: Compensatory Education at the Crossroads*

DeCarvalho • *Rethinking Family-School Relations: A Critique of Parental Involvement in Schooling*

Peshkin • *Permissible Advantage? The Moral Consequences of Elite Schooling*

Spring • *The Universal Right to Education: Justification, Definition, and Guidelines*

Nieto, Ed. • *Puerto Rican Students in U.S. Schools*

Glander • *Origins of Mass Communications Research during the American Cold War: Educational Effects and Contemporary Implications*

Pugach • *On the Border of Opportunity: Education, Community, and Language at the U.S.-Mexico Line*

Spring • *Education and the Rise of the Global Economy*

Benham/Heck • *Culture and Educational Policy in Hawai'i: The Silencing of Native Voices*

Lipka/Mohatt/The Ciulistet Group • *Transforming the Culture of Schools: Yu'pik Eskimo Examples*

Weinberg • *Asian-American Education: Historical Background and Current Realities*

Nespor • *Tangled Up in School: Politics, Space, Bodies, and Signs in the Educational Process*

Peshkin • *Places of Memory: Whiteman's Schools and Native American Communities*

Spring • *The Cultural Transformation of a Native American Family and Its Tribe 1763–1995*

For additional information on titles in the Sociocultural, Political, and Historical Studies in Education series, visit **www.routledge.com/education.**

U.S. LATINOS AND EDUCATION POLICY

Research-Based Directions
for Change

Edited by Pedro R. Portes, Spencer Salas,
Patricia Baquedano-López, and Paula J. Mellom

Routledge
Taylor & Francis Group

NEW YORK AND LONDON

First published 2014
by Routledge
711 Third Avenue, New York, NY 10017

and by Routledge
2 Park Square, Milton Park, Abingdon, Oxon OX14 4RN

Routledge is an imprint of the Taylor & Francis Group, an informa business

Library of Congress Cataloging-in-Publication Data
U.S. Latinos and education policy : research-based directions for change /
    edited by Pedro R. Portes, Spencer Salas, Patricia Baquedano-López, &
Paula J. Mellom.
        pages cm. — (Sociocultural, political, and historical studies in education)
    Includes bibliographical references and index.
    1. Hispanic Americans—Education.   2. Hispanic Americans—Education—
Case studies.   3. Education and state—United States.   4. Hispanic
Americans—Education—Social aspects.   5. Educational change—United
States.   I. Portes, Pedro.
    LC2669.U27 2014
    371.829′68073—dc23
    2013039410

ISBN: 978-0-415-74782-0 (hbk)
ISBN: 978-0-415-74783-7 (pbk)
ISBN: 978-1-315-79682-6 (ebk)

Typeset in ApexBembo
by Apex CoVantage, LLC

CONTENTS

Foreword by Sonia Nieto   *xi*

Editors' Introduction   *xv*

SECTION I
Policy Concerns about Praxis and Cultural
Capital Preservation   **1**

1 National Myopia, Latino Futures, and Educational Policy   3
   Pedro R. Portes and Spencer Salas

2 Thinking through the Decolonial Turn in Research
   and Praxis: Advancing New Understandings of the
   Community–School Relation in Latina/o Parent
   Involvement   16
   Patricia Baquedano-López, Sera J. Hernandez,
   and Rebecca A. Alexander

3 Cultivating a Cadre of Critically Conscious Teachers
   and "Taking This Country to a Totally New Place"   35
   Angela Valenzuela and Patricia D. López

SECTION II
Children of Immigrants in Schools—Global
and U.S. Policy Research 45

4 Immigration and the American School System:
The Second Generation at the Crossroads 47
Alejandro Portes

5 Divergent Paths to School Adaptation among Children
of Immigrants: New Approaches and Insights into
Existing Data 69
*Cecilia Rios-Aguilar, Manuel S. Gonzalez Canché,
and Pedro R. Portes*

6 Recommendations from a Comparative Analysis of
Educational Policies and Research for the Achievement
of Latinos in the United States and Latin Americans in
Spain toward Smarter Solutions 92
Martha Montero-Sieburth and Lidia Cabrera Perez

7 Development and Its Social, Economic, and Educational
Consequences: The Case of the Zimapán Hydroelectric
Project 115
Sergio Quesada Aldana

8 Transnational Mobility, Education, and Subjectivity:
Two Case Examples from Puerto Rico 126
Sandra L. Soto-Santiago and Luis C. Moll

SECTION III
A Closer Look at Families, Classroom Learning,
and Identity Development 147

9 Finding a Place: Migration and Education in Mixed-Status
Families 149
Ariana Mangual Figueroa

10 Talking the Walk: Classroom Discourse Strategies That
Foster Dynamic Interactions with Latina/o Elementary
School English Learners 173
Ruth Harman

11 Changing the Pedagogical Culture of Schools with Latino
    English Learners: Reculturing Instructional Leadership   192
    Noni Mendoza Reis and Barbara Flores

12 Beyond Educational Standards? Latino Student Learning
    Agency and Identity in Context   204
    Richard P. Durán

    Afterword   215
    Eugene E. García

    Contributors   *221*
    Index   *223*

FOREWORD

As a Puerto Rican educated in New York City schools from first through twelfth grades, and later as a teacher in that same school system, my life has been indelibly marked by these experiences. As a child, I remember both caring and uncaring teachers, dilapidated schools and new ones, demanding courses and not so demanding ones. Most of all, I remember the expectations that teachers had of me and my sister and our classmates. Our first neighborhood was a poor working-class community in Brooklyn populated principally by African Americans, Puerto Ricans, other folks from the Caribbean, and a small remaining but quickly disappearing European immigrant community. In the elementary and junior high school we attended, it was clear that not much was expected of us, that we would be lucky to graduate from high school, and that we would most likely follow in the footsteps of our hardworking but largely unschooled parents.

When my family moved to a more middle-class neighborhood, things changed dramatically. In my new junior high school, and later in our high school—one of the most highly regarded in the city—expectations were considerably higher, but it was only years later that I realized why this was so: In these schools, almost all of our classmates were middle class and White, primarily Jewish but also Italian American and Irish American, among other assimilated European ethnic groups. There, teachers made it clear to us that we were expected to learn; there was also no question that we would attend college and become professionals. These were new messages for me. Years earlier, when I had been the only child in my fourth-grade class to raise her hand when my teacher asked who among us wanted to go to college, my teacher had said that it was all right "because we always need people to clean our toilets."

In my new neighborhood, things were quite different. There, families helped their children with homework (something that my parents could not do, although they cared deeply about our education), and when they couldn't, these parents hired tutors to help their children (one of my classmates in high school had to explain to me what a tutor was). Parents also helped their children fill out college applications, walked them through the process of asking for letters of recommendation, and even took them to visit colleges. In sum, these parents generally expected that their children would be shining examples of the equalizing power of U.S. public education, an equalization that was, and continues to be, elusive for many Latinos/as. Although our parents could not or did not know how to do most of these things, looking back, my sister and I were fortunate to have landed in that high school because, without it, we probably would not have gone on to college or to study for advanced degrees in our fields.

I was one of a small minority of Latinas/os fortunate to get a good education. Yet here we are, more than 60 years after I started first grade in New York City, and most Latinos/as in the country today still face an "uncertain future," to quote the title of a 1976 report, one of the dozens of committee and commission reports written in the intervening years about the education of Latinos/as in the United States (U.S. Commission on Civil Rights, 1976). It is an uncertain future still because policies concerning the education of Latino/a students have remained for the most part stagnant and unimaginative; because the assets that Latino/a students bring to their education are still generally unrecognized or dismissed; because persistent and widely held stereotypes and racist attitudes and behaviors continue to place roadblocks in the way of Latino/a students' academic success; and because, although many recent efforts at delineating the problems and proposing solutions have been made (Gándara & Contreras, 2010; Nieto, 2013; Pedraza & Rivera, 2005), most have been disregarded by policy makers at the local, state, and national levels.

U.S. Latinos and Education Policy: Research-Based Directions for Change is an attempt to respond to the question of how schools can change to truly serve Latino/a students, which until now has been an elusive goal. It is a significant question for a number of reasons, not the least of which is the fact that within a few decades, it is estimated that Latinos will constitute a full quarter of the U.S. population. It is no exaggeration to say that if Latino/a students continue to be underserved and undereducated, they will be unable to become productive citizens of society. That being the case, the standard of living that many Americans currently enjoy will be a thing of the past. Even more important is the reality of the young people themselves: if the situation does not change, many Latino youngsters now living in poverty will continue to face lives of disappointment and unfulfilled dreams because of an education that prepares them neither for college nor for work. On the contrary, as research studies and reports have documented for many years, Latino/a youngsters have experienced a *subtractive education* (Bartlett & García, 2011; Valenzuela, 1999) that not only robs young people of a future, but also robs our nation of the tremendous assets that these young people have to offer.

The editors and authors of this volume loudly proclaim, "Basta ya!" Enough, the authors say: enough of unresponsive schools and limiting pedagogy, enough of false starts (such as is the case with bilingual education, now almost abandoned after a hopeful start a few decades ago), and enough of uncaring educators and unrelenting racism. It is time for us to help shape the policy arena in ways that "we can believe in." We may have reached the historic moment when the dreadful state of Latino education will no longer be tolerated. This compilation of chapters written by some of the most important Latino/a scholars working on issues of public education today—joined by others who are not Latino/a but work with and care about our students—is both a hopeful sign and a shift in focus to proposing policy changes that might indeed make a difference.

The chapters in this volume do not simply propose policy changes, however; their work continues in the tradition of the resistance begun so many years ago by scholars such as George Sanchez (1940/1996), Antonia Pantoja (2002), and others who championed our young people and attempted to change the appalling conditions in which they were being educated. Like previous researchers and scholars, the authors here insist on progressive and decolonizing approaches to Latino/a education, approaches that while differing dramatically from what most Latinos/as have experienced in their education, are nevertheless firmly rooted in the stated, although still unfulfilled, U.S. ideals of democracy, equality, and fair play.

Two elements distinguish this volume from others: one is its laser focus on policy, and another is its interdisciplinary and multinational nature. In terms of the first, the editors have wisely recognized that without changes in policy at both the micro- and macrolevels, little will change for Latino/a students. The policies they describe and critique range from current standardized testing policies, to the elimination of native language instruction in many states, to teacher education approaches that fail to include a Latino focus and perspective. The text also describes promising efforts as diverse as transforming classroom practice to become more culturally responsive, to respectful school-wide policies promoting parent engagement, to the need for policy changes to eliminate the deleterious effects of standardized testing and privatization.

The interdisciplinary focus of the volume is evident in its concern not only with where Latinos/as come from, but also with how those home contexts might influence their reception and experiences in the United States. The text also includes a range of disciplinary perspectives from areas as disparate as anthropology, economics, history, linguistics, sociology, and ethnic studies. Moreover, the research in the volume ranges from studies focusing on a small number of participants to large multiyear studies of thousands of students. The methods used are also diverse, from quantitative to ethnographic to historical analyses, all of which lead to important evidence-based understandings about the education of Latinos/as that can significantly alter policy.

The sum effect of the chapters in this book is to offer a more hopeful vision of education for Latinos/as while at the same time recognizing the difficult struggle that lies ahead. Changing the trajectory of education for Latinos/as will mean transforming policies and practices at all levels, including frameworks, approaches, and pedagogy, as well as reconceptualizing the role of teachers, principals, families, and communities. The road ahead is certainly not an easy one, but those of us who have been in the field for decades know that the education of our young people is a struggle worth the effort.

—Sonia Nieto

References

Bartlett, L., & García, O. (2011). *Additive schooling in subtractive times: Bilingual education and Dominican immigrant youth in the Heights.* Nashville, TN: Vanderbilt University Press.

Gándara, P. C., & Contreras, F. (2010). *The Latino education crisis: The consequences of failed social policies.* Boston: Harvard University Press.

Nieto, S. (Ed.). (2013). Charting a new course: Understanding the sociocultural, political, economic, and historical context of Latino/a education in the United States. *Journal of the Association of Mexican American Educators, 6*(3).

Pantoja, A. (2002). *Memoir of a visionary: Antonia Pantoja.* Houston, TX: Arte Público Press.

Pedraza, P., & Rivera, M. (Eds.). (2005). *Latino/a education: An agenda for research and advocacy.* Mahwah, NJ: Lawrence Erlbaum.

Sanchez, G. I. (1996). *Forgotten people: A study of New Mexicans.* Albuquerque, NM: University of New Mexico Press. (Original work published 1940)

U.S. Commission on Civil Rights. (1976). *Puerto Ricans in the continental United States: An uncertain future.* Washington, DC: Author.

Valenzuela, A. (1999). *Subtractive schooling: U.S.-Mexican youth and the politics of caring.* Albany, NY: State University of New York Press.

EDITORS' INTRODUCTION

U.S. Latinos and Education Policy: Research-Based Directions for Change, through collectively hypothesizing in a blend of empirical and conceptual writing, considers intelligent and pragmatic policy alternatives for the current state of U.S. Latino education and for other multicultural contexts. This collection is intended for policy makers, elected officials, and those who elect them, including scholars, researchers, and graduate students whose work intersects the cultural, social, academic, and psychological needs of U.S. Latinos and other nondominant communities. Similarly, it serves as a theoretical or methodological must-have resource for educators and decision makers. Because many of the chapters address the social nature of achievement, the volume complements teacher and leadership preparation in educational policy areas, sociology, developmental psychology, and also the related fields of linguistics, literacy, and ethnic studies. It is also designed and appropriate for use in graduate-level seminars as a primary text. It is our hope that it will also serve as a resource for scholars and practitioners across disciplines.

Carrying forward an interdisciplinary conversation that began at a conference held in Athens, Georgia, in October 2009, this volume is motivated by our collective discontent with contemporary educational policy for Latino schoolchildren—policy that has done little to dismantle achievement disparities at the group-based level (P. R. Portes, 2005; P. R. Portes & Salas, 2007, 2009). Indeed, current paradigms of accountability have fueled "subtractive" understandings of how and what U.S. Latinos might achieve in schools by undermining the resources that an additive cultural identity might otherwise enable. Scholarship for Latinos in education has been largely focused on exposing inequalities within local contexts and, at times, offering examples of change stemming from the lived experiences of scholars, activists, and practitioners. We value these contributions. However, we argue in this volume the need for going further to translate how understandings generated therein might be realized incrementally at a macrolevel and over the sustained K–12 experience of Latino children. In unchaining the gridlock of structured inequality in education for this group, other students also gain in attaining a common goal. To that end, this work distinguishes itself from others in that the aim is not only to expose educational inequalities as related to U.S. Latinos. Rather, the volume aims to provide policy makers with research-based policy directions (tools) for change we can all believe in and that can actually begin to be implemented.

Notably, the volume does not attempt a synthesis of Latino policy scholarship. Neither can we as editors seek to forge a unified voice across its chapters. Rather, the chapters advance a diverse set of emic perspectives challenging the status quo in proposing more intelligent alternatives to No Child Left Behind and Race to the Top, both misnomers that impede real changes in deterring "group-based inequality" (P. R. Portes, 2005). The volume is reflective of tensions and differences in our communities that are both cultural and the result of the culturing process itself as a new decade of testing-based ideology engulfs educational policy. Long-standing narratives of assimilation posited that the success of U.S.-born Latinos and their immigrant peers depended on their willingness to discard all things foreign with K–12 public education historically mediating their absorption into a separate-but-unequal national, Anglo-led culture (see, P. R. Portes, Gallego, & Salas, 2009). A discourse of normalization continues to dismantle bilingual education, legitimize reductive models of learning and literacy in historic Latino communities, and fuel a high-stakes testing movement in U.S. public education (Gutierrez, Asato, Santos, & Gotanda, 2002; Gutiérrez, Baquedano-López, & Alvarez, 2000; Moll & Ruiz, 2002; Orfield & Kornhaber, 2001; Valenzuela, 2004). Although we can all agree on higher standards, the costs by the measurement community of practice continue to strip resources for equity in learning and teaching outcomes.

Equity in Latino achievement in U.S. schools is still trying to become a national policy concern. Presidential Advisory Commissions on Educational Excellence for Hispanic Americans and entities such as the Pew Research Center, Migration Policy Institute, The Center for Latino Achievement and Success in Education (CLASE), National Latina/o Education Research and Policy Project (NLERAP), and the Tomás Rivera Institute have been focused on various aspects of the state of Latino achievement in K–16 education. More recently, monographs centered on various aspects of Latino educational achievement have recently appeared through Teachers College Press (Contreras, 2011) and Harvard University Press (Gándara & Contreras, 2010). This volume enhances existing discussions by showcasing how researchers, both from within and working with Latinos communities, have employed multiple analytic frameworks and by informing readers how the present scholarship can serve equity-oriented practice.

Thus, key questions of how culturally oriented theory might be deployed in praxis to advance the education and potential of dual-language children bring together the chapters in this volume. The reader can see how interdisciplinary scholarship is valuable in sharing a public concern regarding families and communities in shaping the intersecting roles of language and other semiotic means. With the authors' attention to the semiotic relations concerning culture, language, and mind to the role that significant, lived experiences may be available to individuals or not, decision makers can appreciate how our interdependent future depends on a shared cultural vision for effecting a sound policy change.

Together, we see how social contexts can be restructured and how what we decide to do about leveling complex unfair social conditions can determine the quality and security of our shared future. The volume thus differs from others in the field through its attention to ethnicity directly in context and in relation to the interaction of developmental and cultural factors. In so doing, an array of theoretical and methodological perspectives helps integrate policy research for practice from multiple disciplines. This array brings policy research directly into focus in advancing human development. Our hope then is to contribute toward a platform from within an inclusive platform to apply, interpret, contextualize, and bridge best with better decisions across the nation's states and school districts.

Overview

This volume is organized into three parts. The three chapters in Section I take as their point of departure a view of education as both product and process of social and historical events and practices. The first chapter by P. R. Portes and Salas repositions educational policy as a mediational tool. They argue that although cultural historical theory has been taken up in distinct ways in educational research that emphasizes the social mediation of human development and learning, policy has been overlooked as a social and cultural psychological device motivated and shaped over time by individuals and collectivities. As the authors suggest, counteracting the achievement gap for Latinos requires leveraging policy for mediation across the life span of youth most at risk. Expanding on the role of policy in the lives of youth and their families, the second chapter by Baquedano-López and colleagues examines the ways in which government and school-based parent involvement policies, as well as public discourses about Latino parents, have controlled the participation of parents in schools, limiting them, for example, to surveillance roles on behalf of the school as chaperones, monitors of homework, or school attendance. These authors call for a "decolonial turn" (following Maldonado-Torres, 2011) in education that reimagines and repositions parents as knowledgeable and legitimate social actors who are integral to educational projects for social change. The final chapter in this section provides an integrative view of institution, community, and education through the work of the NLERAP and their affiliate teacher preparation initiatives. Valenzuela and López discuss the organizational aspects of NLERAP and their grow-your-own teacher education institutes initiative in the context of cultivating community capacity as a broad-scale approach to teacher preparation and the transformation of public education. This chapter also reveals how scholars in our community are attempting to influence equity and change on the ground through a national organization of veteran and emerging scholars. Seeking to engage and educate dominant policy communities together with new ways of addressing local, statewide and national-level changes, these authors speak from ongoing efforts that include a critique of business-as-usual practices based on often ambiguous goals for Latinos.

The five chapters in Section II examine the experiences of young immigrants in schools and both U.S. and global policy approaches. One of the many insights readers will enjoy is from an important longitudinal study of children of immigrants that has provided a most solid, evidence-based grounding for social policy analysis regarding academic achievement as far as contexts and student characteristics are concerned. A. Portes summarizes the gist of numerous studies that forged what is now incorporated into the broader literature as his theory of segmented assimilation. Based on follow-up interviews from the large original study of middle school students from more than 70 ethnic enclaves in San Diego and Miami, the reader will find his conclusions and recommendations useful. This is a landmark set of data from which others have examined some of the conclusions in greater detail. For example, in this collection, Rios-Aguilar and her colleagues employ those data to derive and examine a novel approach that transcends long-standing dichotomies regarding melting-pot assimilation or integration categories for understanding immigrant student's adaptation to school. The chapter employs Berry's (1997) modes of cultural adaptation model in relation to segmented assimilation examining academic achievement and its usual predictors. Significant intragroup differences exist within the 1.5 generation of students that mediate academic success. A surprise here is mainly that those who assimilate (as the host society would wish in melting-pot fashion) do not necessarily do as well in school as those who seem to reject a total American identity and attempt to venture from their ethnicity. Their achievement is comparable to those who prefer to integrate or negotiate both American and family ethnic culture during the storm and stress of adolescence. In this section too, the context of Latinos in a different but monolingual culture (Spain) is described empirically by Montero-Sieburth and Cabrera Perez with the previously discussed models in mind. For example, what happens to children of immigrants schooled in a system with their first language not playing as major of a block, although literacy in either standard Spanish or English might play comparable roles? How does the context of reception measured indirectly in the previous two studies play a part in the European context?

The international flavor of this section includes Quesada Aldana's narrative, in which the reader begins to appreciate the global backlash aspects of the North American Free Trade Agreement and the economic grid's impacts on families and the communities that then fill U.S. classrooms later. But the real gem of this chapter is its discussion of human costs that U.S.-backed projects extract from Mexican peasant communities that become displaced and dispossessed. To understand policy decisions about Latinos and U.S. education, we must understand the national and international consequences of development, especially in the Mexican context. These are the consequences that, ironically, force immigrants to "break the law" of the country that has imposed and created the very conditions for their exile. Hence, the semiotic impact of global economics, workforce issues, and education policy and praxis are jointly considered in ways that allows us all to reexamine if teaching and learning is well and equitably organized. Our future depends to a great extent then on decision makers having an interdisciplinary lens and respecting evidence-based recommendations.

The transnational lens of this book includes the experiences of *minoritized* Latino groups in the United States. Soto-Santiago and Moll present case studies of the educational "repositioning" of two students experiencing transnational mobility between the United States and Puerto Rico. The authors offer an important comparative perspective on Puerto Rican students as a *minoritized* Latino group (but with U.S. citizenship) who because of the cultural, racial, and linguistic differences have many similar experiences of migration and dynamics integration with other Latino groups.

The four chapters in Section III offer situated perspectives of learning among immigrant students across school, home, and community. The first chapter by Mangual Figueroa is based on a 23-month ethnographic study and examines the educational opportunities and challenges experienced by children in one mixed-status family of the Latino diaspora in the Rust Belt region of the United States. Without policies that support them, undocumented family members, whether adults or children, experience invisibility and an increasing threat of criminalization by immigration laws. Harman takes us to a classroom in an underperforming Massachusetts school district where the effects of policy are also felt. Taking the classroom as a case study, Harman examines the tensions generated when a federally funded university–school alliance is invested in preparing teachers to "teach against the grain," yet top-down policies put pressure on these teachers to teach to the test and follow mandated curricula. The role of school leadership in mediating the effects of top-down policy on teachers and the most at-risk students is taken up in the chapter by Mendoza Reis and Flores. The authors present a model for reculturing instructional leadership as a necessary step to advance the academic achievement of English learners. And as they note, without vision, pedagogical knowledge, understanding, and wisdom, educational transformation cannot take place. Success, they argue, depends on leaders and professionals enacting an advocacy stance toward English learners. In the final chapter, Durán discusses how select theories and findings from sociocultural, critical pedagogy, and learning sciences research can create a different foundation for learning, instruction, and assessment—a foundation that ought to be more effective for educational policies attempting to improve educational outcomes for underserved students. The chapter discusses how becoming an effective learner is coupled with participation in a local community of learners that introduces and reinforces social identities of learners as participants and transformers of the world around them.

In sum, with the American dream progressively elusive for and exclusive of large numbers of Latinos, a serious question remains: How can and will schools serve them and, by consequence, the nation? This volume's intent is to inform collectively, in a blend of empirically and conceptually derived responses, smarter policy alternatives for Latino education as a means to educational excellence in general. Despite their diverse range of cultural histories, broadly speaking, first- and second-generation Latino youth are subject to massive educational and workforce underrepresentation stemming from faulty educational policies that deter our national interests and potential. As Valenzuela (1999, 2002) has argued, subtractive schools take much away from children of nondominant communities and give little in return. However, such understandings of the subtractive nature of Latinos' experiences in education must also recognize the subtractive underpinnings of education research and policy and systems of educational accountability that continue to legitimize and perpetuate deficits for U.S.-born Latinos. Contemporary "deculturalization" (Spring, 2004) stems from "the inherent tendency of nation-states to use their educational systems to create uniform culture and language usage as a means of maintaining order and social control" (p. 124) and has been the historic modus operandi of U.S. public schools. Although the deculturalization of Latinos by U.S. schools has been historic, so too has been Latino resistance to it. This volume continues in that tradition of resistance that seeks a fair future for all youths in our schools.

References

Berry, J. W. (1997). Immigration, acculturation, and adaptation. *Applied Psychology, 46*(1), 5–68.

Contreras, F. (2011). *Achieving equity for Latino students.* New York: Teachers College Press.

Gándara, P. C., & Contreras, F. (2010). *The Latino education crisis: The consequences of failed social policies.* Boston: Harvard University Press.

Gutierrez, K. D., Asato, J., Santos, M., & Gotanda, N. (2002). Backlash pedagogy: Language and culture and the politics of reform. *Review of Education, Pedagogy, & Cultural Studies, 24*(4), 335–351.

Gutiérrez, K. D., Baquedano-López, P., & Alvarez, H. H. (2000). The crisis in Latino education: The norming of America. In C. Tejeda, C. Martinez, & Z. Leonardo (Eds.), *Charting new terrains of Chicana(o)/Latina(o) Education* (pp. 213–232). Cresskill, NJ: Hampton Press.

Maldonado-Torres, N. (2011). Thinking through the decolonial turn: Post-continental interventions in theory, philosophy, and critique—an introduction. *Transmodernities: Journal of the Peripheral Cultural Production of the Luso-Hispanic World, 1*(2), 1–15.

Moll, L. C., & Ruiz, R. (2002). The schooling of Latino children. In M. M. Suárez-Orozco & M. Páez (Eds.), *Latinos: Remaking America* (pp. 362–374). Berkley, CA: University of California Press.

Orfield, G., & Kornhaber, M. L. (2001). *Raising standards or raising barriers? Inequality and high-stakes testing in public education.* New York: The Century Foundation Press.

Portes, P. R. (2005). *Dismantling educational inequality: A cultural-historical approach to closing the achievement gap.* New York: Peter Lang.

Portes, P. R., Gallego, M. A., & Salas, S. (2009). Dismantling group-based inequality in a NCLB era, effective practices, and Latino students placed at risk. In E.G.J. Murillo, S. A. Villenas, R. T. Galvan, J. S. Munoz, C. Martinez, & M. Machado-Casas (Eds.), *Handbook of Latinos and education: Research, theory and practice* (pp. 438–449). Mahwah, NJ: Lawrence Erlbaum.

Portes, P. R., & Salas, S. (2007). Dreams deferred: Why multicultural education has failed to close the achievement gap: A cultural historical analysis. *Cultura y Educacíon, 19*(4), 365–377.

Portes, P. R., & Salas, S. (2009). Poverty and its relation to development and literacy. In L. Morrow, R. Rueda, & D. Lapp (Eds.), *Handbook of research on literacy instruction: Issues of diversity, policy, and equity.* New York: Guilford Press.

Spring, J. H. (2004). *Deculturalization and the struggle for equality: A brief history of the education of dominated cultures in the United States* (4th ed.). Boston: McGraw-Hill.

Valenzuela, A. (1999). *Subtractive schooling: U.S.-Mexican youth and the politics of caring.* Albany, NY: State University of New York Press.

Valenzuela, A. (2002). Reflections on the subtractive underpinnings of education research and policy. *Journal of Teacher Education, 53*(3), 235–241.

Valenzuela, A. (2004). *Leaving children behind: Why Texas-style accountability fails Latino youth.* Albany, NY: State University of New York Press.

SECTION I

Policy Concerns about Praxis and Cultural Capital Preservation

1

NATIONAL MYOPIA, LATINO FUTURES, AND EDUCATIONAL POLICY

Pedro R. Portes and Spencer Salas

This chapter originates from a general discontentment with contemporary educational policy as a whole for future generations of Latino schoolchildren, in particular, the accumulation of "reform" initiatives that have done relatively little to dismantle mounting disparities in learning and teaching at a group-based level. Such disparities are, of course, instrumental in keeping most children from some groups stuck in a caste-like society. The current "common core standards" reform paradigm is, again, rooted in a shortsighted accountability logic and a test-driven political economy that perpetuate historically stereotyped understandings of U.S. Latinos and cap their potential in most schools. Not only is schooling subtractive and hazardous to some groups, but so too is the actual cultural and developmental grasp of this nation's silent crisis. The crisis lies in the fact that in spite of decades of tinkering with reforms and new legislated measures, the majority of poor children from Spanish-speaking families remain in the lowest quartile of academic achievement and are often blamed for the systems' failure to meet Academic Yearly Progress (AYP). Two basic problems persist at this juncture: First, although we know how to educate children more effectively and evidence-based alternatives are available, the knowledge base and actions necessary are not brought to bear at the front lines of professional development and in the preparation of educators. Second, schools remain structured politically to educate and graduate most students subject to group-based inequality below grade level and to house most until they, as a whole, populate the nation's underclass. This same system continues to empower those with significant socioeconomic status advantages to qualify for advanced placement in higher education and the workforce. Nowhere is this problem clearer than in the severe underrepresentation of Latinos in postsecondary STEM areas (Chapa & De La Rosa, 2006; U.S. Commission on Civil Rights, 2010).

Of course, some exceptions apply and are given disproportionate media attention generally in ways that distort unresolved fundamental issues. At the heart of this lies the following question: Why can't we, after decades, organize a better system that actually and systematically reduces group-based inequality (GBI; P. R. Portes, 2005) in education outcomes? A central idea in this chapter is that this undereducation is by design a dialectical program. Not only is it about the cumulative undereducation that underlies repeated failures to meet at least minimum core standards for the neediest groups, but of equal concern is the pervasive undereducation of the dominant group and its leadership in making headway in restructuring a deficient system to produce both greater equity and excellence nationally. The latter group ultimately governs policy decisions that reproduce the current situation at various levels. According to the annual Condition of Education reports based on The National Assessment of Educational Progress (NAEP) scores, we find after several decades that the performance of middle school students' from the dominant group exceeds or is comparable to Latino and Black high school seniors.

Critical to understanding this chapter is the fact that Latinos, including English learners (ELs), are at least three times likelier to live in poverty than members of the dominant group. Latinos comprise a complex ethnicity that our institutions are just beginning to understand. Surely, poverty is concentrated in this young group that is and will remain in flux, unlike traditional European and African immigration. This is largely because of geographic proximity and related economic interests.

Ethnogenesis is an active process that is historically and economically situated (P. R. Portes, 1996). What is needed is a transcultural lens to see Latinos and ELs dynamically as a group of incoming immigrants and their children led by a powerful Mexican presence (along with Asian, Caribbean, and Central and South American groups). They represent a self-replenishing sector economically—one that produces wealth and that furthermore extends the nation's collective intelligence through additive bilingualism. In addition to Asians, of course, as one of the fastest-growing but overall smaller groups that immigrates with greater (relatively) social capital, Latinos replenish the United States with educated and less educated human capital that contributes to maintaining many of our national advantages. We know this, yet for myopic reasons, we implement educational norms and policies unwisely or contrary to our best interests as a nation. Those policies often compromise the extent to which educational excellence can be defined—primarily by evidence of ethnic group equity in student outcomes.

Having missed educational opportunities to learn in the formative years, learning outcomes from the public education system become business as usual and mirrored by teacher quality shortfalls and after-school differentials that ensure an average four-year gap in student learning. This gap is also constructed in schools and remains permanent for too many of the nondominant groups' children. Latinos in the educational system today, some of whom require four to six years to develop basic academic English levels to benefit from regular instruction (Thomas & Collier, 1996; Valdés, 2001, 2010), are facing a tracked system that by design effectively creates deficits and gaps. In effect, public schooling is constrained by shortsighted policies from educating the neediest in systemic violations of the least restrictive (learning) environment (PL-92).[1] As a consequence, for example, in 2009, only 19.2 percent of Latinos between the ages of 25 and 34 had earned a two- or four-year degree, compared with 41 percent nationally (see College Board Advocacy and Policy Center, 2013; Johnson, 2011). Subsequent public laws dismantled bilingual education (which, along with dual immersion, is a proven way to shorten academic gaps), and somehow the Supreme Court allows the rights of these children to an equitable education that does not leave most in this group behind to continue to be violated. Routinely, resources are drawn away from evidence-based alternatives that can and do improve teaching and learning at all levels (P. R. Portes & Salas, 2009, 2010). We thus ask how our democratic society can maintain this collective attention-deficit disorder, ignoring the issues mentioned previously while continuing the hypocritical facade of *seeming* concerned with equity.

We write this chapter using a lens of cultural historical theory, a rich metaparadigm that is especially relevant for reimagining the educational policy for children from nondominant communities—and U.S. Latinos in particular (P. R. Portes & Salas, 2011). Cultural historical scholarship for Latinos in U.S. schools has been largely local in nature, exposing, often through careful microanalysis of social interactions in classrooms and communities, the disparities therein and offering examples of grassroots change emerging from the agency of individual actors and coalitions of the willing. Achievement has often been located at the school or, more generally, at the classroom level—focusing on one child at a time. In contrast, cultural historical theory allows us to see decades of political rhetoric while the usual suspects (vulnerable children of poverty) have their odds for success tripled against them by status, language/cultural history, and the selfish corporatization of education as a whole. A most conservative impact analysis of the aforementioned easily reveals not simply a lack of progress in disarming severe GBI, but actually an intensification of a virtual apartheid in the United States.

We embrace, value, and recognize the dynamic trajectories that a scholarship of engagement has paved, especially in the areas of language and literacy education. However, our intent here is to argue the need for scholarship and research to translate how understandings generated therein might be realized at a macrolevel—over the sustained K–12 experience of Latino children. Moving beyond the role of whistle-blowers, we attempt an outline of how policy makers at local, regional, and national levels might dismantle the increasingly restrictive environments that U.S. Latino and other schoolchildren and young adults experience in our institutions. This analysis is informed by concerns about the inability of the educational research to reduce practical and statistically significant achievement gaps. The gaps in STEM learning outcomes in K–16 offer the best evidence of a silent crisis and the resulting disparities in rates of poverty and college completion. The latter, in turn, is reproduced in subsequent decades combined with national discourse surrounding schoolchildren that in real time has given way to a "return to the Mexican room" (Gándara & Orfield, 2010)—segregated teaching and learning across many institutional contexts.

Beyond Multicultural Education

As we have argued previously, until recently, an individualism grounded in a Darwinian legacy worked to legitimize the assumptions that male, middle-class, English monolinguals were the only learners that mattered (P. R. Portes & Salas, 2007, 2009). That is to say, an ethnocentric movement drawn from so-called scientific evidence was employed in the literature controlled by this community to brand nonmajority groups intellectually deficient and their families pathological (see, e.g., Herrnstein & Murray, 1994). Damaged families, in turn, produced damaged children simultaneously subject to a combination of contempt and pity (see, Scott, 1997). Rather than focusing on what families do or don't do, we argue that Latino children's legal entitlement to quality public schooling is routinely violated. Dysfunctional, nativist educational policy that underfunds schools is frequently ill equipped to leverage the diversity brought to classrooms. In sum, a continuation of disparate practices that sustain massive inequalities remains robust in the new century through the mechanism of undereducation. The latter affects not only new generations of poor children, but also those being prepared in higher education. For example, when Latino educators in Arizona sought to redress this blatant exclusion from the educational system by creating social studies programs to reeducate Latino and other students about this history and neglected contributions, they were met with repression and even legal sanctions (see Santa Ana & Gonzalez de Bustamante, 2012).

Today, in semiotic fashion, the damaging, myopic policy misunderstandings persist rooted in the consciousness of our system's new generations of educators and decision makers at state and national levels. Although individual and local "success" stories of teachers and school communities that "stand and deliver" periodically capture national attention, the achievement of Latinos in U.S. schools at the group-based level remains severely constrained, with current and future generations of Latino children perpetually at risk in an educational sense and in a cycle of intergenerational urban poverty (Chapa & De La Rosa, 2004; A. Portes & Zhou, 1993). Since President Johnson's war on poverty ended, there has been no significant progress in terms of reducing the percentile of Latino children living in poverty or in NAEP scores (cf. P. R. Portes, 2005). We suggest that the group-based economic and educational disparities that we describe are more than a bipartisan problem and one that we hope can be clarified for policy makers at various levels.

Mediating Achievement

With Johnson's Great Society and a national awakening at the policy level of the societal structures perpetuating inequality, resulting equity-oriented educational reforms embraced student-centered pedagogies—breaking out temporarily from a testing and measurement headlock (see P. R. Portes & Salas, 2007). Student-centered teaching was one of several focuses that included early childhood education, multicultural education for both dominant and nondominant groups, and school-to-work initiatives. Inspired by the 1960s civil rights movement and pushing against discriminatory schooling practices, severe underrepresentation at all levels that matter, and racist research, activist scholarship responded with the two-factor conjecture that the standardized tests used to categorize minority students as underachieving were biased and that teachers routinely held lower expectations for minority students. Groundbreaking social justice–oriented scholarship exposed the inherent racism in the ways minority children had been framed previously. Activist, equity-oriented scholarship demanded the elimination of segregation and insisted on the inclusion of cultural history in the curriculum. Scholars argued for examination of political, social, and historical events from multiple perspectives, with teacher education embracing diversity-oriented coursework for preservice and in-service educators for its ethical significance. Multicultural education in its various forms has since been the conceptual cultural framework or pedagogy of choice for advancing equity in culturally and linguistically complex schools (for a recent review, see, e.g., Paris, 2012). Unfortunately, it has not been sufficient to impel large-scale improvements in student outcomes. We believe that the multicultural "spring" failed in organizing equity of outcomes and has been replaced by the political economy of testing, which has had its "makeover" (Nichols & Berliner, 2007). Somehow testing is being sold as snake oil for reducing GBI in educational outcomes. The results are reprehensible because resources are diverted away from improving teacher leadership preparation and maximizing student learning.

Even as we too are fervently committed to social justice, access to/equity in education, science, and a pluralistic society, the persistence of large-scale proportional GBI reveals that reforms oriented to reframing teachers' dispositions to diversity has had limited impact on teaching and learning or achievement gaps, particularly for Latino and Black students. Indeed, larger policy-generated, test-centric "accountability" paradigms essentially perpetuate unfairness and restructured disparities of an increasingly un-American educational system. Ironically, the dominant political economy based on higher (common core) standards and more testing tends to distract us from implementing needed structural changes. That is, testing continues to confirm with annual reports that we are still on the wrong track regarding the reduction of significant group-based inequalities. This is, in large part, because the Race to the Top discourse, like No Child Left Behind (NCLB) before it, and its inventors miss the issues raised here.

Grounding a Policy Alternative

Our understandings of the sociogenesis, or intergenerational and societal development, of GBI as it applies to Latino children are informed by a cultural historical framework drawing from the translated works of Vygotsky and his contemporaries (see P. R. Portes & Salas, 2011). Cultural historical theory is useful in its analysis of language as a mediational tool linked with thinking, mediated action, and development and, therefore, is particularly insightful with respect to the ways that the emerging Latino and other nondominant minorities are less well educated or undereducated.

For Vygotsky (1978) and the interdisciplinary cultural psychology he helped inspire, "all the higher functions originate as actual relations between human individuals" (p. 57)—in meaningful and volitional social interaction whereby interpersonal processes are transformed into intrapersonal processes through the "helping means" of material tools and symbolic artifacts. As Holland and Valsiner (1988) explain, such tools and/or artifacts are often "psychological mediational devices between one's mental states and processes and one's environment" (p. 248)—something that can be applied to policy-based practices at the collective level. Thus, the "mind in society" (Vygotsky, 1978) is distributed across "helping means"—material tools and social and cultural psychological devices that women and men have shaped over time and that have, in turn, shaped them (see Salomon, 1993).

Who and what is available routinely in activity settings over time influences learning—combinations that can, in turn, empower individuals to master new tools for adaptation. Social class, for example, interacts with the cultural histories of various groups in ways that constrain those settings for some relative to others (P. R. Portes, 1999). As a result, differences related to language and other tools that mediate learning opportunities in school and other settings translate into insurmountable challenges for some children year after year. Thus, numerical comparisons of school performance among groups and teacher variables require that attention be given to the contextualized and particular cultural history of each group. Such contexts might include, for example, obvious differences in student populations, physical structures, and the communities surrounding these campuses; considerable variations in resources, mutuality of teacher-student acceptance, and treatment of children, including teacher quality, appropriateness, and accessibility of curricular materials; and the nature of pedagogical decisions based on the ways educators identify, evaluate, and respond to student cultural competencies. Furthermore, the cultural competencies and socialization patterns children acquire in their homes and communities may or may not be linked directly to what is required in school or to their potential to make successful adaptations to outside demands made by schools (González, Moll, & Amanti, 2005; Heath, 1983; Valdés, 1996).

From a cultural historical view of human development, sustained acceleration of these schoolchildren's academic development depends on the organization of mediational tools at the macrolevel—deep structural changes in the education system. The latter can be informed by a transformation of how we prepare educators and the public in general, as well as through evidence-based professional development for school personnel. We argue that a truly systemic reform effort would integrate such elements along with other powerful "helping means" strategically and developmentally to counteract the systemic constraints imposed today on Latino and other children and youth placed at risk

Counteraction: A Guiding Policy Avenue for Change

To counteract means to make ineffective, restrain, or neutralize the usually ill effects of an influence by means of an opposite force, action, or influence. From our theoretical lens, development is mostly driven by the *vivencias*, or lived experiences, organized in and out of the home (see González Rey, 2011). *Vivencias*, in some cases, lead not only to cognitive or academic savvy, but also to positive cultural identities (CID+) that are linked with motivation and affective drivers of development (P. R. Portes & Salas, 2010). When development is structurally or sufficiently constrained, creating "deficits" at both the individual and societal level, external counteractions need to restructure those conditions that unnecessarily create learning and teaching gaps, damaged identities, and severe underrepresentation in higher education and work. For Latinos, this counteracting process necessitates opposing the very mechanisms that produce below-grade-level learning and subsequent achievement gaps through tools that might include but are not limited to effective early childhood education, improved teacher pedagogy and leadership in public schools, and higher education in general. Dual-immersion bilingual education is also a potent means in many communities in spite of a national shortage of bilingual teachers. A policy strategy that intentionally weaves *helping means* or provides responsive teaching to the most needy for a sustained period of related counteractions would help reverse the current institutionalization of group-based inequities borne by these children. Hence, our analysis includes the interaction of both the students and those who structure and carry out teaching and learning in semiotic fashion. The achievement gap that, in reality, represents a complex network of gaps developing over time in various groups has different parts. One part, between U.S. Latinos and their non-Latino White peers, is to a great extent located in and perpetuated by the deficit thinking of a dominant non-Hispanic White middle-class majority largely reacting, from a "sociogenesis" standpoint (Vygotsky, 1978), on nativist premises framing children of immigrants as a potential threat to national stability (Brimelow, 1995; O'Reilly, 2006). Policy makers could become more knowledgeable in better understanding the value of emerging bicultural identities and the advantages of bilinguals as national assets that could be applied and developed as between-group cultural gaps are reduced to insignificance. Such is also part of a U.S. Jeffersonian pluralistic concept of a democratic and just society.

Capable new generations of potentially bilingual U.S. children need not be shortchanged or their academic learning and aspirations diminished through labeling such as non/limited English proficient. In routing them for the de facto remediation that English-as-a-second-language programming leads to, most fall and remain behind regardless of evidence that better options exist. Instead, we contend that a broader view of identity at the intercultural level founded on the principles of additive bilingualism is possible in our schools. To that end, promoting positive linguistic and cultural identities of bilinguals in the K–12 pipeline is foundational for the CID+ framework we propose (P. R. Portes & Salas, 2010). Additionally, who and what is (or is not) available routinely in activity settings over time influences how developing children and adolescents eventually perceive themselves (P. R. Portes & Salas, 2009).

Policy Recommendations and Conclusions

In brief, our recommendations call for a more cogent organization of P-20 *vivencias*, or affective/cognitive learning experiences in educational settings for those most at risk. More empowering educational cultural programs need to be offered strategically to undo GBI. In essence, this is what the middle-class consistently organizes with its social capital and funds in and out of school, valuing and enforcing English only/English first as one canon. In a global society, that thinking is shortsighted in preparing our workforce, including educators. The promotion of learning and teaching within a CID+ framework has powerful implications for the nation as a whole and for transforming gaps into social capital in particular. Second, the current attacks on ethnic studies and dual-language curricula and programs are myopic. It is as important for both dominant and nondominant generations to understand our collective history as it is to have culturally responsive teaching practices that are evidence and equity based.

Thus, we believe that CID+ is instrumental in reducing academic gaps and part of a coordinated comprehensive restructuring of education that is immediately needed. As a general strategy, CID+ represents a departure from current "pull-out" or other remedial basic skill programs in which some ethnic groups' children are coconstructed as deficient English speakers rather than treated as potential additive bilinguals. The evidence from the intelligence of such students and the exceptional bilingual schools where the community supports dual-immersion practices is compelling (Valdés, 2003). At minimum, in high-density (Latino) districts, such options should be available to all students whose parents support the interrelated outcomes of a broader cultural (self) identity and ability to thrive with more than one sign system of language in a global society. We know that after elementary school, a time when gaps are still minimal, the primary task of individuals is to define a positive identity before all else across various domains. A broader identity counters violence and is the mark of an ethical society (Erikson, 1968)—especially in times when racial hatred and undereducation are used as means to foment a caste-like society. We also need to consider how much of the group-based inequality that alarms us all is situated in the undereducation of dominant group members in this domain, particularly at policy levels. Dialectically, the latter may be considered equally as opportunities or liabilities to be countered in the future.

A preventive counteraction approach at the individual level begins at an early age, ensuring that culturally mediated activities occur routinely with high intensity in and out of schools while not sacrificing or destroying native culture or first-language means. Counteraction is a culturally organized and additive approach characterized by the layering of teaching and learning responsive interactions for optimal academic and social-emotional development. Such an approach transforms future generations toward both greater equity and excellence that may include, but is not defined by, test scores. More than multicultural celebrations of diversity, counteraction involves the systemic pursuit of equity in learning opportunities and achieving grade-level (test) outcomes for future generations of children living in poverty in particular. Moreover, unlike NCLB that safeguards a failed system focused more on accountability and test scores than equity and development, counteraction must increasingly narrow the existing educational gaps in a sustained fashion.

For example, a sociolinguistic support system of interwoven learning experiences for children reared in poverty needs to be in place to empower concept development in valued literacy or school content areas. A comprehensive counteracting strategy would represent a departure from current stopgap, choral, restrictive approaches in transitional language basic programs in which ethnic groups remain undereducated in often-hostile school environments. Furthermore, school cultures must involve "communities of learners" across levels (students, teachers, and leaders) that activate higher-level thinking and continuous enrichment in the very ways that supportive, everyday classroom activities are mediated. Additionally, rigorous, challenging academic environments, designed for continuity, need to be supplemented with human resources comparable to the other more "established or institutionalized" programs, such as in Special Education, Drug Free programs, or even more expensive programs involving incarceration or alternative schools for minors. In short, formal education needs to reinforce these poor children's development in valued areas with regard to school success in both formal and informal settings (P. R. Portes, 2005). Our communities can promote self-regulation and motivation and guide young Latinos and others living in poverty toward academic equity and success when counteractions are structured in the system and sustained as long as necessary. A preventive counteraction approach at the collective level begins with initiatives to prepare more bilingual educators in teacher and principal/counselor education programs, as well as Latino college graduates in STEM areas. This requires broadening the scope of teacher quality at the college level where deficient instruction prevails in discouraging the few Students Placed at Risk who are admitted from graduating in the fields with the grossest disparities (P. R. Portes, 2005).

Conclusions

The conundrum of Latinos in education is that for the majority of Americans, the status quo makes perfectly good sense and "feels" safer. First, few want to invest in the changes that are perceived to be invested solely in other people's children.

Those who do understand the socioeconomic advantages of broader language education and rigor also see the benefits of a CID+ paradigm. Popular mythology insists, however, that each group of immigrants waits its place in line—more specifically, at its place in a cultural historical time line as its non-Anglo European predecessors did when the value of educational research and helping means were unknown. As Haberman (2002) noted,

> The achievement gap is not an aberration of American society nor is it an unintended consequence . . . It reflects the will of the overwhelming majority of Americans who believe that education is a personal not a common good and that the highest quality education is a scarce resource. (p. 1)

Regardless of the resources and knowledge we now have, structured GBI in education and society constitutes a most significant policy crisis. Few understand that we are already paying more dearly by not investing in human capital development for more culturally competent citizens. Mastering a variety of tools or helping means contributes to the common social interest and educational excellence through greater equity. Underlying this historical situation is a complex set of national identity issues. From our cultural historical analysis, the structural conditions have already been organized for a polarized future unless dismantling inequality becomes a higher national priority. The results have already been coming in for decades as we shift to an increasingly caste-like oligarchic society. What is most wrong with this picture is the senseless waste of human capital and the lost opportunity in this historical "moment" to shift gears in a more intelligent direction. Inevitably, prolonged social injustice must weigh short-term benefits with historical consequences in society.

From a sociogenetic stance, when a society is becoming increasingly multicultural, the primary function of the educational system is to empower its most valuable resource—the minds of children from all groups—and to maximize children's development for the nation as a whole. Thinking as a united state has far to go. We still segregate public schools; we fail to challenge and educate the most disadvantaged while enriching the learning conditions of only the most advantaged students. This remains subtle to most policy makers but true. With a deculturalization policy in effect (Spring, 2004), our society strays from basic equity principles in financing a system that is designed to undereducate children of nondominant communities in part because of their diminished political status and voice, as well as sitting on an inert knowledge base. In effect, to deculturalize "other people's children" (Delpit, 1995), the system indirectly conveys the superiority of the monocultural, Anglo-centric hegemony as ideal while tolerating or "dealing" with diversity. It is fashionable now to celebrate difference as long as it does not require equity-oriented actions for all children meeting minimum standards for grade-level proficiency. Testing seems to be mainly an added cost to monitor and ensure that the status quo model is still "working." The current approach focuses on raising a few test points for all groups with no understanding of GBI. A system that inhibits the development of Latinos by structured differentials in teacher quality, learning support, tracking, and minimizing challenging learning opportunities results in predictable deficits. These are concentrated in key areas, of course, in mediational tools such as reading, math, and science, so by the end of high school, a massive inequality prevails in STEM and teacher education (U.S. Commission on Civil Rights, 2010; Villegas, Strom, & Lucas, 2010).

Thus, a strategic cultural historical praxis may help restructure society toward a just norm not steeped in group conflict, greed, and violence. It would have to recognize a long-standing national myopia and mobilize resources in this decade to prevent the massive inequality now being structured particularly for this fast-growing student population. One initial policy goal then is to remove the means that produce and sustain gross socioeconomic disparities by enforcing the least restrictive environments for schoolchildren. This one is already public law.

Note

1. The violation is disguised by the accommodations inherent in transitional English for Speakers of Other Languages (ESOL)-based programs that, unlike dual immersion or bilingual education, are not evidence based yet have been institutionalized in ways that produce and sustain gaps. The evidence-based alternatives are ruled out in spite of meeting the least restrictive principle. This unethical and hypocritical praxis has thus become business as usual in most districts.

References

Brimelow, P. (1995). *Alien nation: Common sense about America's immigration disaster* (1st ed.). New York: Random House.

Chapa, J., & De La Rosa, B. (2004). Latino population growth, socioeconomic and demographic characteristics, and implications for educational attainment. *Education and Urban Society, 36*(2), 130–149.

Chapa, J., & De La Rosa, B. (2006). The problematic pipeline: Demographic trends and Latino participation in graduate science, technology, engineering, and mathematics programs. *Journal of Hispanic Higher Education, 5*(3), 200–202.

College Board Advocacy and Policy Center. (2013). *The college completion agenda: Latino edition.* Retrieved from http://completionagenda.collegeboard.org/latino/

Delpit, L. (1995). *Other people's children: Cultural conflict in the classroom.* New York: The New Press.

Erikson, E. (1968). *Identity, youth, and crisis.* New York: Norton.

Gándara, P., & Orfield, G. (2010). *A return to the "Mexican room": The segregation of Arizona's English learners.* Retrieved from http://civilrightsproject.ucla.edu/research/k-12-education/language-minority-students/a-return-to-the-mexican-room-the-segregation-of-arizonas-english-learners-1/

González, N., Moll, L. C., & Amanti, C. (2005). *Funds of knowledge: Theorizing practices in households, communities, and classrooms.* Mahwah, NJ: Lawrence Erlbaum.

González Rey, F. (2011). The path to subjectivity: Advancing alternative understandings of Vygotsky and the cultural historical legacy. In P. R. Portes & S. Salas (Eds.), *Vygotsky in 21st century society: Advances in cultural historical theory and praxis with non-dominant communities* (pp. 32–49). New York: Peter Lang.

Haberman, M. (2002). *Can teacher education close the achievement gap?* Paper presented at the AERA, New Orleans, LA.

Heath, S. B. (1983). *Ways with words: Language, life, and work in communities and classrooms.* New York: Cambridge University Press.

Herrnstein, R. J., & Murray, C. A. (1994). *The bell curve: Intelligence and class structure in American life.* New York: Free Press.

Holland, D. C., & Valsiner, J. (1988). Cognition, symbols, and Vygotsky's developmental psychology. *Ethos, 16*(3), 247–272.

Johnson, L. (2011). Latinos need more support to raise lagging graduation rates, report says. *The Chronicle of Higher Education.* Retrieved from http://chronicle.com/article/Latinos-Need-More-Support-to/129247/

Nichols, S. L., & Berliner, D. C. (2007). *Collateral damage: How high-stakes testing corrupts America's schools.* Cambridge, MA: Harvard Education Press.

O'Reilly, B. (2006). *Cultural warrior.* New York: Broadway.

Paris, D. (2012). Culturally sustaining pedagogy: A needed change in stance, terminology, and practice. *Educational Researcher, 41*(3), 93–97.

Portes, A., & Zhou, M. (1993). The new second generation: Segmented assimilation and its variants. *Annals of the American Academy of Political and Social Science, 530*(Nov.), 74–96.

Portes, P. R. (1996). Ethnicity and culture in educational psychology. In D. Berliner & R. Calfee (Eds.), *The handbook of educational psychology* (pp. 331–357). New York: Macmillan.

Portes, P. R. (1999). Social and psychological factors in the academic achievement of children of immigrants: A cultural history puzzle. *American Educational Research Journal, 36*(3), 489–507.

Portes, P. R. (2005). *Dismantling educational inequality: A cultural-historical approach to closing the achievement gap.* New York: Peter Lang.

Portes, P. R., & Salas, S. (2007). Dreams deferred: Why multicultural education has failed to close the achievement gap—a cultural historical analysis. *Cultura y Educación, 19*(4), 365–377.

Portes, P. R., & Salas, S. (2009). Poverty and its relation to development and literacy. In L. Morrow, R. Rueda, & D. Lapp (Eds.), *Handbook of research on literacy instruction: Issues of diversity, policy, and equity.* New York: Guilford Press, pp. 97–113.

Portes, P. R., & Salas, S. (2010). In the shadow of Stone Mountain: Identity development, structured inequality, and the education of Spanish-speaking children. *Bilingual Research Journal, 33*(2), 241–248.

Portes, P. R., & Salas, S. (Eds.). (2011). *Vygotsky in 21st century society: Advances in cultural historical theory and praxis with non-dominant communities.* New York: Peter Lang.

Salomon, G. (Ed.). (1993). *Distributed cognitions: Psychological and educational considerations.* Cambridge, UK: Cambridge University Press.

Santa Ana, O., & Gonzalez de Bustamante, C. (Eds.). (2012). *Arizona firestorm: Global immigration realities, national media and provincial politics.* Lanham, MD: Rowman & Littlefield.

Scott, D. M. (1997). *Contempt and pity: Social policy and the image of the damaged Black psyche, 1880–1996.* Chapel Hill, NC: University of North Carolina Press.

Spring, J. H. (2004). *Deculturalization and the struggle for equality: A brief history of the education of dominated cultures in the United States* (4th ed.). Boston: McGraw-Hill.

Thomas, W. P., & Collier, V. P. (1996). *Language minority student achievement and program effectiveness.* Fairfax, VA: Center for Bilingual/Multicultural/ESL Education, George Mason University.

U.S. Commission on Civil Rights. (2010). *Encouraging minority students to pursue science, technology, engineering and math careers.* A briefing before the U.S. Commission on Civil Rights held in Washington, DC. Washington, DC: Author.

Valdés, G. (1996). *Con respeto: Bridging the distances between culturally diverse families and schools: An ethnographic portrait.* New York: Teachers College Press.

Valdés, G. (2001). *Learning and not learning English: Latino students in American schools.* New York: Teachers College Press.

Valdés, G. (2003). *Expanding definitions of giftedness: The case of young interpreters from immigrant communities.* Mahwah, NJ: Lawrence Erlbaum.

Valdés, G. (2010). *Latino children learning English: Steps in the journey.* New York: Teachers College Press.

Villegas, A. M., Strom, K., & Lucas, T. (2010). Closing the racial/ethnic gap between students of color and their teachers: An elusive goal. *Equity & Excellence in Education, 45*(2), 283–301.

Vygotsky, L. S. (1978). *Mind in society: The development of higher psychological processes* (M. Cole, V. John-Steiner, S. Scribner, & E. Souberman, Trans.). Cambridge, MA: Harvard University Press.

2

THINKING THROUGH THE DECOLONIAL TURN IN RESEARCH AND PRAXIS

Advancing New Understandings of the Community–School Relation in Latina/o Parent Involvement

Patricia Baquedano-López, Sera J. Hernandez, and Rebecca A. Alexander

This volume's focus on policy presents us with both an exciting opportunity and an exceptional challenge. It offers us the possibility to build on the work of many scholars who have critiqued the deficit framings of Latino parents in our schools. Our challenge lies in accepting the place of "policy" as a generating force of change and improvement in the educational conditions of Latina/o students and their families in schools. Although we know that existing policies cannot sufficiently address the diversity and complexity of involvement of Latino parents in our schools, as we will argue in this chapter, the notion and practice of parental involvement not only have derived from policy, but also constitute policy. Our chapter seeks to problematize this bind and offer a way to rethink the ways we approach Latino parental involvement as policy. It does so by engaging and advancing decolonial theory and praxis in education to shed light on schooling issues related to parental involvement. We also draw from our various experiences working with policy makers, our teaching and service in Latino communities, and our long-term research addressing educational issues related to Latinas/os.

The Decolonial Turn and Latino Parent Involvement in Schools

Many studies on Latino parental involvement have critiqued policy efforts that construct schools as the sites of privileged knowledge and which restrict parents to minimal supporting roles (Nakagawa, 2000). We add our voices to the call to continue to advance decolonial approaches to educational research and practice.

Our educational curricula, policies, and activities have emerged from and continue to uphold Eurocentric values and ideologies that minimize and erase the knowledge, experiences, and values of those who do not have positions of power (see also Delgado Bernal, 1998; Delgado Bernal, Elenes, Godinez, & Villegas, 2006; Paperson, 2010; Tuck, 2009). We find Maldonado-Torres' (2011) conceptualization of *thinking through the decolonial turn* important for understanding the double reach of colonial legacies in education, which have enabled subjugating practices for those deemed educable through schools as institutions functioning as ideological (and repressive) state apparatuses (Althusser, 2001). Thinking through the decolonial turn entails tracing and employing distinct expressions of decolonial thought across established bodies of knowledge and seeking critical intersections and intertextuality of approach and purpose. This means to also break down disciplinary silos and break away from, to use Sandoval's (2000) words, the "apartheid of disciplinary knowledge" (p. 69). The field of education, already conceived as interdisciplinary, stands to further benefit from other perspectives and approaches that critically engage the current educational apparatus and move us away from complicit participation in it through research, practice, or policy. Educational change requires the destabilization of a constant racist relation that endorses a benevolent educative or "civilizing function" (Césaire, 1956/2010) aimed at Latino students and other students from nondominant groups.[1] This civilizing function reinforces the dominant group's ideologies expressed through educational policies that define what is best for Latina/o students and their parents. In our public education system, these policies have built a conceptual and practical architecture that sustains itself on the false notion of excellence rooted in individualism and supported through (biased) testing as a measure of individually achieved merit. And when students fail to achieve excellence defined in this way, a concatenation of remedial actions is mobilized to place them under tighter forms of surveillance to solve the "educational crisis" brought about by (nondominant) students' "failure" to succeed in our schools. Many have offered important critiques of this manipulation of a crisis in education (Berliner & Biddle, 1995; Gándara & Contreras, 2009; Gutiérrez, Baquedano-López, & Alvarez, 2000; Varenne & McDermott, 1999). The manufactured educational crisis, as a sociohistorical expression of colonial administration, implicitly blames parents of nondominant students for contributing to these students' failure and penalizes them through restrictive parental roles in schools.

Much debate inside and outside our academic conversations continues to unsettle the rigidity and closeness of an educational system that engages in exclusionary practices through racisms and other *-isms*. We believe it is imperative to continue to do so in order to bring about the change this book anticipates. Our chapter contributes to this effort a perspective that disrupts what we see as a benign framing of the relationship between school and the Latino home. Our focus on Latino parents illustrates deep inequities tied to the history of Latino families in the United States, yet it also helps us understand more broadly the relationship of parents to schools. Our chapter argues for multiple locations and repositioning of knowledge systems—those of the school and those of parents. Latino parents (as all parents do) have knowledge that is valuable and necessary for their children's education. Consistent with the framing of our chapter, we consider this repositioning of knowledge as a decolonial act that is not merely a (romantic) retrieval of lost knowledge but, instead, as Grande (2004) notes, speaking from the condition of oppression of Native Americans, entails critical and "active recovery" that recognizes what communities have historically and culturally reimagined and reinvested (p. 175). We understand this to mean that knowledge recovery as a decolonial act must be sensitive to both historical and local circumstance. The knowledge that circulates in nondominant communities as critically and actively recovered by educational practitioners and researchers is dynamic and creative; it is the result of tensions within the system, and it is, above all, necessarily an unsettling process. In Fanon's (1963) words, "Decolonization never takes place unnoticed, for it influences individuals and modifies them fundamentally" (p. 36). This transformative and decolonizing potential in educational theorizing and practice can shape the way we recognize and bring back complexity to the experiences of Latino parents with schools and the potential influence of these parents on the educational trajectories of their children.

Thinking through the decolonial turn in education requires that we take up local positions on issues to critically examine and act in ways that change the everyday materiality and conditions of a history of control and subordination in the education of Latinos and their families. It requires that we challenge the Eurocentrism that has materialized in an agenda of modernity and development (Mignolo, 2010), which we argue finds its expression in public education as the long history of remedial educational policy for Latino students and their families has demonstrated. The reduction of cultural complexity characteristic of colonial systems requires our local efforts today to recover fragmentary knowledge and history (see also Dussel, 2003; Smith, 1999). Decolonization work in schools must also be concerned with the active recovery and the repositioning of subjugated knowledge.

Our chapter has two principal aims. First, it seeks to advance ways to identify and examine dominant modes of parental involvement. To accomplish this goal, we discuss models of Latino parental involvement and their relationship to federally funded educational policy. Our second goal is to discuss existing frameworks that could be useful to theorize and engage through decolonial action in order to create liberated spaces for learning and teaching where teachers and parents as social actors work on the joint goal of educating children and youth. To accomplish this, we discuss examples of policies derived from social action, including organizing and coalition work. In earlier work, we examined the vast array of parental involvement approaches in schools, highlighting those that employ a decolonial approach in the ways parents and schools work the boundaries imposed by the dichotomy of home and school (Baquedano-López, Alexander, & Hernandez, 2013). Here we review examples of decolonial and Freirian approaches to participation in school and examples from parent organizing through labor unions. We also offer examples from our own ethnographic research projects to illustrate how mainstream parental involvement paradigms and policies for immigrant parents do not always adequately address the particular situation of immigrant mothers. We hope that the themes we engage in this chapter prove useful to reexamine the relationship between educational policies on parent involvement and critically engage the home–school binary.

The Discourse on Parents as Problems and Educational Policy

Though Latino and other nondominant parents have always been actively involved in their children's schooling in school-sanctioned and nonsanctioned ways, a grand narrative of the uninvolved parent circulates in the public discourse on education. We illustrate how this narrative is created and promoted through social and educational policies that base the parameters of the home–school relationship on White middle-class values that have been supported by a century of developmental science that normalizes the family unit according to these values (Kainz & Aikens, 2007). Turning a blind eye to deep social inequities and disparate educational conditions, these policies regard nondominant *parents as problems*, a narrative that supports the dominant ideology of federal education policy making.

The Latina mother has historically been constructed as both a problem and an obstacle in the educational and social mobility processes. We trace this ideological position starting with early legislation such as the Civilization Fund Act of 1819 and the "Americanization" programs at the turn of the 20th century. Striving to assimilate Native Americans and Mexicans, respectively, into mainstream America by separating children and their families (G. G. González, 1997; Spring, 2001), these programs led to a focus on the foreign mother as the primary socialization agent within the home. The California's Home Teacher Act of 1915 placed teachers into Mexican students' homes with the goal of bringing educational opportunities directly to the mother because the goal of having Mexican families adopt American values was believed to be at risk if mothers were not explicitly socialized into those values. It was believed that the Mexican mother would lose her authority over her children as they were being educated in U.S. schools (outside of the home) and she remained within the home, uneducated and in need of the intervention of White home teachers. The Home Teacher Act also spelled out the role of the Parent-Teachers Association in supporting home teachers as they were confronted with the many "problems" of the foreign family home:

> Suppose a home teacher went forth, merely with her unaided resources, to do the work outlined by this law. In each home she would find a problem; in one, economic difficulties; in another, sickness; in a third, perhaps, that Americanized children have slipped from the control of their un-Americanized parents. What could she do alone but break her heart over the ills she could not help? She needs behind her, not only the school system,

but all organized helpfulness—in which the Parent-Teachers Association holds an important place. (Gibson, Hanna, Scharrenberg, McBride, & Lubin, 1916, para. 4)

Though the Home Teacher Act was written in the early part of the 20th century, these interventionist government policies and practices still continue under the guise of social policies, including parental involvement initiatives. We further discuss this *parent as problem* ideology by examining policies and programs that intervene as remedies for the "uninvolved" and "uncivilized" parent such as early learning programs, family literacy programs, and Title I Parent Compacts. In doing so, we introduce three parental tropes: parents as first teachers, parents as learners, and parents as partners. These parental tropes subject parents to particular educational roles that although they appear to be innocuous, are ideologically grounded in the "parent as problem" narrative and often interpreted at the school level in ways that maintain the status quo and serve to disempower parents that are willing to enter the system prepared to be leaders and actively engaged participants.

The Parents-as-First-Teachers Trope

Federally funded early intervention programs prescribe a set of pedagogical practices that low-income parents are to implement as early as the birth of a child. As their children's "first teachers," parents are expected to prepare their children for academic success with these prescribed practices between the ages of zero to five, a time period that is deemed critical to cognitive growth. Messages from organizations such as First Five in California, implore a particular parenting style that includes talking, interacting, and being in the world in ways that are culturally and socially incongruent with many parents' lived realities. This narrow approach ignores the knowledge—both linguistic and cultural—that parents hold and are able to pass on to their children in authentic and meaningful ways. Still, federal preschool and other early learning programs have been established to target non-dominant parents for failing to prepare their children for a schooling process; one that beginning in kindergarten, standardizes early learning (Fuller, Bridges, & Pai, 2007) at the school site and contributes to subtractive pedagogical approaches (Valenzuela, 1999) that might disempower both students and their families.

These programs that evaluate parenting styles and support a homogenous approach to early learning are reiterated in more recent federally funded initiatives, which turn the national attention to families of color. President Johnson's War on Poverty, supported by the Moynihan report on the deterioration of the African American family (Moynihan, 1965) claimed that the country's economic stability was at risk and implied that low-income people of color were to blame. In response, a set of federally funded programs were developed, including the Elementary and Secondary Education Act (ESEA) of 1965 and its provision for Head Start and

Title I (low-income) programs. Serving to repair the historical construction of deficient families, these initiatives targeted poor parents as problems, incapable of providing a culturally and linguistically rich environment to help their children transition successfully to school. By adhering to a normalized view of the White middle-class family (Kainz & Aikens, 2007), these policies obtained public support but failed to recognize the complexity of family arrangements and the economic limitations impacting many low-income parents of color (Hill Collins, 1990). Thus, the construction of the parent-as-first-teacher trope enlists parents into a set of funded programs that transfers educational responsibilities from parents to these programs.

The Parents-as-Learners Trope

Under President Johnson's War on Poverty, the Workforce Investment Act, the ESEA, and the Head Start Act promoted family literacy programs (Caspe, 2003) as initiatives designed to address the documented literacy incongruencies between ethnically and linguistically diverse homes and schools (Rodríguez-Brown, 2009). Programs that focus on family literacy are utilized to engage and teach minority parents (especially Latino immigrants) a variety of skills deemed necessary to be successful parents with children in school (Auerbach, 1989). Although the focus is on enhancing parent literacy "to improve the developmental capacity and educational options available to family members" (Gadsden, 1994, p. 2), it is not unusual for programs to explicitly teach parents how to navigate the school system, establish a home reading routine, or provide English-as-a-second-language classes.

Although the philosophical frameworks for family literacy program models differ, in many cases, deficit assumptions about nondominant families and their cultural practices tend to drive the purpose, design, and practices of these interventions (Valdés, 1996; Whitehouse & Colvin, 2001). Today, many family literacy programs strive to mitigate the cultural and linguistic divide between diverse homes and schools, and the need for such interventions is legitimized through the deficit discourse on Latino children and families commonplace in the field of education (Valencia, 1991, 2011). To counter such deficit notions, many family literacy educators follow a more progressive stance toward Latino communities that locates and builds on their cultural and linguistic strengths (e.g., funds of knowledge discussed in N. González, Moll, & Amanti, 2005). This "antideficit rhetoric" is still problematic in those cases in which educational practices are still grounded in a framework that operates as a neodeficit ideology (Auerbach, 1995).

The Parents-as-Partners Trope

Parent involvement provisions of Title I require that schools share information with parents on school programs, academic standards, and assessments, in order for parents to be more "knowledgeable partners" (Epstein & Hollifield, 1996). This explicit stance, however, regards parents with children in schools that receive

Title I funding as ill-informed, positioning them at the receiving end of partnership efforts. Additionally, the federally mandated use of School-Family Compacts for Title I schools that outline how families, school staff, and students are required to share responsibility for improved student academic achievement (U.S. Department of Education, 1996) also regards racially and linguistically diverse parents as problems that need to be fixed. The provisions relegate parent responsibility to marginal educational spaces that include monitoring attendance, homework completion, and TV watching, thereby limiting a parent's role to one of surveillance or "compliance officer or watchdog of the school system" (Mapp, 2011, p. 11).

This shift in the discourse to parents as partners attempts to put accountability on schools to better serve nondominant families, but the narrow and rigid approaches to parent involvement ultimately erode meaningful interactions between the home and school. Also problematic is that the push for partnerships is prominent only in schools that serve communities that qualify for Title I funding and are not mandated in middle- and upper-class communities where partnerships between home and school are believed to already exist. Because the notion of partnerships is constructed under a perceived lack of parent involvement in racially and linguistically diverse communities, meaningful and authentic partnerships between the home and school in low-income areas are compromised at the expense of mandated compacts and school-sanctioned "involvement."

These three parent tropes are aligned with an ideological stance that parents are problems that must be overcome or remediated. The *parents-as-first-teachers* trope acknowledges that all parents are their children's first teachers, yet deems low-income parents of color as incapable of fulfilling this role. The *parents-as-learners* trope promotes changing the diverse home/family to accommodate the school's agenda and regards only nondominant parents as "uneducated" and in need of direct instruction. The *parents-as-partners* trope relies on a discourse of partnerships that is misleading, for it acknowledges and sustains relationships with middle-class parents (as the norm), while implicitly targeting parents of color as needing to be "engaged" and "involved" as partners. These educational policies and programs not only define a set of possibilities for parent involvement practices that are narrow and limited, but also present us with an irreconcilable paradox: it is through these very policies that the social distance between diverse homes and schools widens as parents are perceived to be problems. Moreover, the knowledge and contribution of racially and linguistically diverse families is disregarded. Finally, these parental tropes allow for a mainstream narrative that continues to ignore social inequities by blaming parents (both implicitly and explicitly) for a manufactured educational crisis, ultimately sustaining colonial relationships between families of color and the state.

Moving beyond the Deficit Narrative

Much of the work of parents of color entails addressing this reality and preparing their children for life amidst racism (Burton, Bonilla-Silva, Ray, Buckelew, & Freeman, 2010; Howard & Reynolds, 2008; Reynolds, 2010). These efforts and tasks are demonstrably important for young people's educational success (Constantine & Blackmon, 2002; Scott, 2003). The historical and present exclusion of Latino families from schools and the demands for continued Americanization have generated a palpable social distance between Latino families and schools (Moll & Ruiz, 2002). In recent years, a "Latino threat" narrative (Chávez, 2008) targeted at immigrants but affecting all Latinos has contributed to this distance. The response of many Latino families to these challenges has been to become engaged in a diversity of educational practices and interventions not generally captured by the deficit-focused literature on parent engagement. In this section, we examine three approaches that attempt to decolonize the relationship between Latino families and schools that we feel go beyond this deficit narrative: an educational sovereignty approach, an empowerment approach, and a community organizing approach.

The determination of what constitutes valid and useful knowledge and who possesses this knowledge—what Foucault calls knowledge-power (Foucault, 1976/2000, 1995)—is one of the primary mechanisms through which colonizing relationships between Latino families and schools are perpetuated. Moll and colleagues have attempted to upend educational institutions' traditional focus on White middle-class homes, families, and institutions as the locus of knowledge through an emphasis on what they call educational sovereignty and funds of knowledge (N. González et al., 2005; Moll, Amanti, Neff, & González, 1992). Arguing that educators must understand the sociopolitical, historical, and economic context of households to recognize the intellectual knowledge present in Latino households, they advocate countering subtractive schooling paradigms (see also Valenzuela, 1999) by addressing teachers' lack of knowledge about their students' homes and families and providing teachers tools to incorporate their students' intellectual resources into their curriculum. This educational sovereignty approach seeks to make visible the unequal social structures underlying public education and integrate and build on the resources of Latino families to address these inequities. The perspective from cultural historical activity theory offers a model for understanding scales of multiple actors working within educational activity systems and how these systems conspire to create the achievement gap, but they may also be critically engaged to close the achievement gap (Portes, 2005; Portes & Salas, 2011). Durán (2011) reviews approaches that draw on cultural historical activity theoretical models that create contexts for interaction among parents and students, school practitioners, and university researchers to close the serious digital gap experienced by Latino families. To the extent that they serve to destabilize a normative approach to education, culturally relevant approaches (Gay, 2000; Ladson-Billings, 1994, 1995; Lee, 1995, 2001) and work that has redefined the value of immigrant Latino parents and their families' linguistic and cultural legacies (Farr, 2004, 2006; N. González, 2001; Guerra, 1998; Orellana, 2009; Valdés, 2003; Zentella, 1997) have contributed to ways to rethink the importance of Latino families' cultural legacies in curriculum development. There is also a growing body of research that problematizes the exclusion of LGBTQ = Lesbian, Gay, Bisexual, Transgender or Questioning (LGBTQ) students of color and their life and school experiences (Cruz, 2001; McCready, 2004). This work advances the shift that is necessary to reconceive the location of knowledge and thinking as heterogeneous and multiple (Tlostanova & Mignolo, 2009).

A second approach to addressing colonizing relationships between Latino families draws on the work of Paulo Freire (1973) and works to empower parents.[2] Such approaches counter the narrative of traditional family literacy models and affirm diverse family practices (as also efforts to upgrade parents to standard) by repositioning parents as social actors and agents of change. In this regard, these approaches engage decolonial work to shift the location of knowledge from social institution to social actors. However, many Freirian-based approaches do not always operationalize how power operates structurally within the foundations of their programs and ignore the racial dynamics that still uphold the divide between those in power and those who are not. Similarly to the educational sovereignty approach, Freirian work with parents is based on the recognition of social, economic, and political oppression as foundational to the relationship between schools and Latino families (De Gaetano, 2007; Torres & Hurtado-Vivas, 2011). Instead of focusing on training and transforming teachers through their entry into Latino homes, this approach seeks to organize parents to demand and assume positions of agency within educational structures, so their knowledge is not just something brought into the classroom, but also something that forms, constructs, and defines the educational space (Reyes and Torres, 2007). Delgado-Gaitan (1993) and Villenas (1996) ground this field in the complex relationships of domination that have shaped not only Latino parent organizing, but also themselves as researchers (see also Villenas & Deyhle, 1999). Although both Delgado-Gaitan and Villenas describe the work of parents to collectively articulate and act on ideologies that counter their marginalization, both researchers also describe the powerful pressure they felt, explicitly or implicitly, from both the school and the broader research community, to situate these parents as deficit. In describing how this deficit framing is implicit in the need to organize parents and still possible despite their organization, these researchers raise questions about the extent to which empowerment projects might reproduce exploitive relationships, drawing on the labor and cultural practices of Latino families without enabling structural change. As strong advocates for empowering projects enabling the elaboration of critical consciousness, cultural community, and political action, they also raise the haunting question around parent organizing in schools: Is this enough?

Although both of the previous two approaches address parent relationships with schools, a third approach works more broadly with parents as members of multiple communities (professional, regional, or national) to align schools with these communities. Warren, Hong, Rubin, and Uy (2009) describe how community-based schools support the economic, social, and cultural needs of families and communities with wraparound services (see also Warren, 2011). Hong (2011) suggests that work with parents should extend to broader community issues (i.e., affordable housing, immigration reform, and health care) as a means of both building strong relationships and holistically addressing the needs and concerns of families of color—only some of which are centered around schools. Rogers and Terriquez (2009) similarly describe the ways in which labor unions can become critical sites of educational organizing for Latino families and schools can become important sites of civic involvement for families that are particularly politically marginalized, such as those who are undocumented.

All of these approaches work to address pressing issues facing Latino families, to unite and strengthen their political voices, and to counter the deficit narratives common in schools; however, these approaches also have limits. These limits lie in the ways in which these approaches have been adopted as solutions to what are, in reality, deep problems of political, economic, and social power—problems not easily addressed by isolated projects, no matter how individually empowering. As Fuentes (2009–2010) shows, the extent to which such projects receive the endorsement of educational and political institutions often depends on the extent to which they withhold or moderate their critiques. Dyrness (2009), commenting on the exclusion of Latino parents from a school they had helped found, also warns of the ways in which empowerment can quickly become disempowerment as oppositional projects become incorporated into powerful established structures. To the extent to which any of these projects operate from or take up a narrative of inclusion—the inclusion of funds of knowledge, the inclusion of parents, or the inclusion of communities—they may also risk reproducing the "civilizing function" of educational projects because Whiteness remains centered and gatekeepers, directors, curriculum developers, and researchers remain rooted in Eurocentric paradigms.

The Case of Latina Immigrant Mothers in U.S. Schools: A Cautionary Note about Empowerment

The critical work on Latino parent involvement we have discussed previously refocuses the site of intervention from the parent to the school. By recognizing schools, not Latino parents and children, as deficient, such approaches work to develop parent power and community as a tool for resisting, transforming, and addressing oppressive and marginalizing aspects of both schools and education systems. A danger in this work, however, is that it becomes focused on self-empowerment, or on the transformation of the power/consciousness of individual Latino parents, instead of being focused on structural empowerment—the transformation of institutions, apparatuses, and controlling processes. In the ethnographic research of both Sera J. Hernandez and Rebecca A. Alexander, Latina mothers shared stories of being deeply involved in both parent organizing and in their child's schools and yet simultaneously disempowered. Here we share two anecdotes that describe these parents' experiences with schools.

Sera J. Hernandez worked with Justa García (pseudonym), a first-generation mother from Mexico. Justa was socialized into the politics and everyday functioning of

U.S. public schools rather quickly. Actively involved in her daughter's bilingual classroom at a school in Northern California, she eventually became the president of the school's English Learner Advisory Committee, a parent group that helps make decisions about programs, services, and funding for students learning English as an additional language. Her daughter, who was in middle school at the time of the study, was a student who had not been able to be reclassified as a fluent English speaker by the state's language policies. Justa, aware of the implications of the label "language learner," worried about her daughter's access to college-bound classes once she transitioned to high school. Over conversations at her home, Justa stressed the ways in which the policies, such as the high-stakes testing of language learners, were inequitable. The subsequent quote[3] illustrates Justa's understanding of the racial and class differences between "language learners" because the White students are not subjected to the same rigid language practices that the Latino children must endure to prove they are "ready" for untracked classes:

> ¿Por qué a los niños que están en inmersión y hablan inglés, Americanos, no le hacen el test en español? Nada más se los hacen a los Latinos? ¿Por qué si están en el mismo programa todos, y están luchando para aprender ese idioma, por qué a todos no les hacen el mismo examen? ¡Y ellos pobrecitos ahí en la librería[4] todos! Y los demás que estaban en el mismo grupo . . . jugando. Entonces pues es así.

> *Why are the children that are in immersion and speak English, Americans, don't take the test in Spanish? They only make the Latinos. Because if everyone is in the same program, and they are fighting to learn this language, why doesn't everyone take the same exam? And those poor kids there in the library all of them! And the rest of them from the same group . . . playing. Well, that's the way it is.*

Although Justa had found an expression of empowerment in working within the walls of the public school system, her objections to racialized schooling practices never reached public spaces. Despite her role in her child's education, Justa was still a parent who could only act within the confines of roles that were expected to be supportive of school policies and not to challenge them.

Rebecca A. Alexander noted a similar dynamic. She noted that even when the school administration was Latino and sensitive to the concerns of Latino parents, a broader set of structural forces including neighborhood violence, the criminal justice system, and inadequate support services severely impacted families and shaped their relationship with the school. Constrained by its own marginalization by working in a stigmatized neighborhood in a low-performing school serving poor families of color, the school administration was also limited in its response to Latina mothers' explicit requests and concerns. The following excerpt from Rebecca A. Alexander's field notes is based on an interview with María Zavete, a

Latina mother of two teenage boys, and presents an account of María's involvement in school:

> *María was in room 7 when I came in, talking with Araceli. Apparently Niño, her son, had broken a window over at the elementary school but María said she went and looked and there was no broken window. She said that, as a result of the school's report, the police had come to her house and had Niño, who is developmentally disabled, sign a paper when she was not present. She was trying to figure out where to get help because the police didn't leave a copy of the paper and wouldn't answer questions for her when she called. She said, "Niño just signs his name Niño, that's it." She says she has about 15 social workers from different agencies all working with her, watching her, all of whom do nothing . . . María explained that she has been involved in parent organizing for a long time, that she was part of a group that was so successful they did a study on a school's treatment of parents. She is at the school constantly, as a volunteer at recess, working with other mothers on creating cultural performances, teaching the kids dance, working with the teachers. She still, however, is very frustrated . . . The tangle of social service agencies does not help.*

María's frustration illustrates the very severe limits of individual empowerment. She is well connected to the school and her local government, she is adept at negotiating these institutions, and she is embedded in a well-organized community of mothers that she has played a substantial role in creating; however, in the face of her son's mental disabilities, trapped between a social-service system that surveils him (but does nothing to help), a criminal justice system that criminalizes him (but does nothing to help), and a school that prohibits him (but does nothing to help), she is consumed with the endless problem of trying to get help. Our recounting of María's experiences illustrates the reality that for empowerment to be significant, it must touch and transform the structures that make state, institutionalized, and community violence an everyday part of these families' lives.

The examples from ethnographic research presented here describe two mothers' participation in empowerment projects. The projects simultaneously cater to the neoliberal state through the responsibilization of parents and transform relations of power through collective organization that pushes back on individualizing and marginalizing schools of the repressive state. The accounts of Justa and María illuminate the hard limits of these projects. As "empowered" parents, they are resubsumed into individualized battles against racialized schooling practices and the criminalization of their children. Their actions do not reach the public space or become the collective battles of these empowerment projects. These parents have learned to work together to shout at the system, so to speak, so that they might be heard. This has not, however, changed the fact that they still must shout when others may whisper.

"Empowerment" efforts cannot always bridge the epistemic gap. Freire's *conscientização* is not about trying to learn the systems, strategies, modes, techniques, and practices of the oppressors, but about trying to unlearn them (Freire, 1970/2003). It is aimed not at incorporating people into institutions, but at disrupting the violence those institutions perpetrate—be it physical or structural. There are, thus, very real constraints on the possibility of empowerment when organized through either state-funded educational institutions or (foundation-funded) nonprofits. The limits of both (except through the disobedience that occurs within them) are defined by those who will profit from violence against the oppressed. These empowerment projects can barely dent the broader institutional structures within which parents like Justa and María must be empowered before they can participate effectively in the education of their children—a perverse inversion of the original intent of the concept.

What Does It Take, and How Do We Get There?

The necessary relocation of epistemic force, a necessity that we might, for lack of a better term, call "radical democracy" or perhaps sovereignty, prevents us from offering policy solutions. Neither we nor the policy makers who may read this could create decolonial policy for Latino students and their families. Indeed, the term "decolonial policy," if we take policy to mean sets of rules crafted by elected powers who only in very limited respects represent those they govern, is in itself a contradiction. We have been arguing that decolonial work is aimed at undoing the dominance and violence of colonization—violence that is implicit in the imposition of unilateral policy.

"Going Beyond Words": The Latina/o Academy of Arts and Sciences

In more than one way, the ideas presented in this chapter also respond to calls that have been put forth by a group of Latina/o scholars to advance scholarship and praxis that bring about epistemic justice and whose aims are to influence and restructure the means and ends of research to advocate for Latino youth. In 2007, the University of California, Berkeley, was the site of a working conference aimed at establishing a Latina/o Academy of Arts and Sciences, whose goals are to build on Latino intellectual and sociopolitical knowledge by increasing understanding (and like other academies) of this knowledge across a range of disciplinary fields. Inspired by the youth uprisings and political mobilization in 2006 in response to the Specter bill in California, which made it illegal for persons or institutions to provide assistance or services to anyone who might be illegally in the United States, a group of Latina/o scholars met to begin to estimate capacity for the creation of the academy and what aims this would serve.[5] Following this first event, there have been publications and presentations at public venues to add signatories and garner support to launch the effort more formally.[6] Ramona Hernández (2012) describes the effort as the "academy that goes beyond words" and as an academy that "does not accommodate itself in the ivory tower and remain indifferent to the everyday struggles of peoples the Academy claims to represent" (p. 280). This organism would be a place of intervention, and as such, it would seek to inform government decision making and public policy on issues that are of interest and concern to Latinos in this country and beyond. It is our hope that educational researchers join the efforts of the academy to find strength in a collective voice against the invalidation of multiple experiences, knowledges, and abilities across educational spaces.[7]

The need to create critical conceptual spaces that could broaden the scope of policies and practices of parental involvement is great. In the spirit of generating dialogue with researchers and policy makers, we offer a list of approaches to helps us find ways to redefine parental involvement in schools so that we have equitable divisions of labor. We believe it is necessary for our current educational leaders and practitioners to:

- Recognize Latino parents as legitimate knowers through processes that integrate parents' knowledge to transform existing power dynamics in schools. We are aware that this is a process that requires the professional input from parents in school decisions, a process that changes the ways schools view Latino parents not just as examples or sources of cultural and linguistic knowledge but as actors shaping the course of education in this country.
- Revise policies on parent involvement at the school level that construct minimal participatory roles for Latino parents (chaperone roles, food preparation, or other manual-service roles) and that may fall across class lines. This means also expanding school resources to support parents to design and attend seminars to promote the place of parents as knowledgeable and true partners in education.
- Avoid reductionist discourses on the Latina/o experience that often lead to simplistic binaries in education, such as Latino parents as "problems" or "partners," or Latino students as "at risk" of school failure or filled with untapped "cultural and linguistic resources" needing to be leveraged.
- End the discourse of remedial or "catch-up" education that justifies the relegation of Latino and other nondominant students and their families to the margins of public education and that further amplifies the myth of the achievement gap.
- Engage a radical interrogation of the self (the professional educator, policy maker, or researcher) as a powerful, racialized actor within a highly inequitable system and as one who is responsible less for creating policy than for creating space where those who are currently disempowered may find the means to do so.

On this last point, as Quijano (2000) has noted, power in relationships of dominance is not based on wealth or class; rather, it is based on a racial classification that defined colonial relations in much of European expansion, including the United States, and we add, a classification that is still in place today across our social

Baquedano-López, Hernandez, and Alexander

institutions, including schools. Without a critical examination of how this classification operates in our educational system, we risk justifying a history of exclusion of parents from their children's education. We hope that the approaches we have discussed in this chapter contribute to dialogue on the ways we conceptualize and engage notions of parent involvement. The transformation of our school system requires that we change the way we think about practices of education, and more importantly, that we consider how educational policies contribute in explicit and implicit ways to the perpetuation of social inequalities.

Notes

1. Fanon's (1967) discussion of the relationship between the colonizer and colonized lays bare the fact that to be civilized means to lose one's culture and identity: "Every colonized people—in other words, every people in whose soul an inferiority complex has been created by the death and burial of its local originality—finds itself face to face with the language of the civilizing nation" (p. 18). See also Spring (2001) and Willinsky (1998) on the reach of colonialism in today's social institutions.
2. Many of these approaches have been instrumental in promoting ways to conceptualize the general notion of "involvement" as "critical involvement" and advance the empowerment of parents.
3. These data are taken from a longer transcript of interactions that were audio recorded by Sera J. Hernandez at Justa's house.
4. Consistent with local usage, Justa was referring to the school library when she said librería.
5. The organizing committee in 2006 was composed of Patricia Baquedano-López, Rachel Moran, Nelson Maldonado-Torres, and Christine Trost from University of California, Berkeley, and Paula Moya from Stanford University. A panel at the 2011 presentation at the XVI LatCrit conference in San Diego included many of the original participants of the conference at University of California, Berkeley.
6. The following sources might of interest to readers: Maldonado-Torres, N. (2011). The Latina/o Academy of Arts and Sciences: Decolonizing knowledge and society in the context of neo-apartheid. Harvard Law Review, 14, 285–293; Moya, P. (2011). Why Latina/o? Why academy? Harvard Law Review, 14, 295–300.
7. Like other interventions in education, in particular critical race theory and Latina/o critical theory, the Latina/o Academy of Arts and Sciences' aims seek to investigate the inequities in society that lead to the achievement gap, among other outcomes.

References

Althusser, L. (2001). Lenin and philosophy and other essays. New York: Monthly Review Press.
Auerbach, E. R. (1989). Toward a social-contextual approach to family literacy. Harvard Educational Review, 59(2), 165–181.
Auerbach, E. R. (1995). Deconstructing the discourse of strengths in family literacy. Journal of Reading Behavior, 27(4), 643–661.
Baquedano-López, P., Alexander, R., & Hernandez, S. (2013). Equity issues in parental and community involvement in schools: What teacher educators need to know. In C. Faltis & J. Abedi (Eds.), Extraordinary pedagogies for working within school settings serving non-dominant students [Special issue]. Review of Research in Education, 37(1), 161–194.

Berliner, D. C., & Biddle, B. J. (1995). *The manufactured crisis: Myths, frauds, and the attack on America's public schools.* Redding, MA: Addison-Wesley.

Burton, L. M., Bonilla-Silva, E., Ray, V., Buckelew, R., & Freeman, E. H. (2010). Critical race theories, colorism, and the decade's research on families of color. *Journal of Marriage and Family, 72,* 440–459.

Caspe, M. (2003). *Family literacy: A review of programs and critical perspectives.* Retrieved from the Harvard Family Research Project website: www.hfrp.org/publications-resources/browse-our-publications/family-literacy-a-review-of-programs-and-critical-perspectives

Césaire, A. (2010). Culture and colonization. *Social Text, 28*(2), 127–144. (Reprinted from Aimé Césaire's speech at Le Premier Congrès International des Ecrivains et Artistes Noirs, Paris, September 1956)

Chávez, L. (2008). *The Latino threat: Constructing immigrants, citizens, and the nation.* Stanford, CA: Stanford University Press.

Constantine, M. G., & Blackmon, S. M. (2002). African American adolescents' racial socialization experiences: Their relations to home, school and peer self-esteem. *Journal of African American Studies, 32,* 322–335.

Cruz, C. (2001). Toward an epistemology of a brown body. *International Journal of Qualitative Studies in Education, 14*(5), 657–669.

De Gaetano, Y. (2007). The role of culture in engaging Latino parents' involvement in school. *Urban Education, 42,* 145–164.

Delgado Bernal, D. (1998). Using a Chicana feminist epistemology in educational research. *Harvard Educational Review, 68*(4), 555–579.

Delgado Bernal, D., Elenes, A., Godinez, F., & Villegas, S. (Eds.). (2006). *Chicana/Latina education in everyday life: Feminista perspectives on pedagogy and epistemology.* Albany, NY: State University of New York Press.

Delgado-Gaitan, C. (1993). Researching change and changing the researcher. *Harvard Educational Review, 63*(4), 389–412.

Durán, R. (2011). Development of Latino family-school engagement programs in U.S. contexts: Enhancements to cultural historical activity theory accounts. In P. Portes & S. Salas (Eds.), *Vygotsky in 21st century society: Advances in cultural historical theory and praxis with non-dominant communities* (pp. 229–246). New York: Peter Lang.

Dussel, E. (2003). *Beyond philosophy: Ethics, history, Marxism, and liberation theology* (E. Mendieta, Ed.). Lanham, MD: Rowman & Littlefield.

Dyrness, A. (2009). Cultural exclusion and critique in the era of good intentions: Using participatory research to transform parent roles in urban school reform. *Social Justice, 36*(4), 36–53.

Epstein, J. L., & Hollifield, J. H. (1996). Title I and school-family-community partnerships: Using research to realize the potential. *Journal of Education for Students Placed at Risk, 1*(3), 263–278.

Fanon, F. (1963). *The wretched of the earth* (C. Farrington, Trans). New York: Grove Press.

Fanon, F. (1967). *Black skin/white masks* (C. L. Markmann, Trans.). New York: Grove Press.

Farr, M. (2004). *Ethnolinguistic Chicago: Language and literacy in the city's neighborhoods.* Hillsdale, NJ: Lawrence Erlbaum.

Farr, M. (2006). *Rancheros in Chicagoacán: Language and identity in a transnational community.* Austin, TX: University of Texas Press.

Foucault, M. (1995). *Discipline and punish: The birth of the prison* (2nd ed., A. Sheridan, Trans). New York: Vintage Books.

Foucault, M. (2000). Truth and power. In P. Rabinow (Ed.), *The Foucault Reader* (pp. 51–75). New York: Pantheon. (Original work published in 1976)

Freire, P. (1973). *Education for critical consciousness.* New York: Seabury Press.

Freire, P. (2003). *Pedagogy of the oppressed.* New York: Continuum. (Original work published in English in 1970)

Fuentes, E. (2009–2010). Learning power and building community: Parent-initiated participatory action. *Social Justice, 36*(4), 69–83.

Fuller, B., Bridges, M., & Pai, S. (2007). *Standardized childhood: The political and cultural struggle over early education.* Stanford, CA: Stanford University Press.

Gadsden, V. L. (1994). *Understanding family literacy: Conceptual issues facing the field* (National Center on Adult Literacy Technical Report TR94–02). Retrieved from www.eric. ed.gov/PDFS/ED374339.pdf

Gándara, P., & Contreras, F. (2009). *The Latino education crisis: The consequences of failed school policies.* Cambridge, MA: Harvard University Press.

Gay, G. (2000). *Culturally responsive teaching: Theory, practice, and research.* New York: Teachers College Press.

Gibson, M. S., Hanna, E. J., Scharrenberg, P., McBride, J. H., & Lubin, S. J. (1916). *The home teacher: The act with a working plan and forty lessons in English.* Commission of Immigration and Housing of California. Retrieved from http://archive.org/stream/hometeacheract00cali/hometeacheract00cali_djvu.txt

González, G. G. (1997). Culture, language, and the Americanization of Mexican children. In A. Darder, R. D. Torres, & H. Gutiérrez (Eds.), *Latinos and education: A critical reader* (pp. 158–173). New York: Routledge.

González, N. (2001). *"I am my language": Discourses of women and children in the borderlands.* Tucson, AZ: University of Arizona Press.

González, N., Moll, L. C., & Amanti, C. (Eds.). (2005). *Funds of knowledge: Theorizing practices in households, communities and classrooms.* Mahwah, NJ: Lawrence Erlbaum.

Grande, S. (2004). *Red pedagogy: Native American social and political thought.* Lanham, MD: Rowman & Littlefield.

Guerra, J. (1998). *Close to home: Oral and literate practices in a transnational Mexicano community.* New York: Teachers College Press.

Gutiérrez, K., Baquedano-López, P., & Alvarez, H. (2000). The crisis in Latino education: The norming of America. In C. Tejeda, Z. Leonardo, & C. Martínez (Eds.), *Charting new terrains in Chicano(a) and Latina(o) education* (pp. 213–232). Cresskill, NJ: Hampton Press.

Hernández, R. (2012). Dominicans and the National Latino/a Academy of Arts and Sciences. *Harvard Law Review, 14,* 277–281.

Hill Collins, P. (1990). *African American feminist thought: Knowledge, consciousness, and the politics of empowerment.* New York: Routledge.

Hong, S. (2011). *A cord of three strands: A new approach to parent engagement in schools.* Cambridge, MA: Harvard Education Press.

Howard, T. C., & Reynolds, R. (2008). Examining parent involvement in reversing the underachievement of African American students in middle class schools. *Education Foundation, 22*(1–2), 79–98.

Kainz, K., & Aikens, N. L. (2007). Governing the family through education: A genealogy on the home/school relation. *Equity & Excellence in Education, 40*(4), 301–310.

Ladson-Billings, G. (1994). *The dreamkeepers: Successful teachers of African American children.* San Francisco, CA: Jossey Bass.

Ladson-Billings, G. (1995). That's just good teaching! The case for culturally relevant pedagogy. *Theory into Practice, 34*(3), 159–165.

Lee, C. D. (1995). A culturally based cognitive apprenticeship: Teaching African American high school students skills in literary interpretation. *Reading Research Quarterly, 30*(4), 608–631.

Lee, C. D. (2001). Is October Brown Chinese? A cultural modeling activity system for underachieving students. *American Educational Research Journal, 38*(1), 97–141.

Maldonado-Torres, N. (2011). Thinking through the decolonial turn: Post-continental interventions in theory, philosophy, and critique—an introduction. *Transmodernities: Journal of the Peripheral Cultural Production of the Luso-Hispanic World, 1*(2), 1–15.

Mapp, K. L. (2011, June). *Title I and parent involvement: Lessons from the past, recommendations for the future.* Paper presented at the "Tightening Up Title I" Conference, Center for American Progress and the American Enterprise Institute, Washington, DC. Retrieved from www.americanprogress.org/events/2011/03/

McCready, L. (2004). Understanding the marginalization of gay and gender non-conforming Black male students. *Theory into Practice, 43*(2), 136–143.

Mignolo, W. (2010). *The darker side of the renaissance: Literacy, territoriality, and colonization* (2nd ed.). Ann Arbor, MI: Michigan University Press.

Moll, L., Amanti, C., Neff, D., & González, N. (1992). Funds of knowledge for teaching: Using a qualitative approach to connect homes and classrooms. *Theory into Practice, 3*(2), 132–141.

Moll, L., & Ruiz, R. (2002). The schooling of Latino children. In M. Suárez-Orozco & M. Páez (Eds.), *Latinos: Remaking America* (pp. 362–374). Berkeley, CA: University of California Press/David Rockefeller Center for Latin American Studies.

Moynihan, P. (1965). The Negro family: The case for national action. Office of Planning and Research, United States Department of Labor. Retrieved from www.AfricanAmericanpast.org/?q=primary/moynihan-report-1965

Nakagawa, K. (2000). Unthreading the ties that bind: Questioning the discourse of parent involvement. *Educational Policy, 14,* 443–472.

Orellana, M. F. (2009). *Translating childhoods: Immigrant youth, language, and culture.* New Brunswick, NJ: Rutgers University Press.

Paperson, L. (2010). The postcolonial ghetto: Seeing her shape and his hand. *Berkeley Review of Education, 1*(1), 5–34.

Portes, P. R. (2005). *Dismantling educational inequality: A cultural-historical approach to closing the achievement gap.* New York: Peter Lang.

Portes, P. R., & Salas, S. (Eds.). (2011). *Vygotsky in 21st century society: Advances in cultural historical theory and praxis with non-dominant communities.* New York: Peter Lang.

Quijano, A. (2000). Coloniality of power, Eurocentrism, and Latin America. *International Sociology, 15*(1), 215–232.

Reyes, L. V., & Torres, M. N. (2007). Decolonizing family literacy in a culture circle: Reinventing the family literacy educator's role. *Journal of Early Childhood Literacy, 7*(1), 73–94.

Reynolds, R. (2010). "They think you're lazy," and other messages African American parents send their African American sons: An exploration of critical race theory in the examination of educational outcomes for African American males. *Journal of African American Males in Education, 1*(2), 144–163.

Rodríguez-Brown, F. V. (2009). *Home-school connection: Lessons learned in a culturally and linguistically diverse community.* New York: Routledge.

Rogers, J., & Terriquez, V. (2009). "More justice": The role of organized labor in educational reform. *Educational Policy, 23*(1), 216–241.

Sandoval, C. (2000). *Methodology of the oppressed.* Minneapolis, MN: University of Minnesota Press.

Scott, L. D. (2003). The relation of racial identity and racial socialization to coping with discrimination among African American adolescents. *Journal of African American Studies, 33,* 520–537.

Smith, L. T. (1999). *Decolonizing methodologies: Research and indigenous peoples.* London: Zed Books/University of Otago Press.

Spring, J. (2001). *Deculturalization and the struggle for equality: A brief history of the education of dominated cultures in the United States* (3rd ed.). Boston: McGraw Hill.

Tlostanova, M., & Mignolo, W. (2009). Global coloniality and the decolonial option. *Kult, 6,* 130–147.

Torres, M. N., & Hurtado-Vivas, R. (2011). Playing fair with Latino parents as parents, not teachers: Beyond family literacy as assisting homework. *Journal of Latinos and Education, 10*(3), 223–244.

Tuck, E. (2009). Suspending damage: A letter to communities. *Harvard Educational Review, 79*(3), 409–427.

U.S. Department of Education. (1996). *Policy guidance for Title I, Part A: Improving basic programs operated by local educational agencies.* Retrieved from www2.ed.gov/legislation/ESEA/Title_I/parinv2.html

Valdés, G. (1996). *Con respeto: Bridging the distances between culturally diverse families and school: An ethnographic portrait.* New York: Teachers College Press.

Valdés, G. (2003). *Expanding definitions of giftedness: The case of young interpreters from immigrant communities.* Mahwah, NJ: Lawrence Erlbaum.

Valencia, R. (1991). *Chicano school failure and success: Research and policy agendas for the 1990s.* New York: Falmer Press.

Valencia, R. (2011). *Chicano school failure and success: Past, present, and future* (3rd ed.). New York: Routledge.

Valenzuela, A. (1999). *Subtractive schooling: U.S.-Mexican youth and the politics of caring.* Albany, NY: State University of New York Press.

Varenne, H., & McDermott, R. (1999). *Successful failure: The school America builds.* Boulder, CO: Westview Press.

Villenas, S. (1996). The colonizer/colonized Chicana ethnographer: Identity, marginalization, and co-optation in the field. *Harvard Educational Review, 66*(4), 711–731. Retrieved from http://her.hepg.org/content/3483672630865482/fulltext.pdf

Villenas, S., & Deyhle, D. (1999). Critical race theory and ethnographies challenging the stereotypes: Latino families, schooling, resilience and resistance. *Curriculum Inquiry, 29*(4), 413–445.

Warren, M. R. (2011). Building a political constituency for urban school reform. *Urban Education, 46*(3), 484–512.

Warren, M. R., Hong, S., Rubin, C. L., & Uy, P. S. (2009). Beyond the bake sale: A community-based relational approach to parent engagement in schools. *Teachers College Record, 111*(9), 2209–2254.

Whitehouse M., & Colvin, C. (2001). "Reading" families: Deficit discourse and family literacy. *Theory into Practice, 40*(3), 212–219.

Willinsky, J. (1998). *Learning to divide the word: Education at empire's end.* Minneapolis, MN: University of Minnesota Press.

Zentella, A. C. (1997). *Growing up bilingual: Puerto Rican children in New York.* Malden, MA: Blackwell.

3

CULTIVATING A CADRE OF CRITICALLY CONSCIOUS TEACHERS AND "TAKING THIS COUNTRY TO A TOTALLY NEW PLACE"

Angela Valenzuela and Patricia D. López

With President Barak Obama winning more than 70 percent of the Latino vote in the 2012 presidential election, a figure that also represents the necessary margins that helped to lead him and unprecedented numbers of Latinos to Congress, this was indisputably a watershed moment for Latinos. Echoing this, Vice President Joe Biden addressed members of the Congressional Hispanic Caucus Institute (CHCI) in a swearing-in ceremony on January 3, 2013, describing Hispanics as at "the center of the nation's future" and reminding all that their political power would only grow after the last presidential election. He further added that "the way to make the mark . . . is for the Hispanic community to step up and step out and let the world know, let the Republicans know, let others know that if you ignore the needs and concerns of the Hispanic community, you will not win." Described as reminiscent of John F. Kennedy's 1961 inaugural address, Biden's parting comment was, "It's no longer about what can be done for the Hispanic community . . . The question is what the Hispanic community is going to do to take this country to a totally new place" (see CHCI, 2013).

The National Latino/a Education Research and Policy Project (or simply NLERAP, pronounced like "nel-rap") seeks to heed Biden's call and take this country to a totally new place. Moreover, we want our families, communities, and progressive, community-based organizations to have a catalytic and substantive role in this process. If such a trajectory is to be effective, however, this requires an organizational framework that matches Vice President Biden's high-sounding rhetoric. NLERAP harbors precisely such seeds of change.

With support from the Ford and Kellogg Foundations and numerous partners, NLERAP has been building an infrastructure for educational change to address from a research-based perspective the crisis of Latino/a underachievement in our nation. Originally headed by Pedro Pedraza and Melissa Rivera (2000–2008) and currently by Angela Valenzuela and Patricia D. López (2009–present), we are a 35-member collectivity, or brain trust (referred to internally as the "NLERAP Council"), composed of scholars, research faculty, public school educators, community leaders, and advocates that have convened for well over a decade for this purpose (for a current list of the NLERAP Council membership, visit the NLERAP website at http://nlerap.org).

Our strategic goals are twofold: first, to promote a "grow-your-own" (GYO) educational pipeline for Latino/a youth into higher education that is community centered and university connected; and second, to cultivate a critical mass of critically conscious, civically engaged, globally literate educators throughout the country that embodies a collectivist, community-centered ethos in their pedagogy and praxis. This approach is invested in transforming education in a way that that involves both community, family, and Latino/a youth as equal, respected partners rather than as how they are frequently regarded in the educational process—that is, as the objects, rather than the subjects, of reform.

Accordingly, our partnership model connects schools and districts to community-based organizations and universities in the following five cities and states: Sacramento, California; Chicago, Illinois; Milwaukee, Wisconsin; Dallas, Texas; and Brooklyn, New York. The act of convening a constituency around public schooling and GYO teachers across our five sites reveals how our initiative positions the community to take ownership of our GYO teacher preparatory pipeline model so that once teachers enter the profession, they also enter into our nation's neighborhoods as critically conscious agents of change. For this to occur, teachers need a constituency, or support network, in those instances when they become politically involved in acts of social justice and transformational change.

Although most reform efforts are focused on the *content* of change in terms of curricula, programs, models, projects, and policies, our collective efforts additionally emphasize the *structure* and *process* of change. NLERAP has made great strides in developing its infrastructure. Through community forums, we have identified key partners and community leadership within each site that have the capacity to move our GYO initiative forward. These partners are working closely with their public university leadership to create an educational pipeline from select public high schools, as well as through entry points at the postbaccalaureate and paraprofessional levels. They are also working closely together to institutionalize two signature courses developed by our national NLERAP research and curriculum committees for future teacher candidates that foster sociocultural and sociopolitical awareness together with a community-centered, participatory action research (PAR) approach and an engaged approach to policy that we simply term "engaged policy" (López, 2012).

Regarding structure, there are no shortcuts to building NLERAP's infrastructure within which community-based curricula, programs, projects, and policies flourish, in a sustaining manner. This requires very intense, relational work, candid conversations regarding ethical motivations and shared principles, transparency, and *confianza* (trust). Aside from the broad, nonnegotiable parameters like the integration of our two signature courses into teacher preparation curricula and promoting a pipeline from within traditional public school settings that help teacher graduates return to their home communities (or school sites that are relatively similar and geographically proximate), each site enjoys a high degree of autonomy. Regional sites have diverse advisory boards that consist of partners that each play an integral part in providing the resources and capital needed to transform both K–12 *and* postsecondary, higher education institutions. These regional infrastructures also have their respective fiscal agents that connect to the national office at the University of Texas at Austin and our NLERAP Inc. nonprofit in Dallas, Texas, the organization's fundraising arm (see the NLERAP website at http://nlerap.org).

Regarding process, our collective wisdom, experience, and knowledge yields the four overarching components that facilitate the educational success of Latino/a students: first, community and family engagement and advocacy that honors funds of knowledge and pedagogies of the home; second, sociocultural and sociopolitical theoretical foundations that are the bases for critical pedagogy; third, community-based PAR that prepares teachers to work alongside their students on research projects that situate them at the center of the inquiry process;[1] and fourth, engaged policy that inserts communities' ways of knowing into political debates and policy-making processes.

Taken together, these four components recognize the importance of collaborative knowledge creation and how communities are best positioned to generate context-specific funds of "legitimate" knowledge that can inform curricular content, research foci, and pedagogical practices. Several decades of research findings by members of our NLERAP Council have demonstrated how one or more of the previously mentioned components has positively impacted the education of Latino/a students on the national level (García & Baetens, 2009; García & Kleifgen, 2010; Nieto, 2005, 2013; Villegas, 2007), as well as in specific contexts such as Arizona (Cammarota, 2008; Casanova, 2010; Moll, Amanti, Neff, & Gonzalez, 1992), California (Berta-Ávila, Tijerina Revilla, & López Figueroa, 2011; Conchas & Rodriguez, 2008; Flores, 2005; Lindquist Wong & Glass, 2009), Chicago (Antrop-González, 2011; Flores-González, 2002), Connecticut (Irizarry, 2011), Massachusetts (Nieto, 2003), New York (García & Kleifgen, 2010; Mercado & Brochin-Ceballos, 2011; Noguera, 2007; Pedraza & Rivera, 2005; Rivera, Medellin-Paz, & Pedraza, 2010; Torre, 2009), and Texas (López, 2012; López, Valenzuela, & Garcia, 2011; Reyes, Scribner, & Paredes Scribner, 1999; Romo & Falbo, 1996; Valenzuela, 1999, 2004).

Community and Family Engagement

As university-based educators, we unfortunately, albeit typically, enter into the fray of educational change with limited conceptions of the role of community and parents as agents of change. In contrast, we seek to center parent, family, and community engagement in educational reform. For us, this means that our part-nering community-based organizations (CBOs) and parents play a leading role in developing and cultivating our GYO pipeline. Our conceptualization of parent involvement is an unconventional one. Typically, parent involvement is limited to helping children and youth develop reading and mathematics skills, spelling, homework, vocabulary, and so on (Olivos, Jiménez-Castellanos, & Ochoa, 2011). Or, as Baquedano-López et al. (Chapter 2, this volume) find, their participation is frequently controlled and limited to surveillance roles as chaperones and moni-tors. As important as these are, NLERAP views parent involvement as a politi-cal act and seeks to therefore cultivate family, parent, and community agency in ways that are enmeshed within a larger agenda of school, community, and societal transformation.

Other than in narrowly prescribed ways such as in research projects or part-nerships where alumni can facilitate the goals of our universities or through con-tinuation learning structures, the academy devalues engagement outside of the university with parents and community as a part of normal university practice. Despite the fact that our public universities rely, in part, on the local taxpayer base, collaborations with parents and community are, at best, episodic—and mostly related to filling the terms of a given grant—or, at worst, an afterthought.[2] This helps to account for a systemic disconnect between research, researchers, and the communities in whose name this very research gets conducted.

Investigating the process of securing and implementing government National Science Foundation grants in a higher education institution, Daza (2013) launches an implacable critique against what she aptly terms "grant-science," referring to the values and ethics that inform research and knowledge production in universi-ties. Her work demonstrates how historically and socioculturally engrained forms of power reproduce meaning, subjects, identity, and truths because of the time-honored, taken-for-granted material and discursive parameters that define and legitimate scientists' "worldings," or worldviews (see also Spivak, 1985).

Daza maintains that what results is a technocratic imaginary that reproduces neoliberal scientism's positivist and managerial ways, eliminating the presumptive "messiness" of race, culture, language, power, and difference. Against this artifice, authentic partnerships with family and community are inconvenient and poten-tially compromising. As members of university culture, it should therefore come as no surprise that our teacher preparation programs mostly pay lip service to the notion that we need to incorporate community and parents into our curriculum development and praxis.

Although Daza (2013) points to the important and complex role that pro-gressive university researchers can play as both beneficiaries of and "infiltrators" to these regimes of knowledge production, NLERAP further offsets this pat-tern of scientism by empowering an already powerful set of community leaders nationwide to assume ownership of the GYO initiative. These are individuals with long-standing track records of working with parents and communities toward progressive educational change in their respective communities but whose voices are frequently marginal to university-based efforts at reform.

Our approach also helps incubate a learning community that is home to, and nurtures, the pipeline, alongside enabling social justice and communitarian values and orientations through its partnering, educative role in the preparation of future GYO Latino/a teacher cohorts. The fruit of this labor is the eventual return of critically conscious GYO graduates to our nation's secondary schools, armed with a different worlding premised on the fertile soil of shared histories of struggle that our partnering CBOs themselves signify and into which our GYO pipeline gets rooted.

Curriculum as Praxis

In many respects, curriculum rests at the heart of NLERAP's GYO teacher preparation pipeline initiative. Our curriculum is critical of, and seeks to remedy, existing sterile standards-based approaches that objectify youth, families, and communities by privileging reductive educational outcomes like tests scores and a narrowing of the achievement gap via test-based measures of success. More often than not, this kind of focus aligns with curricula that eviscerate students' histories, cultures, languages, community-based identities, and thus, their sense of self-worth and how to be a change agent in the world (Valenzuela, 1999, 2004). Many youth subsequently internalize pejorative attitudes of the dominant culture toward their own groups (Valenzuela, 1999).

To reverse this trend, we have devised a curriculum that both honors and strengthens students cultural and community-based identities while simultaneously illuminating the way that power and privilege work in a capitalist society to reproduce asymmetries of power in institutions like schools, as well as in the workforce and the economy. This curriculum finds expression in the two above-mentioned signature courses that each partnering university will offer its teacher candidates. Whether these courses involve either the development of new courses or accommodate to existing ones, their respective content will cultivate sociocultural and sociopolitical awareness.

In a monograph produced by our group (Nieto, Rivera & Quiñones, 2012) these core forms of awareness were identified as necessary requirements for all teacher preparation programs that develop graduates with career trajectories that include the teaching of underserved, ethnic, and linguistic minority youth. While immersing students in scholarship pertaining to critical multicultural studies, sociocultural learning theory, politics, policy, local, community, and hemispheric histories and struggles, candidates will engage in constant self-reflection regarding their own views on, and attitudes toward, race, class, gender, sexual orientation, language, and ability. What makes our curriculum dynamic is how it is situated philosophically within an understanding of curriculum as praxis and the transformative role that critically conscious teachers can and should play (hooks, 1994; Solorzano & Delgado Bernal, 2001).

Specifically, these courses will get taught in the very community contexts from which they emanate where teacher candidates will learn from traditional methods like lectures and discussions but also engage in PAR that attaches to real-world issues that impact communities, thereby providing immediate benefits to the very communities to which they shall eventually return as teachers. Our approach thus intentionally blurs the boundaries between teaching, research, and advocacy. It is not sufficient for us to grow a nominal pipeline of Latino/teacher candidates; we must also foster in them the critical-thinking skills that they need to be full, participating members of a democratic society. Although our curriculum as praxis approach sets a very high bar for our teacher candidates, their learning is never separate from the support of a community that eagerly awaits their return upon graduation and certification.

PAR and Critical Methodologies

Embedded within our signature courses are the theoretical and practical elements that equip teachers with the tools to engage in a community-based process for examining pressing issues that are relevant to their students (see Ayala, forthcoming). A core contribution of PAR to teacher preparation is its role in cultivating strong relationships between teachers and their students (Irizarry, 2011). That is, research and "the researched" are partners to any particular given inquiry, a process that partly consists of joint decision making regarding what gets studied, how it gets studied, and what was learned from the study via a collectively deliberated process.

For example, our GYO curriculum engages candidates in problem-posing dialogues (Freire, 1990) that encourage them to rely on their own life experiences for naming the problems that they face, giving them the tools to determine the causes of these problems so that they can act as effective change agents. This should culminate into a deeper, critical reflection on the politics of being a teacher of Latino/a students. As teachers gain confidence in engaging in PAR projects that are important to their communities, they, too, will gain self-assurance in taking ownership of their role as political actors that engage policies and practices at multiple levels (García & Menken, 2010; López, 2012; López & Valenzuela, forthcoming).

Our approach contrasts with most research designs that make these decisions at a distance from the very communities that serve to justify this research (Daza, 2013). Consequently, PAR is, of necessity, a collectivist and inclusive endeavor that seeks to partner all of our teacher candidates with youth, other educators, and community members in carrying out specific research projects that are co-constructed. Data or research evidence gathered can consist of standard instruments like surveys, interviews, focus group information, and so on, but they may also consist of cultural and artistic productions accomplished through poetry, dance, theater, and other forms of expression.

This approach fosters meaningful relationships, activism, and community betterment and well-being. Settings for this research are found nationwide, and all generate interdisciplinary bodies of knowledge that directly address the exploitative and oppressive conditions within which youth are schooled, work, and live. Although this research approach will get folded into our signature courses, it is our hope and expectation that it gets folded into other aspects of the teacher preparatory curriculum and possibly even institutionalized as a separate third course.

Engaged Policy

The final component is a relatively new element embraced by NLERAP that we term "engaged policy" and its role in redefining what is possible for schools, families, and communities. Engaged policy is concerned with "extending the political reach" (López, 2012) of those persons who are committed to being agents of social change beyond the classroom, school, and community settings into the realm of the state. Hence, governmentality (Lather, 2004) is an important, orienting concept with respect to engaged policy.

Too often, much of the research and knowledge generated either from local communities or university researchers does not find its way into policy-making discourses. Consequently, policy-making bodies are absolved of their responsibility to consider the needs of marginal communities—sometimes because policy makers are unaware of such research and, in other instances, because the issues are either too politically contentious or minoritarian (see López, 2012; Valenzuela & Maxcy, 2011). In this framing, policies like high-stakes standardized testing that are detached from, and alienating to, marginal communities can be thought to exist not because of a lack of evidence, but rather because of the political aspects of educational policy making (López, 2012).

Except perhaps through student internships—termed "service learning"—in the government sector or in think tanks that do participate in state affairs, higher education institutions generally do not equip undergraduate or graduate students with the knowledge, skills, and predispositions that they need to have in order to be effective agents of change at these levels (Benneworth, 2013). Knowing how to pass, amend, or defeat legislation, for example, requires not only an array of specific kinds of skill sets, but also a particular kind of investment in, and understanding of, politics, power, and governmentality in order to be either reactive against or proactive toward harmful or constructive policy agendas, respectively (López, 2012). In short, we have theorized engaged policy as academic researchers putting their research-based knowledge to work within state policy-making arenas (Foley & Valenzuela, 2005; López, 2012; López et al., 2011).

In the context of teacher preparation, engaged policy focuses on providing teachers with historical and tangible understandings of the broad roles that they play in policy processes. Engaged policy brings to life the multiple, often competing, dimensions that embody policy as both text and processes (for elaboration, see López, 2012). Therefore, the act of interrogating conventional ideas of what is policy and placing an eye on decision-making bodies complements the knowledge generated either through our NLERAP curriculum or PAR projects that critically analyze issues that are impacting them and the students that they teach. This is an important contribution because it is not enough to know either what is wrong or to only address what is wrong at the microcontext of the classroom, school, or district level. If classrooms, schools, and districts are largely an artifact of state- and federal-level policy making, engaged policy helps to take us there.

Conclusion

Because teachers have to negotiate multiple realities in and out of the classroom, many of which are associated with external forces, it is important for them to see themselves as having a sense of responsibility and varied forms of agency that can lead to significant social change. The idea here is not for NLERAP's GYO teacher education institutes (TEI) teachers themselves to take our country "to a totally new place" as expressed by Vice President Biden, but rather for them to get the experience that they need in working with the community so that they can come to see themselves as integral to larger, historic, community-based emancipatory projects to which our teacher preparatory programs have heretofore mostly been incognizant. The latter is a consequence of historic institutional arrangements that exclude our communities' participation in teacher preparation as a matter of custom and norms, abetted by the role of the state through grant-science. By centering our GYO-TEI initiative in the community and not universities, NLERAP has effectively inaugurated a new set of institutional arrangements that not only disrupts institutionalized ways of knowing and doing business, but also breathes life into a new set of institutional arrangements that hold great promise for Latino/a students, their families, and communities. And to help the Latino/a community is to help our nation.

Notes

1. For example, with NLERAP's inaugural 2012–2013 cohort at California State University, Sacramento, all GYO students are placed at a partnering secondary school site from the onset. They will go through a practicum that will offer them a mentorship opportunity with a cooperating teacher where they will learn how to foster a safe and engaging classroom, as well as how to develop curricula in a progressive, sensible manner in ways that allow them to assume greater responsibilities over time. They will implement and make adjustments to curricula devised by members of the NLERAP Council that consist of a participatory action research approach that builds on, and extends, real-life, community-based efforts and concerns. GYO teachers are expected through this process to evolve into critically conscious agents of change with a community-anchored identity grounded in principles of social justice.
2. Area studies like Mexican American and African American studies are potentially important exceptions to this overall trend because of their unique histories of struggle as a consequence of community pressures and enduring constituencies.

References

Antrop-González, R. (2011). *Schools as radical sanctuaries: Decolonizing urban education through the eyes of youth of color and their teachers.* Charlotte, NC: IAP.

Ayala, J., Cammarota, J., Rivera, M., Rodriguez, & Berta-Avila, M.T. (unpublished manuscript). *Red Dawns of Hope: Developing a PAR Entremundos for Education with Latin@ Communities.*

Benneworth, P. (2013). *University engagement with socially excluded communities.* Dordrecht, The Netherlands: Springer Verlag.

Berta-Ávila, M., Tijerina Revilla, A., & López Figueroa, J. (2011). *Marching students: Chicana and Chicano activism in education, 1968 to the present.* Reno, NV: University of Nevada Press.

Cammarota, J. (2008). *Sueños Americanos: Barrio youth negotiating social and cultural identities.* Tucson, AZ: University of Arizona Press.

Casanova, U. (2010). *¡Sí se puede! Learning from a high school that beats the odds.* New York: Teachers College Press.

Conchas, G. Q., & Rodriguez, L. F. (2008). *Small schools and urban youth: Using the power of school culture to engage students.* Thousand Oaks, CA: Corwin Press.

Congressional Hispanic Caucus Institute Inc. (CHCI). (2013). Vice President Joe Biden joins CHCI swearing-in ceremony to welcome Hispanic members of the 113th Congress. Retrieved from www.chci.org/news/pub/vice-president-joe-biden-joins-chci-swearing-in-ceremony-to-welcome-hispanic-members-of-the-113th-congress-

Daza, S. L. (2013). A promiscuous (feminist) look at grant-science: How colliding imaginaries shape the practice of NSF policy. *International Journal of Qualitative Studies in Education, 26*(5), 580–598.

Flores, B. (2005). The intellectual presence of the deficit view of Spanish-speaking children in the educational literature during the 20th century. In P. Pedraza & M. Rivera (Eds.), *Latino education: An agenda for community action research.* Mahwah, NJ: Lawrence Erlbaum.

Flores-González, N. (2002). *School kids/street kids: Identity development in Latino students.* New York: Teachers College Press.

Foley, D. E., & Valenzuela, A. (2005). Critical ethnography: The politics of collaboration. In N. K. Denzin & Y. Lincoln (Eds.), *The Sage handbook of qualitative research* (3rd ed., pp. 217–234). Thousand Oaks, CA: Sage.

Freire, P. (1990). *Pedagogy of the oppressed.* New York: Continuum.

García, O., & Baetens, B. H. (2009). *Bilingual education in the 21st century: A global perspective.* Malden, MA: Wiley-Blackwell.

García, O., & Kleifgen, J. A. (2010). *Educating emergent bilinguals: Policies, programs, and practices for English language learners.* New York: Teachers College Press.

García, O., & Menken, K. (2010). Stirring the onion: Educators and the dynamics of education policies (looking ahead). In K. Menken & O. García (Eds.), *Negotiating language policies in schools: Educators as policymakers* (pp. 249–261). New York: Routledge.

hooks, b. (1994). *Teaching to transgress: Education as the practice of freedom.* New York: Routledge.

Irizarry, J. G. (2011). *The Latinization of U.S. schools: Successful teaching and learning in shifting cultural contexts.* Boulder, CO: Paradigm.

Lather, P. (2004). Scientific research in education: A critical perspective. *British Educational Research Journal, 30*(6), 759–772.

Lindquist Wong, P., & Glass, R. D. (Eds.). (2009). *Prioritizing urban children, teachers, and schools through professional development schools.* Albany, NY: State University of New York Press.

López, P. D. (2012). *The process of becoming: The political construction of Texas' lone STAAR system of accountability and college readiness* (Doctoral dissertation). University of Texas at Austin, Austin, TX.

López, P. D., & Valenzuela, A. (forthcoming). Resisting epistemological exclusion and inserting La Clase Mágica into state-level policy discourses.

López, P. D., Valenzuela, A., & Garcia, E. (2011). The critical ethnography for public policy. In B. A. Levinson & M. Pollock (Eds.), *Companion to the anthropology of education* (pp. 547–563). Malden, MA: Blackwell.

Mercado, C. I., & Brochin-Ceballos, C. (2011). Growing quality teachers: Community-oriented preparation. In B. Flores, R. H. Sheets, & E. R. Clark (Eds.), *Teacher preparation for bilingual student populations: Educar para transformar* (pp. 217–229). New York: Taylor & Francis/Routledge.

Moll, L. C., Amanti, C., Neff, D., & Gonzalez, N. (1992). Funds of knowledge for teaching: Using a qualitative approach to connect homes and classrooms. *Theory into Practice, 31*(2), 132–141.

Nieto, S. (2003). Identity, personhood, and Puerto Rican students: Challenging paradigms of assimilation and authenticity. *Scholar-Practitioner Quarterly, 1*(1), 41–62.

Nieto, S. (2005). Schools for a new majority: The role of teacher education in hard times. *New Educator, 1*(1), 27–43.

Nieto, S., Rivera, M. & Quiñones, S. (guest eds.) (2012). Charting a new course: Understanding the sociocultural, political, economic and historical context of Latino/a education in the United States. *[Special Issue] AMAE: Association of Mexican American Educators 6*(3).

Nieto, S. (2013). Latino/as and the elusive quest for equal education. In B. Flores & R. Roslado (Eds.), *A companion to Latina/o studies.* Malden, MA: Blackwell.

Noguera, P. (2007). "¿Y qué pasará con jóvenes como Miguel Fernández?" Education, immigration, and the future of Latinas/os in the United States. In J. Flores & R. Rosaldo (Eds.), *A companion to Latina/o studies* (pp. 202–216). Malden, MA: Blackwell.

Olivos, E. M., Jiménez-Castellanos, O., & Ochoa, A. M. (Eds.). (2011). *Critical voices in bicultural parent engagement: Advocacy and empowerment.* New York: Teachers College Press.

Pedraza, P., & Rivera, M. (Eds.). (2005). *Latino/a education: An agenda for research and advocacy.* Mahwah, NJ: Lawrence Erlbaum.

Reyes, P., Scribner, J. D., & Paredes Scribner, A. (Eds.). (1999). *Lessons from high-performing Hispanic schools: Creating learning communities.* New York: Teachers College Press.

Rivera, M., Medellin-Paz, C., & Pedraza, P. (with El Puente Academy for Peace and Justice). (2010). *Imagination for the imagined nation: A creative justice approach to human development.* New York: Ford Foundation.

Romo, H., & Falbo, T. (1996). *Latino high school graduation: Defying the odds.* Austin, TX: University of Texas Press.

Solorzano, D. G., & Delgado Bernal, D. (2001). Examining transformational resistance through a critical race and LatCrit theory framework: Chicana and Chicano students in an urban context. *Urban Education, 36*(3), 308–342.

Spivak, G. C. (1985). Three women's texts and a critique of imperialism. *Critical Inquiry, 12*(1), 243–261.

Torre, M. E. (2009). Participatory action research and critical race theory: Fueling spaces for nos-otras to research. *Urban Review, 41*(1), 106–120.

Valenzuela, A. (1999). *Subtractive schooling: U.S.-Mexican youth and the politics of caring.* Albany, NY: State University of New York Press.

Valenzuela, A. (2004). *Leaving children behind: Why Texas-style accountability fails Latino youth.* Albany, NY: State University of New York Press.

Valenzuela, A., & Maxcy, B. (2011). Limited English proficient youth and accountability: All children (who are tested) count. In D. L. Leal & K. J. Meier (Eds.), *The politics of Latino education.* New York: Teachers College Press.

Villegas, A. M. (2007). *Profile of new Hispanic teachers in U.S. public schools: Looking at issues of quantity and quality.* Paper presented at the Annual Meeting of the American Education Research Association (AERA), Chicago, IL.

Children of Immigrants in Schools—Global and U.S. Policy Research

4

IMMIGRATION AND THE AMERICAN SCHOOL SYSTEM

The Second Generation at the Crossroads[1]

Alejandro Portes

The rapid growth of the immigrant populations in the United States and Western Europe represents one of the most important demographic and social phenomena confronting these societies. Close to 13 percent of the U.S. population today is foreign born. In 2010, 1 million were admitted for legal permanent residence, and another 73,000 as refugees. Although the flow of unauthorized immigration slowed down in the wake of the economic crises beginning in 2007, the resident unauthorized population approaches, according to the best estimates, 11 million (Office of Immigrant Statistics, 2011; Passel, 2009).

Among the most important social consequences of this large immigrant flow are the reconstitution of families divided by migration and the procreation of a new generation. Unlike adult immigrants, who are born and educated in a foreign society and whose outlook and plans are indelibly marked by that experience, the children of immigrants commonly become full-fledged members of the host society with outlooks and plans of their own. If their numbers are large, socializing these new citizens and preparing them to become productive and successful in adulthood becomes a major policy concern.

Although public discourse and some academic essays treat this young population in blanket terms, the truth is that the term *migrant children* conceals more than it reveals because of the heterogeneity of its component groups. First, there is a significant difference between children born abroad and those born in the host society. The former are immigrant children, whereas the latter are children of immigrants—the first and second immigrant generations, respectively. Research points to major differences in the social and cultural adaptation of the two groups (Rumbaut, 2004). Another distinct group, the "1.5 generation," includes children born abroad but brought to the host society at an early age, making them sociologically closer to the second generation. These young immigrants also differ by their countries of origin and their socioeconomic background. It turns out, though, that the two characteristics overlap to a large degree because immigration to the United States has divided into two streams. One is made up of highly skilled professional workers coming to fill positions in high-tech industry, research centers, and health services. The other is a larger manual-labor flow seeking employment in labor-intensive industries such as agriculture, construction, and personal services (A. Portes & Rumbaut, 2006).

Professional migration, greatly aided by passage of the H1-B program by Congress in 1990, comes primarily from Asia, mainly from India and China, with smaller tributaries from the Philippines, South Korea, and Taiwan. Manual labor migration comes overwhelmingly from adjacent Mexico, and secondarily from other countries of Central America and the Caribbean. To the disadvantages attached to their low skills and education are added those of a tenuous legal status, as many of these migrants have come surreptitiously or with short-term visas (A. Portes & Rumbaut, 2006).

To the extent that migrant workers, either professional or manual, return promptly to their countries of origin, no major consequences accrue to the host society. In reality, however, many of them, professionals and manual workers, stay and either bring their families or create new families where they settle. Over time, the divide in the major sources of contemporary migration has given rise to two distinct pan-ethnic populations in the United States—"Asian Americans," by and large the offspring of high-human-capital migrants, and "Hispanics," the majority of whom are manual workers, and their descendants (Massey, 1998; Massey, Durand, & Malone, 2002; A. Portes & Fernández-Kelly, 2008). Vast differences in the human-capital origins of these populations and in the way they are received in the United States translate into significant disparities in the resources available to families and ethnic communities to raise a new generation in America. Naturally, the outcomes in acculturation and social and economic adaptation vary accordingly.

Theoretical Perspectives on the Future of the Second Generation

Past research into this bourgeoning population has shown that a conventional assimilation model based on a unilinear process of acculturation followed by social and economic ascent and integration does not work well in depicting what takes place on the ground. Instead, several distinct paths of adaptation have been identified, some of which lead upward as portrayed by the conventional assimilation model; other paths, however, lead in the opposite direction, compounding the spectacle of poverty, drugs, and gangs in the nation's cities. *Segmented assimilation* is the concept coined to refer to these realities. This alternative model has both charted the main alternative path of contemporary second-generation adaptation and identified the main forces at play in that process (A. Portes & Fernández-Kelly,

2008; A. Portes & Zhou, 1993). Specifically, three major factors have been identified: the human capital that immigrant parents bring with them, the social context in which they are received in America, and the composition of the immigrant family.

Human capital, operationally identified with formal education and occupational skills, translates into competitiveness in the host labor market and the potential for achieving desirable positions in the American hierarchies of status and wealth. The transformation of this potential into reality depends, however, on the context into which immigrants are incorporated. A receptive or at least neutral reception by government authorities, a sympathetic or at least not hostile reception by the native population, and the existence of social networks with well-established coethnics pave the ground for putting to use whatever credentials and skills have been brought from abroad. Conversely, a hostile reception by authorities and the public, and a weak or nonexistent coethnic community handicap immigrants and make it difficult for them to translate their human capital into commensurate occupations or to acquire new occupational skills. *Mode of incorporation* is the concept used in the literature to refer to these tripartite (government/society/community) differences in the contexts that receive newcomers (A. Portes & Fernández-Kelly, 2008; A. Portes & Zhou, 1993). Lastly, the structure of the immigrant family has also proved to be highly significant in determining second-generation outcomes. Parents who stay together and extended families where grandparents and older siblings play a role in motivating and controlling adolescents, keeping them away from the lure of gangs and drugs, play a significant role in promoting upward assimilation. Single-parent families experiencing conflicting demands and unable to provide children with proper supervision have exactly the opposite effect (A. Portes & Rumbaut, 2006; Rumbaut, 2004). Figure 4.1 graphically summarizes this discussion by outlining both the discrete paths and the key determinants of segmented assimilation.

Preliminary Evidence

As noted previously, one of the principal characteristics of contemporary immigration to the United States is that, unlike the European flows at the start of the 20th century, the present ones are bifurcated into highly skilled professional immigrants coming to fill engineering, programming, medical, and other occupations in high demand at the top of the labor market and unskilled manual workers coming to fill low-wage labor needs in agriculture, construction, personal services, and other sectors. Differences in immigrant human capital and modes of incorporation translate, in turn, into monthly earnings, annual incomes, and occupational status. Professional-level occupations are rare among Mexicans, Haitians, and Southeast Asians because of very low human capital, but they are common among Filipinos, Chinese, and Cubans. Income figures follow a similar pattern with the same three nationalities at the top and Mexicans and Haitians at the bottom.

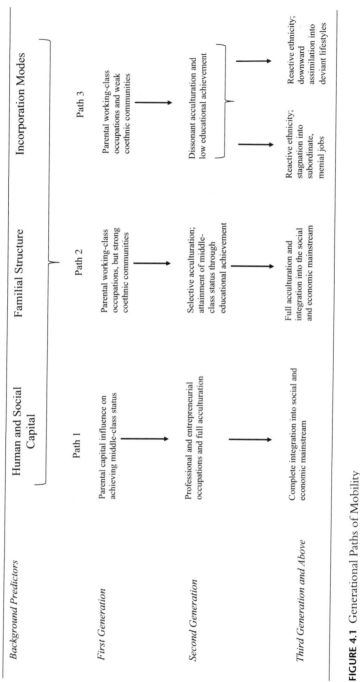

FIGURE 4.1 Generational Paths of Mobility

Adapted from Portes and Fernández-Kelly (2008).

Despite very low average education, Southeast Asians are not particularly disadvantaged in terms of income, a result that reflects their favorable mode of incorporation as refugees from communist regimes who had access to a series of government benefits. These differences among first generation immigrants go on to determine the patterns of adaptation in the second generation (A. Portes & Rumbaut, 2006; Rumbaut, 2004). Two main data sources for the evaluation of these adult outcomes exist. The first is based on a combination of decennial census and quarterly Current Population Survey (CPS) data. The second source is one of the few longitudinal studies conducted so far on the second and higher generations.

One of the pivotal studies based on publicly available census data was conducted by Rumbaut, who used 2000 census data for the foreign-born population and adjusted results on the basis of combined 1998–2002 CPS data to yield estimates for the second generation. Thus defined, the foreign-born population of the United States in 2000 numbered 33.1 million, and the second generation 27.7 million. Some 40 percent of the foreign born arrived in the United States as children under 18 (Rumbaut, 2005). Table 4.1 summarizes the extensive tables constructed by Rumbaut on the basis of these data for the foreign born who arrived as children (under 18) and the native born of foreign parentage—the second generation "proper." The table includes data for three major Latin American national origin groups, including Mexicans, three Asian groups, and, for purposes of comparison, native-parentage Whites and Blacks of the same age cohort.

Results of the Rumbaut study can be summarized as follows. First, all national origin groups make significant progress from the first to the second generation in educational attainment, with second-generation outcomes approaching average outcomes for native Whites. Second, although all national origin groups make educational progress, second-generation Mexicans and Central Americans fall significantly behind native Whites in rates of high school completion and college graduation. Second-generation Cubans are even with Whites, and all Asian national origin groups exceed native-White educational averages in both the first and second generations. Third, male incarceration rates increase for all national origin groups between the first and second generations. Mexican incarceration rates increase the most, and all Latin American second-generation rates significantly exceed the native-White figure. By contrast, Asian incarceration rates are very low in both the first and second generations. Fourth, female fertility rates in adolescence and early adulthood decline across generations for all Latin national origin groups, but they decline least among Mexican Americans. Mexican fertility rates far exceed those of native-White females and are even higher than the native-Black figures, which are the next highest. Fifth, Asian fertility rates are extremely low and decline further between generations. Both rates represent but a fraction of the native-White figures.

As a whole, these findings from the Rumbaut study are congruent with the segmented-assimilation hypothesis. The main source of longitudinal data for

TABLE 4.1 Outcomes of Assimilation across Generations (%)

| | | | | | | | National Origin | | | | | |
| | | | | | Latin American Origin | | | Asian Origin | | | Native Parentage | |
Outcome	Generation			All Children of Immigrants	Cuban	Guatemalan/Salvadoran	Mexican	Chinese	Indian	Korean	Non-Hispanic White	African American (Non-Hispanic)
Education	Foreign Born[1]	High School Dropout	%	31.4	16.9	53.1	61.4	9	6.7	3.2	n/a	n/a
		College Graduate	%	23.2	22.9	6.4	4.3	58	59.4	59.6	n/a	n/a
	Native Born[2]	High School Dropout	%	11.6	9.1	22.5	24.1	3.6	5.9	3.2	9.1	19.3
		College Graduate	%	27.3	36.7	23.8	13	72.5	72	69.4	30.7	14.1
Male Incarceration Rate[3]	Foreign Born[1]		%	1.25	2.79	0.75	0.95	0.3	0.29	0.38	n/a	n/a
	Native Born[2]		%	3.5	4.2	3.04	5.8	0.65	0.99	0.94	1.71	11.61
Female Fertility Rate[4] **Ages**	Foreign Born[1]	15–19	%	3.3	2.3	4.5	5.5	0.3	0.7	0.5	n/a	n/a
		20–24	%	19.7	18.1	22.9	30.2	1.9	4.3	3.9	n/a	n/a
	Native Born[2]	15–19	%	2.6	1.8	3	5	0.4	0.36	0.2	1.9	4.5
		20–24	%	17.4	11.4	16.5	25.2	0.9	1.6	2.8	15.6	22.5

[1] Adults aged 25–39, restricted to those who arrived in the United States as children under 18.

[2] Adults aged 25–39. Data are for individuals with at least one foreign-born parent.

[3] Adult males, aged 18–39, in correctional facilities at the time of the 2000 census.

[4] Females of the indicated ages who had one or more children at the time of the 2000 census.

Data Source: 2000 U.S. Census. Table adapted from Portes and Fernández-Kelly (2008).

evaluating adult outcomes is the Children of Immigrants Longitudinal Study (CILS) conducted between 1992 and 2002 (A. Portes & Rumbaut, 2001). CILS followed a sample of more than 5,200 children of immigrants from early adolescence to early adulthood, interviewing them at three key points of their life cycle: in junior high school, at average age 14; just prior to high school graduation (or dropping out of school), at average age 17; and at the beginning of their work careers (or continuing schooling), at average age 24. Each sample wave retrieved approximately 85 percent of the preceding one. The latest wave produced data on 3,564 respondents, or 68 percent of the original sample. Using data from the baseline survey, it was possible to develop a predictive equation of "presence/absence" in the following ones. Results presented next have been corrected for sample mortality using the Heckman method based on this equation.

Table 4.2 presents results of the last CILS survey on indicators of different adaptation paths. These include educational achievement, employment, income, premature childbearing, and incidents of arrest and incarceration. The table divides the large Cuban American sample according to whether respondents attended public schools or the private bilingual schools set up by exiles arriving in the 1960s and 1970s. Public school Cuban Americans are mostly the offspring of refugees who arrived during the chaotic 1980 Mariel exodus or afterward, whose levels of human capital were significantly lower than the earlier upper- and middle-class exiles and who experienced a much more negative context of reception in the United States. Of all the groups included in the CILS sample, Cubans are the only one to have gone from a positive to a negative mode of incorporation, marked by the Mariel exodus and its aftermath.

Although variations among second-generation nationalities in average educational attainment were minor, those relating to dropout rates or quitting study after high school were not. In South Florida, youths who failed to pursue their studies beyond high school ranged from a low of 7.5 percent among middle-class Cubans to a high of 26 percent among Nicaraguans. Public school Cuban Americans did much worse in this dimension than their better-off compatriots.

In Southern California, Chinese and other Asians had extraordinary levels of educational achievement, whereas close to 40 percent of second-generation Mexicans and Laotian/Cambodians failed to advance beyond high school. A favorable context of reception for Southeast Asians proved insufficient to overcome the heavy educational deficiencies of the first generation. The proportion of second-generation Laotians and Cambodians with more than a high school education was not significantly higher than among their parents (see Table 4.1). Mexican Americans, on the other hand, advanced significantly beyond the parental generation. Their below-average achievements relative to other nationalities reflect the very low family educational levels from which they started (Haller, A. Portes, & Lynch, 2011; A. Portes, Fernández-Kelly, & Haller, 2009).

Family incomes follow these differences closely. In South Florida, middle-class Cuban Americans enjoyed a median family income of more than US$70,000 and

TABLE 4.2 Key Second-Generation Adaptation Outcomes in Early Childhood, 2002–2003

Outcomes		South Florida National Origin							Southern California National Origin						
		Colombian	Cuban (Private School)	Cuban (Public School)	Haitian	Nicaraguan	West Indian	Other	Cambodian	Chinese	Filipino	Mexican	Vietnamese	Other (Asian)	Other (Latin American)
Education	Average Years	14.49	15.32	14.32	14.44	14.17	14.63	14.55	13.3	15.4	14.5	13.4	14.9	15.2	14.4
	High School or Less (%)	17	7.5	21.7	15.3	26.4	18.1	20.8	45.9	5.7	15.5	38	12.6	9.1	25.5
Language	Prefers Language Other than English (%)	2	1.5	1.8	5.2	2.7	0		3.8	0	0.3	6.5	0.5	2.3	4.3
	Prefers English Only (%)	64.9	72.5	62.7	63.5	61.8	90.8		43.2	74.3	90.2	37.9	56.1	86.4	65.2
Incarceration Rate	Total (%)	6	2.9	5.6	7.1	4.4	8.5	4.9	4.3	0	3.9	10.8	7.8	6.7	6.4
	Males (%)	10.4	3.4	10.5	14.3	9.9	20	8.3	9.5	0	6.8	20.2	14.6	9.5	18.8
Family Income (US$)	Mean	58,339	104,767	60,816	34,506	54,049	40,654	59,719	34,615	57,583	64,442	38,254	44,717	58,659	43,476
	Median	45,948	70,395	48,598	26,974	47,054	30,326	40,619	25,179	33,611	55,323	32,585	34,868	40,278	31,500
Unemployment Rate (%)[1]		2.6	3	6.2	16.7	4.9	9.4	7.3	9.3	2.9	7.8	7.3	13.9	4.5	2.2
Has Children (%)		16.6	3	17.7	24.2	20.1	24.3	16.4	25.4	0	19.4	41.5	9	11.4	15.2
n (Total = 3,324)		150	133	670	95	222	148	404	186	35	586	408	194	46	47

[1] Respondents without jobs, whether looking or not looking for employment, except those still enrolled in school.

Data Source: CILS, third survey. Table adapted from Portes and Fernández-Kelly (2008).

mean incomes more than US$104,000, whereas second-generation West Indians had median incomes of just above US$30,000, and Haitians even less. Approximately one-third of these mostly Black groups had annual incomes of US$20,000 or less. In California, similar differences separate second-generation Chinese, Filipinos, and other Asian Americans with average incomes above US$57,000 from Mexicans and Laotian/Cambodians with mean incomes in the mid-30s. Median incomes of these Southeast Asian refugee families were the lowest in the sample.

The dictum that the rich get richer and the poor get children is supported by figures in Table 4.2. Only 3 percent of middle-class Cuban Americans had children by early adulthood. The figure is exactly 0 percent for Chinese Americans. The rate then rises to about 10 percent for the Vietnamese; more than 15 percent for Colombians, public school Cubans, and Filipinos; 25 percent among Haitians, West Indians, Laotians, and Cambodians; and a remarkable 41 percent among Mexican Americans. Hence, the second-generation groups with the lowest education and incomes were those most burdened, at an early age, by the need to support children.

Still more compelling are differences in incidents of arrest and incarceration. Young males are far more likely than young females to be arrested and to find themselves behind bars. Yet, among Chinese males in the CILS sample, no one did so, and among middle-class Cubans, just 3 percent did. The rate then climbs to 1 in 10 among Laotian Cambodians and other Latinos in Florida. 18 percent among Salvadorans and other Latinos in California, and a full 20 percent among West Indians and Mexicans. To put these figures into perspective, they can be compared with the nationwide rate of incarcerated African American males, ages 18 to 40, which is 26.6 percent (Western, 2002; Western, Beckett, & Harding, 1998). With another 16 years to go on average, it is quite likely that second-generation Mexicans, Salvadorans, and West Indians will match or surpass the African American figure.

This is the most tangible evidence of segmented assimilation in the second generation available to date. It shows the durable effects of family and contextual characteristics as they create paths of advantage and disadvantage among children of immigrants. Events indicative of downward assimilation are neither scarce nor random because they concentrate disproportionately among the offspring of poor and poorly received nationalities. Poignant as these results are, they prompt additional questions bearing on theories of immigrant adaptation and on policies toward the second generation. We will turn to these issues in later sections.

Multivariate Findings

Figures 4.2, 4.3, and 4.4 summarize findings from the CILS third survey showing determinants of educational and occupational achievement in early adulthood, as well as events indicative of downward or upward assimilation. For this purpose, a composite scale was built on the basis of all events reported in Table 4.2. Low scores in this index reflect a higher incidence of downward assimilation events (Haller et al., 2011).

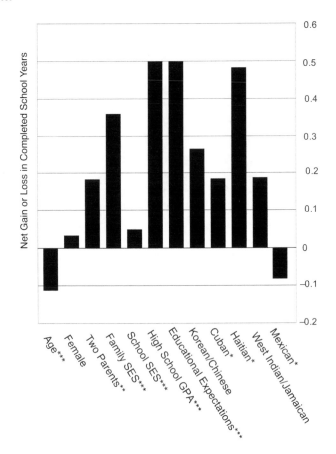

FIGURE 4.2 Determinants of Educational Attainment of Children of Immigrants in Early Adulthood, 2002–2003

Findings from Figures 4.2–4.4 can be summarized in four main points. First, significant and nonrandom differences across second-generation national origin groups generally correspond with the known profile of the first generation in terms of human capital and also the way in which they were received in the United States. Second, good early school grades and positive early educational expectations significantly increase educational attainment and occupational status while preventing downward assimilation. Third, having higher-status parents and being raised by both natural parents also raise educational levels and powerfully inhibit downward assimilation. Fourth, even after controlling for parental variables and early school context and outcomes, there are still differences among national origin groups, especially those associated with a disadvantaged upbringing. Mexican American youths, for example, have a net 19 percent greater chance of experiencing events associated with downward assimilation; the figure rises to

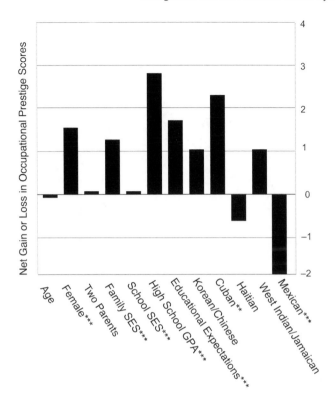

FIGURE 4.3 Determinants of Occupational Attainment of Children of Immigrants in Early Adulthood, 2002–2003

33 percent among second-generation Haitians and to 46 percent among Jamaicans and other West Indians.

Findings in Figures 4.2–4.4 are uncorrected for attrition. Separate analyses showed that mortality for the sample in the final CILS survey was predicted mainly by low family socioeconomic status (SES) and single-parent families—the same two factors that also lower achievement and raise the incidence of downward assimilation. Correcting for sample attrition in these regressions would just inflate the follow-up sample and lead to less rigorous tests of significance of multivariate coefficients.

A second source of longitudinal data in this field is the survey of Mexican Americans across five generations conducted by Telles and Ortiz (2008). Although findings are limited to a single national origin group, they go beyond earlier studies in tracing how the assimilation process unfolds *after* the second generation. The fundamental, and disturbing, finding of this study is that, although there is educational progress between the first and second generations, subsequent generations stagnate educationally and occupationally. They never catch up with the native-White averages.

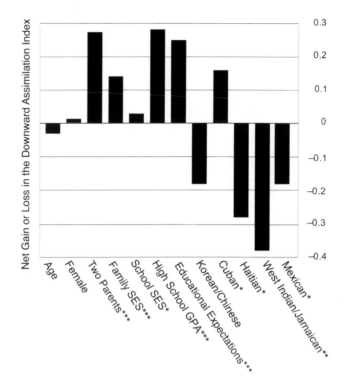

FIGURE 4.4 Determinants of Upward Assimilation among Children of Immigrants in Early Adulthood, 2002–2003

For instance, the odds that the Mexican high school graduation rate would equal the White high school graduation rate rise from only 0.06 among first-generation immigrants to 0.58 among their second-generation children, but then decline to 0.30 among members of the fourth and fifth generations. (Odds less than 1 indicate a lower probability than Whites; 0.58 indicates that second-generation Mexicans are 0.58 to 1 as likely to graduate from high school as Whites.) The odds of achieving a college degree follow a similar course—from 0.12 in the immigrant generation to 0.28 in the second, declining again to 0.12 in the fourth and higher generations (Telles & Ortiz, 2008).

After examining a number of possible determinants of this persistent handicap, Telles and Ortiz (2008) pin primary responsibility on the "racialization" of Mexican American children, who are stereotyped by teachers and school authorities as inferior to White and Asian students and treated accordingly. This treatment becomes a self-fulfilling prophecy, as Mexican-origin youths close ranks to defend themselves against discrimination, abandoning aspirations for high academic achievement and coming to reject members of their own group who retain such aspirations.

Telles and Ortiz (2008) summarize the Mexican experience as follows:

> The signals and racial stereotypes that educators and society send to students affect the extent to which they will engage and persist in school. Racial stereotypes produce a positive self-identity for white and Asian students but a negative one for blacks and Latinos, which affect school success. Racial self-perceptions among Mexican American students generally, endure into the third and fourth generations. (p. 132)

No Margin for Error: Common Trends in Overcoming Disadvantage

Sociology deals with social facts, expressed in rates or averages, rather than with individuals. There are times, however, when the study of individual cases can say something important about how social outcomes come about or about how they can be modified. Segmented assimilation in the second generation offers a case in point. The structural forces leading to alternative paths of adaptation are clear and have been well documented. Yet, not all children advantaged by their parents' human capital, favorable contexts of reception, and stable families manage to succeed educationally, and not all growing up under conditions of severe disadvantage end up in permanent poverty or in jail. Some among the latter may even make it to the top, achieving a college degree and moving into the professional ranks. If this were the case, these individual instances would have sociological significance for the lessons that they could offer in how to overcome the power of structural forces. Put differently, exceptions and outliers are important insofar as they point to alternative social processes, obscured in sample averages, that when present can lead to unanticipated outcomes.

CILS is a uniquely suitable data source to address this issue. Because of its large sample size and longitudinal character, it is possible to identify within it a large number of children who grew up in highly disadvantageous conditions. In agreement with the previous discussion, these can be operationally defined as: (1) very low family SES, (2) a negative context of reception, and (3) a single-parent family. Attending an inner-city, low-SES school in early adolescence is another factor compounding these disadvantages, but, on average, such attendance is highly collinear with low parental SES and context of reception, sending us back to the original determinants.

We may thus ask whether any member of the original sample falling into this category managed to overcome such handicaps to graduate from college and enter graduate school or a professional career. Data from the final CILS follow-up can answer that question. From the 1992–1993 sample of 5,262 cases, we were able to identify only 50 cases of individuals who managed to overcome significant disadvantages in early adolescence to reach college and get their degrees. The number alone is a telling result—less than 1 percent of the original sample. Because these individuals had answered follow-up questionnaires in 2002–2003, it was relatively straightforward to locate most of them again through Internet-assisted searches (A. Portes & Fernández-Kelly, 2008).

When approached, most respondents agreed to cooperate, not surprising given the purpose of the interview: to learn more about reasons for their educational and occupational success. Whenever possible, parents and spouses were also interviewed. CILS cases were supplemented with interviews with additional respondents identified as representative of similar life trajectories in the course of fieldwork. In total, 61 interviews were completed. In this final section, I present and illustrate with narratives four of the common trends found in this extraordinary sample.

Stern Families, Selective Acculturation

The child-rearing and educational psychology literatures in the United States have converged in preaching to parents a tolerant, patient, nonauthoritarian attitude toward their offspring, and in promoting openness to new experiences and intensive socializing among the young. In parallel fashion, schools and other mainstream institutions pressure immigrants and their children to acculturate as fast as possible, viewing their full Americanization as a step forward toward economic mobility and social acceptance (Goyette & Xie, 1999; Hirschman, 2001; Perreira, Harris, & Lee, 2006).

Not really. A *leitmotif* in our interviews was the presence of strong and stern parental figures who controlled, if not suppressed, extensive external contacts and who sought to preserve the cultural and linguistic traditions in which they themselves were reared. Talking back to such parents is not an option, and physical punishment is a distinct possibility when parental authority is challenged. These family environments have the effect of isolating children from much of what is going on outside: they are expected to go to school and return home with few distractions in between. Although such rearing practices will be surely frowned upon by many educational psychologists, they have the effect of protecting children from the perils of street life in their immediate surroundings and of keeping them in touch with their cultural roots.

In other words, while freedom to explore and tolerant parental attitudes may work well in protected suburban environments, they do not have the same effect in poor urban neighborhoods where what there is to "explore" is frequently linked to the presence of gangs and the drug trade. In addition, and contrary to conventional wisdom, full Americanization has the effect of disconnecting youths from their parents and depriving them of a cultural reference point on which to ground their sense of self and their personal dignity. As we shall see, this reference point is also an important component of these success stories.

Maintenance of parental authority and strong family discipline have the effect of inducing *selective acculturation*, as opposed to the full-barreled variety advocated by public schools and other mainstream institutions. Selective acculturation combines learning of English and American ways with preservation of key elements of the parental culture, including language. Previous studies also based on CILS data show that fluent bilingualism is significantly associated with a series of positive outcomes in late adolescence, including higher school grades, higher educational aspirations, higher self-esteem, and lesser intergenerational conflict (A. Portes & Rumbaut, 2001). This final set of interviews confirms the finding, indicating that instances of success out of disadvantage are almost invariably undergirded by strong parental controls leading to selective acculturation. The following narrative illustrates this first common characteristic, while ushering in a second and third.

First Narrative: Raquel Torres, Mexican, Aged 29, San Diego, 2008 (A. Portes & Fernández-Kelly, 2008).[2]

Raquel is the oldest daughter of a Mexican couple who immigrated illegally to San Diego after living for years in Tijuana. The mother has a ninth-grade education and did not work while her three children were growing up; the father has a sixth-grade education. While living in Tijuana, he commuted to San Diego to work as a waiter. At some point, his commuter permit was taken away, and the family simply decided to sneak across the border. They settled in National City, a poor and mostly Mexican neighborhood where Raquel grew up monolingual in Spanish. As the result of her limited English fluency, she had problems at El Toyon Elementary, but she was enrolled in a bilingual training program where children were pulled out of classes for intensive English training. "My teachers were wonderful," she says.

It was while attending elementary school that she noticed how poor her family really was. She wanted jeans, tennis shoes, and popular toys that she saw other children having, but her parents said no. "*No tenemos dinero*" (we don't have any money), they responded. On the other hand, discipline at home was stern: "My parents, they brought us up very strict, very traditional, there was no argument; you just got the look and knew better than to insist." In middle school, she made contact with Achievement via Individual Determination (AVID). While she was still struggling with English, AVID provided her with a college student as a tutor and took her on field trips to San Diego State University. "It was a fabulous field trip; we were paired up with other students and sat in class. Mine was on biology. Still, I hadn't thought of going to college."

The decisive moment came in her first year at Sweetwater Senior High in National City after she enrolled in Mr. Carranza's French class. Carranza, a Mexican American himself and a Vietnam veteran, took a keen interest in his students. "I mean, it wasn't so much the French that he taught, but he would also bring Chicano poetry, and, within the first month, I remember he asked me, 'Where are you going to college?'" At Open House that year, Carranza took her mother aside and asked, "*Usted sabe que su hija es muy inteligente?*" (Do you know that your daughter is very intelligent?) "*De veras, mi hija?*" (Really, my daughter?) answered the mother. "Yes," he said, "she can go to college." "All of a sudden, everything made sense to me; I was going to college."

Raquel graduated with a 3.5 grade point average (GPA) from Sweetwater and applied and was admitted at the University of California, San Diego (UCSD). At the time, her family had moved to Las Vegas in search of work, but Raquel wanted to be on her own. She had clearly outgrown her parents who, at this time, had started to be an obstacle. "When I was studying late at night in senior high, my mother would come and turn off the light. She would say, 'Go to sleep, you'll go blind reading so much.'" Raquel entered UCSD in the last year of the Affirmative Action Program in California. As a result, she got some lip from several fellow students who criticized her for getting an unfair advantage. But she strongly defends the program: "Without Affirmative Action, I probably would not have made it into UCSD. Besides, the Program made me work harder. Other students took their education for granted and didn't study as much, instead going to parties and fooling around."

Raquel graduated from UCSD with a 3.02 GPA and immediately enrolled in a master's program in education at San Diego State. After graduating, she took a job as a counselor in the Barrio Logan College Institute, another private organization helping minority students like herself attend college. She is currently planning to enroll in a doctoral program in education. Her advice for immigrant students: "Stop making excuses; there's always going to be family drama, there's always going to be many issues. But it's what you want to do that matters."

Really Significant Others; Outside Help

Despite these "where there's a will, there's a way," parting words, it is clear that Raquel moved ahead by receiving assistance in multiple ways. First, the stern traditional upbringing noted previously kept her out of trouble, although it set her back in English. Her own selective acculturation had to be nudged along by those "wonderful" teachers at El Toyon Elementary. Then, she encountered the AVID program, which provided her with personalized educational assistance and the first inklings of what college life would be like. Finally, she encountered Carranza, and her future took a decisive turn. The French teacher did not ask *whether* she was going to college, but *what* college she would attend. The fact that he was a coethnic and brought "Chicano poetry" to class surely helped. He went beyond motivating her to recruit the mother in order to support Raquel's new aspirations. Stern immigrant parents may instill discipline and self-control in their children, but they are often helpless in the face of school bureaucracies.

A constant in our interviews, in addition to authoritative and alert parents, is the appearance of a *really* significant other. That person can be a teacher, a counselor, a friend of the family, or even an older sibling. The important thing is that they take a keen interest in the child, motivate him or her to graduate from high school and attend college, and possess the necessary knowledge and experience to guide the student in this direction. Neither family discipline nor the appearance of a significant other is, by itself, sufficient to produce high educational attainment in children, but their *combination* is commonly decisive.

The second element that Raquel's story illustrates is the important role of organized programs sponsored by nonprofits to assist disadvantaged students. Whether it is AVID, the PREUSS Program (also organized by UCSD), Latinas Unidas, the Barrio Logan College Institute, or other philanthropic groups, they can play a key supplementary role by conveying information that parents do not possess: how to fill out a college application, how to prepare for SATs and when to take them, how to present oneself in interviews, how college campuses look and what college life is like, and so forth.

This finding is important because the creation and support of such programs is within the power of external actors and can be strengthened by policy. Although the character of family life or the emergence of a significant other is largely in the private realm, the presence and effectiveness of special assistance programs for minority students is a public matter amenable to policy intervention. The programs and organizations that proved effective were grounded, invariably, on knowledge of the culture and language that the children themselves brought to school and on respect for them. They are commonly staffed by coethnics or bilingual staff. Unlike the full-barreled assimilation approach emphasized by most school personnel, these programs convey the message that it is not necessary to reject one's own culture in order to do well in school. On the contrary, such roots can provide the necessary point of reference to strengthen the children's self-esteem and their aspirations for the future. In that sense, AVID and similar voluntary programs both depend on and promote selective acculturation as the best natural path toward educational achievement.

Second Narrative: Martin Lacayo, Nicaraguan, Aged 29, Miami, 2008 (A. Portes and Fernández-Kelly, 2008).

Martin's mother, Violeta, was a business woman in her native Nicaragua until the Sandinista regime confiscated her properties. His father was a professional and, for a time, mayor of the city of Jinotega. The Sandinistas jailed him as a counterrevolutionary, and he left prison a broken man. When Violeta made the decision to leave the country to escape conscription of her sons in the Sandinista army, the father refused to leave. Violeta managed to send her two oldest sons to Miami in the care of relatives. She then used her last savings to buy tickets to Mexico City for Martin and herself. They then traveled by land to the border and crossed illegally with the help of two "coyotes" (smugglers).

Arriving in Miami, they found themselves without money, without knowledge of the language, and without access to government help because of their illegal status. To survive, Violeta started cleaning houses for wealthy Cuban families. They rented an apartment in the modest suburb of Sweetwater, and Martin enrolled in the local junior high school. Having studied in the private Catholic La Salle School in Jinotega, he found the *One Potato, Two Potato* book he was assigned to read offensive. "It seemed that the teacher wanted us all to go work at the Burger King," Martin said.

At Sweetwater Junior High, he finally came under the protection of Mrs. Robinson, an African American teacher who took interest in the boy. She managed to have him receive a "Student of the Week" award, and his picture was displayed prominently in the school's office. That meant the world to Martin, who had never received any distinction in the United States. The family eventually regularized their legal status under the new NACARA law, engineered by Miami Cuban American congressmen for Nicaraguan refugees. Violeta found a job as a janitor at Florida International University and combined it with her private maid service. The family's economic situation improved, although Violeta never rose above the status of a cleaning woman and her husband never rejoined her.

Martin venerates his mother for the strength and decisiveness that she displayed in these difficult years and for her unwavering support of her sons. Moving to a better part of town, he attended Ruben Darío Senior High School where he excelled, graduating with honors. After this, he immediately enrolled at the University of Miami, completing a bachelor's degree in economics and accounting. He currently works as an accountant for Merrill Lynch and has just bought a luxury condominium in Miami Beach.

The Importance of Cultural Capital

Aside from the elements noted previously, the most important feature illustrated by Martin Lacayo's story is the transferability of social class assets and their use in overcoming extremely trying conditions. The son of a broken family, with a cleaning woman as a mother and living as an illegal migrant, Martin still managed to avoid the lures of gangs and street life, stayed in school, graduated from high school, and then swiftly completed his college education. That LaSalle School that he attended as a young child, plus the memory of the middle-class life that he and his brother enjoyed before escaping to Miami, provided a key point of reference as he confronted poverty and the prospect of going no further than a fast-food job.

He knew the meaning of the dull books put in the hands of limited-English students in public school and set his sights on escaping that environment. His mother not only supported him in that goal, but never allowed him to forget where his family came from. She could be a cleaning woman in Miami, but she did it to save her children from mortal danger, and she remained, despite appearances, an educated, middle-class person.

A recurrent theme in our interviews is the importance of a respectable past, real or imaginary, in the country of origin. Parents repeat stories of who they or their ancestors "really were" as a way to sustain their dignity despite present circumstances. Children exposed to these family stories often internalize them, using them as a spur to achievement. The "cultural capital" (Fernández-Kelly, 2008) brought from the home country actually has two components. The first is the motivational force to restore family pride and status. Regardless of whether the achievements of the past are real or imaginary, they can still serve as a means to instill high aspirations among the young.

The second is the "know-how" that immigrants that did come from the upper or middle classes possess. This know-how consists of information, values, and demeanor that migrants from more modest origins do not have. Regardless of how difficult present circumstances are, former middle-class parents have a clear sense of who they are, knowledge of the possible means to overcome the situation, and the right attitude when opportunities present themselves. These two dimensions of cultural capital converge in cases like Martin Lacayo's where both family lore and the *habitus* of past middle-class life are decisive in helping second-generation youths overcome seemingly insurmountable obstacles.

Policy Implications

From the preceding analysis, it is evident that the assimilation of immigrants and their children into the host societies is not simple, homogeneous, or problem free. Empirical work shows that, on the positive side, much progress is made, on average, from the first to the second generation, both culturally and socioeconomically. On the less rosy side, many individuals and entire groups confront significant barriers to advancement, either because they lack economic resources and skills or because they are received unfavorably by the host community. Segmented assimilation theory emphasizes that immigrants and their descendants can fully acculturate and *still* neither move upward occupationally and economically nor be accepted into native middle-class circles. Immigrant parents generally care much less that their offspring join the American cultural mainstream than that they move ahead educationally and economically.

If this dream of upward mobility is the goal, the data at hand indicate that many migrant children are not making it. The overall advancement of this population is largely driven by the good performance and outcomes of youths from professional immigrant families, positively received in America, or of middle-class refugees who have benefited from extensive governmental resettlement assistance and from strong coethnic communities. For immigrants at the other end of the spectrum, average educational and occupational outcomes are driven down by the poorer educational and economic performance of children from unskilled migrant families who are often handicapped further by an unauthorized or insecure legal status. From a policy viewpoint, these children must be the population of greatest concern.

A first urgent measure is the legalization of 1.5-generation youths who are unauthorized migrants. These children, brought involuntarily into the United

States by their parents, find themselves blocked through no fault of their own from access to higher education and many other everyday needs. This is not an insignificant population. In 2008, it was estimated to number 6 million and included almost half of immigrant youths aged 18 to 34 (Rumbaut & Komaie, 2010). As Rumbaut and Komaie (2010) state:

> For foreign-born young adults, an undocumented status blocks access to the opportunity structure and paths to social mobility. It has become all the more consequential since the passage of draconian federal laws in 1996 . . . and the failure of Congress to pass comprehensive immigration reform. (pp. 55–56)

The CILS results, just reviewed, point to the importance of volunteer programs and other forms of outside assistance to guide the most disadvantaged members of this population and help them stay in school. As we have seen, children who managed to succeed educationally despite having poor and undocumented parents and an otherwise disadvantaged upbringing were consistently supported by volunteers who came to their schools and exposed them to a different social world. We also found that cultural capital brought from the home country provides a significant boon because it anchors adolescent self-identities and strengthens their aspirations.

Cultural capital from the home country sustains and is sustained by selective acculturation. By contrast, dissonant acculturation across generations deprives youths of this form of capital: As they lose contact or even reject the language and culture of parents, whatever resources are embodied in that culture effectively disappear. Rejecting parental cultures may facilitate joining an undifferential mainstream, but often at the cost of abandoning those social and social psychological anchors that assist upward mobility, despite childhood disadvantages. The evidence supports the apparent paradox that preserving the linguistic and cultural heritage of their home countries often helps migrant children move ahead in their new American environment.

A final lesson from the preceding studies is the need to devise incentive schedules to persuade teachers and counselors give up their prejudices and take a more proactive stance toward migrant children. As the case of Raquel Torres, and many others like her, illustrates, the timely appearance of a significant other who takes a keen interest in the child and guides him or her through the intricacies of schools and the college application system can make all the difference. Poor parents, no matter how high their aspirations, seldom can do this by themselves. Schools are the natural setting for such affirmative efforts; if properly implemented, they may reverse the current status of such institutions—from mechanisms for reproducing privilege to sources of greater equality in educational opportunity for children of migrants.

Notes

1. This chapter brings together results presented previously in two articles: Portes, A., & Fernandez-Kelly, P. (2008). No margin for error: Educational and occupational achievement among disadvantaged children of immigrants. *Annals of the American Academy of Political and Social Sciences, 620*(November), 12–36; Portes, A., & Rivas, A. (2011). The adaptation of migrant children. *Future of Children, 21*(Spring), 219–246.
2. Names are fictitious to protect the privacy of respondents.

References

Fernández-Kelly, P. (2008). The back pocket map: Social class and cultural capital as transferable assets in the advancement of second generation immigrants. *Annals of the American Academy of Political and Social Science, 620*(November), 116–137.

Goyette, K., & Xie, Y. (1999). Educational expectations of Asian American youths: Determinants and ethnic differences. *Sociology of Education, 72*(1), 22–36.

Haller, W., Portes, A., & Lynch, S. M. (2011). Dreams fulfilled, dreams shattered: Determinants of segmented assimilation in the second generation. *Social Forces, 89*(3), 733–762.

Hirschman, C. (2001). The educational enrollment of immigrant youth: A test of the segmented assimilation hypothesis. *Demography, 38*(8), 317–336.

Massey, D. S. (1998). March of folly: U.S. immigration policy after NAFTA. *American Prospect, 37*(March/April), 22–33.

Massey, D. S., Durand, J., & Malone, N. J. (2002). *Beyond smoke and mirrors: Mexican immigration in an era of economic integration.* New York: Russell Sage Foundation.

Office of Immigrant Statistics. (2011). *2010 yearbook of immigration statistics.* Washington, DC: Department of Homeland Security.

Passel, J. (2009, March 26). *The economic downturn and immigration trends: What has happened and how do we know?* Lecture, Center for Migration and Development, Princeton University, Princeton, NJ.

Perreira, K. M., Harris, K., & Lee, D. (2006). Making it in America: High school completion by immigrant and native youth. *Demography, 43*(3), 511–536.

Portes, A., & Fernández-Kelly, P. (2008). No margin for error: Educational and occupational achievement among disadvantaged children of immigrants. *Annals of the American Academy of Political and Social Science, 620*(November), 12–36.

Portes, A., Fernández-Kelly, P., & Haller, W. (2009). The adaptation of the immigrant second generation in America: A theoretical overview and recent evidence. *Journal of Ethnic and Migration Studies, 35*(7), 1077–1104.

Portes, A., & Rumbaut, R. G. (2001). *Legacies: The story of the immigrant second generation.* Berkeley, CA: University of California Press and Russell Sage Foundation.

Portes, A., & Rumbaut, R. (2006). *Immigrant America: A portrait* (3rd ed.). Berkeley, CA: University of California Press.

Portes, A., & Zhou, M. (1993). The new second generation: Segmented assimilation and its variants. *Annals of the American Academy of Political and Social Science, 530*(November), 74–96.

Rumbaut, R. (2004). Ages, life stages, and generational cohorts: Decomposing the immigrant first and second generations in the United States. *International Migration Review, 38*(Fall), 1160–1205.

Rumbaut, R. G. (2005). Turning points in the transition to adulthood: Determinants of educational attainment, incarceration, and early childbearing among children of immigrants. *Ethnic and Racial Studies, 28*(November), 1041–1086.

Rumbaut, R. G., & Komaie, G. (2010). Immigration and adult transitions. *Future of Children, 20*(1), 39–63.

Telles, E., & Ortiz, V. (2008). *Generations of exclusion: Mexican Americans, assimilation, and race.* New York: Russell Sage Foundation.

Western, B. (2002). The impact of incarceration on wage mobility and inequality. *American Sociological Review, 67*(August), 526–546.

Western, B., Beckett, K., & Harding, D. (1998). Systeme penal et marche du travail dux Etats-Unis. *Actes de la Recherche en Sciences Sociales, 124*(September), 27–35.

5

DIVERGENT PATHS TO SCHOOL ADAPTATION AMONG CHILDREN OF IMMIGRANTS

New Approaches and Insights into Existing Data

Cecilia Rios-Aguilar, Manuel S. Gonzalez Canché, and Pedro R. Portes

Introduction

The United States is home to a fifth of the world's migrant population (United Nations, 2006). By 2006, about 38 million foreign-born persons were living in the United States, 56 percent of whom had immigrated since 1990, primarily from Latin America and Asia (U.S. Census Bureau, 2007a). The U.S.-born second generation totaled more than 30 million in 2006, so that immigrants and their children today add up to some 70 million persons, constituting 23 percent of the national total (Rumbaut, 2008). As today's children of immigrants—which include children who were born in the United States or who arrived at an early age—reach adulthood, their impact will be broadly felt throughout society. The largest influence will be experienced in the educational system, where 20 percent of youths in American schools are children of immigrants (Feliciano, 2006). Because of the increasing presence of children of immigrants in the American socioeconomic life, the educational adaptation and success of this young generation has significant implications in the economic and social development of the United States (Feliciano, 2006). The educational achievement of immigrants, thus, should be of increasing interest to educators, researchers, and policy makers.

Never before has the educational system been pressed so hard to serve such large numbers of diverse second-generation and immigrant students (Carhill, M. Suárez-Orozco, & Páez, 2008; A. Portes & Rumbaut, 2001). These children and youth come from highly diverse backgrounds, and they (together with their families) bring extraordinary strengths and resources, including strong family ties, deep-rooted beliefs in education, and hope about the future (C. Suárez-Orozco, Pimentel, & Martin, 2009). However, as stated by C. Suárez-Orozco et al. (2009), they also face a variety of challenges associated with the migration to a new country, including high levels of poverty (Capps, Fix, Ost, Reardon-Anderson, & Passel, 2005), hostile "contexts of reception" (A. Portes & Rumbaut, 2001), experiences of racism and discrimination, and exposure to school and community violence (C. Suárez-Orozco & M. Suárez-Orozco, 2001). These barriers complicate immigrant students' adaptation to school, thus leaving them at risk for educational and social disadvantages.

The majority of the studies published to date have examined the academic achievement and educational trajectories of these children and youth by relying on specific conceptual frameworks—adaptation (Berry & Sam, 1997) and assimilation (A. Portes & Rumbaut, 2001; A. Portes & Zhou, 1993)—and on distinct models of school adaptation (Fuligni, 1997; Kao & Tienda, 1995; Padilla & González, 2001; A. Portes & Hao, 2004; P. R. Portes, 1999; and C. Suárez-Orozco et al., 2009). Findings from these studies, mostly (if not exclusively) based on linear regression analytic techniques, have confirmed the critical role that language proficiency (Carhill et al., 2008; A. Portes & Hao, 2002; A. Portes & Rumbaut, 2001; Schmid, 2001), parental socioeconomic status (SES) (Rumbaut, 2008), students' culture (Ogbu, 1989, 1992; Warikoo & Carter, 2009), school SES (Lee & Bryk, 1989) and composition (Callahan, Wilkinson & Muller, 2008), and other psychosocial factors (Fuligni, 1997; P. R. Portes, 1999) play in determining school outcomes. Although these findings are of great importance, existing conceptual frameworks and the methodologies employed to estimate the models have rarely been challenged. Thus, interpretations of any general conceptual model remain guarded in recognition that they essentially sketch of a much more complex process of adaptation (P. R. Portes, 1999). Given the complexity of the school adaptation process, we argue that there is the need to utilize alternative statistical approaches that have the potential to offer more meaningful and valid results that lead to more refined theories and/or conceptual frameworks.

The goal of this study, then, is to test a proposed model of school adaptation among second-generation immigrant children using structural equation modeling (SEM). SEM will allow us to test if the proposed model fits the data or not. Our proposed model is based on existing literature and on theories of acculturation and assimilation. We utilized data from the first wave of the Children of Immigrants Longitudinal Study (CILS) to test our model. Our study is unique and innovative: We estimate the proposed model for different subsamples of students. That is, we take into consideration the fact that students experience different adaptation/assimilation processes to school. Consequently, our study moves existing research forward by providing a more rigorous and comprehensive analysis of the factors that have an influence, both directly and indirectly, on the school adaptation process among different groups of children of immigrants.

Literature Review

Accompanying the increase in the size and diversity of the foreign-born population has been a rise in the number of children from immigrant families attending schools in the United States (Fuligni, 1997). The educational progress of these children and youth appears to be related to the human, economic, social, and cultural capital that their parents brought with them from the home country and the ways in which they are able to mobilize these resources in the United States (A. Portes & Fernández-Kelly, 2008). Given that the literature on the factors that affect immigrant and second-generation students' academic achievement is extensive and that the scope of this chapter is limited, we concentrate our attention on reviewing the literature on what the existing research suggests are the most important factors in determining successful school adaptation among this particular group of students: (1) family SES, (2) family ties/relationships, (3) English proficiency and bilingualism, (4) students' expectations, and the (5) school context.

Family SES

SES is one of the most widely studied constructs in the social sciences (Bradley & Corwyn, 2002). Several ways of measuring SES have been proposed, but most include some quantification of family income, parental education, family structure, and occupational status. Research has established that among native children, their parents' SES has a strong and positive effect on children's and youth's academic achievement (Kao & Thompson, 2003; Schmid, 2001). Indeed, a variety of mechanisms linking SES to children's educational outcomes has been proposed. For example, human capital theory argues that parents make choices about how much time and other resources to invest in their children on the basis of their goals, resources, and restrictions (Haveman & Wolfe, 1994). These investment decisions, consequently, affect their children's educational success. With respect to immigrant and second-generation children, researchers have found that family SES is related in the same way to educational attainment as for native-born children. For example, A. Portes and MacLeod (1996) found that the most powerful predictor of academic achievement is family SES, which contributes directly and indirectly through its effect on intervening variables such as time spent doing homework. Other researchers (e.g., Alba, Massey, & Rumbaut, 1999) have found that immigrant children raised in families with higher educational and income levels tend to do better in school. Unfortunately, recent statistics indicate that children of immigrants are substantially more likely than children with U.S.-born parents to be poor, live in crowded housing, and lack health (Capps et al., 2005). These statistics demonstrate that many immigrant children face difficult challenges that challenge their academic progress. However, as stated by Schmid (2001), the academic achievement of immigrant and second-generation students is not only related to their parents' financial and human capital, but also to other factors (e.g., family, language, and school context).

Family Ties/Relationships

Successfully adapting to the schooling process in the United States can be a difficult and puzzling process for immigrant children, who are frequently caught between pressures to assimilate into American society and pressures to preserve their own cultures of origin (Zhou & Bankston, 1994). Families play an important role in the process of school adaptation of immigrant children. Indeed, some scholars (e.g., Kao, 2004) have argued that members of some ethnic groups may exhibit closer ties to their families, evidenced not only by more frequent contact with family (and extended family), but by being more orientated toward their families. Tienda (1980) found that strong family ties and sense of family and community obligation can help immigrants to adjust to the United States. Similarly, other researchers (i.e., Valenzuela & Dornbusch, 1994) found that a strong sense of *familism*—the expressed identification with the interests and welfare of the family—is an important source of social capital for adolescents of Mexican origin. Moreover, Valenzuela and Dornbusch (1994) found that *familism* affects academic achievement, particularly when combined with higher parental human capital (A. Portes & Zhou, 1993). Other studies have shown that immigrant-specific resources, particularly in the form of social capital within families, are instrumental to success in school (A. Portes, 2000; Stanton-Salazar, 1997; Zhou, 1997). Although it is possible to argue that family relationships can offer a positive basis of identity for many children of immigrants, it is important to keep in mind that family relations can, in some instances, be a source of stress and alienation. For some immigrant and second-generation children and youth, these feelings have led to internal struggles, extreme despair, and low levels of academic achievement (Wolf, 1997).

English Proficiency and Bilingualism

Another key characteristic associated with academic achievement among immigrant children and youth is language background (Carhill et al., 2008; A. Portes & Hao, 2002; Schmid, 2001; White & Glick, 2000). Disadvantages associated with limited English skills among those in the first generation may reduce their ability to negotiate the U.S. school system (Kao & Tienda, 1995; White & Glick, 2000). Extensive research has shown that insufficiently developed academic English-language skills are associated with lower academic achievement, repeating grades, and low graduation rates (Gándara & Hopkins, 2010; Rios-Aguilar, González Canché & Sabetghadam, 2012). Thus, research indicates that low levels of academic English-language proficiency are an important obstacle to academic success (Carhill et al., 2008). Furthermore, research also suggests that there is a positive, if temporary, effect of coming from a bilingual background that may allow immigrant children and second-generation children to tap into the resources available in their families and families' communities (Rumbaut, 1996; White & Glick, 2000; Zhou & Bankston, 1994). For example, A. Portes and Rumbaut (2001) observed a high rate of mother-tongue shift among immigrant and second-generation children and youth but found that the fluently bilingual teenagers in their sample were youths who did better in school, had higher aspirations for the future, enjoyed better mental health and family relations, and were more likely to have friends from abroad (Linton, 2004). Similarly, A. Portes and Hao (2002) found that although complete linguistic assimilation is widely perceived as desirable, a myriad of linguistic adaptation strategies exist in reality and that, among them, fluent bilingualism is consistently preferable.

Achievement Motivation

Researchers (e.g., Fuligni, 1997; Ibañez, Kuperminc, Jurkovic, & Perilla, 2004; P. R. Portes, 1999) have argued that psychosocial factors, such as achievement motivation, self-esteem, and effort optimism (Ogbu, 1992), also affect the process of school adaptation. Unfortunately, research findings along this particular line of inquiry are not consistent. One the one hand, researchers (e.g., Fuligni, 1997; P. R. Portes, 1999) have found that achievement motivation, as measured by students' educational and occupational aspirations and behaviors regarding education, is one of the most important psychosocial predictor of students' academic achievement. On the other hand, researchers (e.g., Goldenberg, 1996; Schneider & Stevenson, 1999) have found that despite the fact that the majority of immigrant students, particularly those from Latin American descent, enter high school with educational and career aspirations as high as those of the majority population, many of these students fail in school.

School Context

More recently, researchers (e.g., Gibson, Gándara, & Koyama, 2004; A. Portes & MacLeod, 1996) have taken parental SES effects on academic achievement as a given and have added to their analyses a set of more complex measures of structural characteristics, such as the school context, to analyze the remaining variation in immigrant students' academic achievement (Kao & Thompson, 2003). For instance, educational researchers have identified school composition as one of the key areas responsible for schools' differences in overall academic success and rates of dropout among immigrant students (A. Portes & Hao, 2004). Although it is widely recognized that school context influences academic achievement in the general population, the prospect that it also shapes immigrant students' achievement has been largely overlooked (A. Portes & Hao, 2004). As argued by Callahan et al. (2008), schools with many immigrant students may offer services and a climate better suited to the particular academic and social needs of immigrants than schools with relatively few immigrant students. Alternately, if a higher concentration of immigrants in a community leads to lower-quality schools, fewer academic opportunities, or, possibly, social marginalization, then immigrant students' needs may be better served in schools serving predominantly nonimmigrant populations. The evidence indicates that institutional and social climates affect immigrant students differently. In essence, Callahan et al. (2008) found that immigrant students placed in English-as-a-second-language (ESL) tracks in schools with a high concentration of immigrant students do better than their non-ESL peers. Moreover, those in schools with a low concentration of immigrants do worse relative to non-ESL peers. These findings clearly indicate that school contexts can either facilitate or impede immigrant students' academic success and higher education opportunities (Callahan et al., 2008).

Theoretical Framework

Berry (1997) argued that the process of acculturation has been widely studied because of researchers' interest in understanding a set of psychological phenomena that arise at the intersection of two cultures—dominant and nondominant. This psychological perspective focuses on examining how individuals who have developed in one cultural context manage to adapt to new contexts that result from migration. In particular, we argue that Berry's conceptual model on the various modes of adaptation—integration, assimilation, separation, and alienation/marginalization—among immigrants can be used to develop a model that explains the school adaptation process of children and youth. Berry (1997) defined these four modes of adaptation (or strategies) as follows. Integration refers to moment when an immigrant identifies with and is involved with *both* cultures—the dominant and the indigenous or nondominant. That is, integration occurs when there is an interest in maintaining one's culture *and* in participating in the culture of other groups in the larger society. When individuals do not wish to maintain their cultural identity and seek daily interaction with other cultures, then assimilation occurs. In other words, assimilation refers to the situation where an immigrant chooses to identify solely with the new culture, thus rejecting his or her own culture. In contrast, when the nondominant group places a value on holding on to their culture, then separation is defined. Finally, when there is little interest in cultural maintenance and little interest in having relations with others from the dominant culture, then marginalization (or alienation) is defined.

Similarly, but from a sociological perspective, researchers (i.e., A. Portes & Rumbaut, 2001) have developed theories—segmented assimilation and selective acculturation—that attempt to capture the difficulties of growing up in America in an immigrant family. *Segmented assimilation* (A. Portes & Rumbaut, 2006; A. Portes & Zhou, 1993) is the concept coined to refer to these complex and multifaceted realities that lead to divergent destinies (Zhou, Lee, Agius Vallejo, Tafoya-Estrada, & Sao Xiong, 2008). Segmented assimilation theory emphasizes the importance of group-level processes in determining the academic, social, and labor market outcomes of immigrants and their children (A. Portes & Zhou, 1993). *Selective acculturation*, on the other hand, is characterized by the presence of ethnic networks and strong communities, which support children as they learn to deal with prejudice, navigate the education system, and find a place in the labor market. The outcome is, usually, upward assimilation combined with bilingualism and biculturalism (Gibson, 2001; Linton, 2004). According to A. Portes and Rumbaut (2001):

> While such a path may appear inimical to successful adaptation in the eyes of conventional assimilationists, in fact it can lead to better psychosocial and achievement outcomes because it preserves bonds across immigrant generations and gives children a clear reference point to guide their future lives. (p. 309)

Primary features of this type or assimilation model are a strong ethnic enclave coupled with the deliberate preservation of the homeland culture, albeit in an adapted form that is a more suitable to the way of living in the host country. A pattern of selective acculturation can lead to rapid mobility into the middle class (Gibson, 2001). Indeed, immigrants face competing and conflicting social and cultural demands when entering into an unfamiliar context. Yet, the difficulties are not always the same for each individual or for different groups of immigrants. The process of growing up American fluctuates between acceptance and confrontation, depending on the characteristics that immigrants and their children bring along and the social context that receives them. Thus, the focus of the sociological approach is on trying to understand the context in which the process of assimilation occurs and how this context intersects with immigrants' characteristics and resources to which they have access.

A Proposed Model of School Adaptation

Based on the existing literature and on both psychological and sociological theoretical frameworks, we developed a model of school adaptation for immigrant and second-generation students (see Figure 5.1). It is also important to highlight that our approach to study school adaptation is innovative in the sense that we disaggregate the statistical analyses. That is, we created mutually exclusive groups of students and tested the proposed model of school of adaptation for the entire sample of students

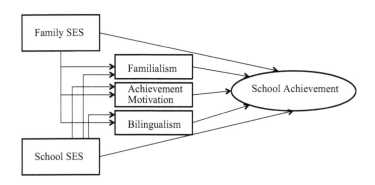

FIGURE 5.1 Proposed Model of School Adaptation

and for each of the newly created groups. More specifically, utilizing the CILS data and relying on P. R. Portes's (1999) factors—ethnic and U.S. pull—we divided the sample of children of immigrants into four groups. The creation of these groups is based on the diverse adaptation strategies that existing conceptual frameworks suggest: (1) integration, (2) assimilation, (3) separation, and (4) alienation.

Table 5.1 contains information about the criteria used to assign students to each of these adaptation modes and about the hypothesized academic achievement outcomes for each mode of adaptation.

Method

Data

The data for this study come from the first wave of the CILS. The CILS was designed to study the adaptation process of the immigrant second generation, which is defined broadly as U.S.-born children with at least one foreign-born

TABLE 5.1 U.S./Ethnic Pull Factors, Adaptation Modes, and Hypothesized Academic Achievement Outcomes

Modes of Adaptation (Berry, 1997)

U.S./Ethnic Pull Factors	*Adaptation Mode*	*Expected Academic Achievement Outcomes*
High U.S. pull/high ethnic pull	Integration	High levels of academic achievement
High U.S. pull/low ethnic pull	Assimilation	Relatively high levels of academic achievement
Low U.S. pull/high ethnic pull	Separation	Relatively low levels of academic achievement
Low U.S. pull/low ethnic pull	Alienation/marginalization	Low levels of academic achievement

Assimilation Theories (A. Portes & Zhou, 1993)

U.S./Ethnic Pull Factors	*Adaptation Mode*	*Expected Academic Achievement Outcomes*
High U.S. pull/high ethnic pull	Selective acculturation	High levels of academic achievement
High U.S. pull/low ethnic pull	Conventional upward assimilation or downward assimilation	Relatively high levels of academic achievement
Low U.S. pull/high ethnic pull	Selective acculturation	High or low levels of academic achievement
Low U.S. pull/low ethnic pull	Downward assimilation	Low levels academic achievement

parent or children born abroad but brought at an early age to the United States (P. R. Portes, 1999). A full description of the CILS's design, sampling, and procedures is available elsewhere (A. Portes & Schauffler, 1995; Rumbaut, 1994). The CILS was conducted with large samples of second-generation immigrant children attending the eighth and ninth grades in public and private schools in the metropolitan areas of Miami/Ft. Lauderdale in Florida and San Diego in California. The response rates were 75 percent for the San Diego group and about 67 percent for the south Florida group (Rumbaut, 1994). Conducted in 1992, the CILS had the purpose of collecting baseline information on immigrant families, children's demographic characteristics, language use, self-identities, and academic attainment. The total sample size was 5,262 immigrant and second-generation students.

Missing Data

Missing data was a concern in this study because some of the variables of interest in this study contained more than 5 percent of missing observations. For these reasons, the authors chose an imputation method—imputation by chained equations (ICE)—to substitute all missing values. This imputation approach is based on each conditional density of a variable given all other variables. The ICE has some clear advantages: (1) no multivariate joint distribution assumption (this reason alone makes it appealing because it allows different types of variables to be imputed together), and (2) it allows for different kinds of weights, as long as the regression models allow them (for details about ICE, see Royston 2007, 2009). After running the ICE, we were able to estimate all missing values, and, thus, the total sample size for this study is 5,262 immigrant and second-generation students.

Sample

The sample for this study, the CILS, includes all immigrant and second-generation children included in the sample. Of all these immigrant and second-generation youth, 46 percent are females and 72 percent of them were born in the United States. Of those students who were not born in the United States, they come primarily from Latin America (Cuba, Nicaragua, Mexico, and Jamaica) and from Asia (Vietnam, Philippines, Laos, and Cambodia). In addition, 92 percent of these students reported that they speak another language. Of those students who speak another language, 64 percent of them say they speak Spanish, and 15 percent of them speak Tagalog or another Philippine language. With respect to these students' parental level of education, it is important to highlight that 17 percent of them reported they finished eighth grade or less, 18 percent are high school graduates, 14 percent finished some college, and 18 percent graduated from college.

Variables

Dependent Variable

The primary outcome measure in the model is students' academic achievement. The outcome is measured by students' combined total score on Stanford reading and math achievement tests. The scales of these standardized tests range between 200 and 800 points.

Independent Variables

Consistent with the existing literature, five independent variables that have shown a strong relationship with immigrant and second-generation students' academic achievement were introduced in the proposed model: (1) family SES, (2) school SES, (3) familism, (4) bilingualism, and (5) achievement motivation. Table 5.2 provides specific information on how each variable was measured and the range of values that all variables included in the study can take.

Data Analyses

SEM is utilized in this paper to evaluate whether the proposed model of school adaptation provides a reasonable fit to the data for the different modes of adaptation. SEM also provides regression coefficients to examine the direction and magnitude of the relationship between the dependent and independent variables. One important advantage of SEM is that it allows for simultaneous estimation of hypothesized relationships using estimated covariance/correlation matrices and generates goodness-of-fit measures to evaluate the overall fit of the proposed model. These fit measures are a corrected version (accounting for sample size and degrees of freedom) of the chi-square test that is frequently recommended. The use of chi-square tests is often criticized because of its sensitivity to sample size (Bentler & Bonett, 1980; Hu & Bentler, 1999), which has led to the proposal of numerous alternative fit indices that evaluate model fit. Following Kleyman and McVean (2008), we report the Root Mean Square Error of Approximation (RMSEA), Incremental Fit Index (IFI), Root Mean Square Residual (RMR), Comparative Fit Index (CFI), Non-Normed Fit Index (NNFI), and Parsimony Normed Fit Index (PNFI). The traditional cutoff points for each of these fit indices suggested by experts in the topic (Bentler & Chou, 1987; Hu & Bentler, 1999; Worthington, & Whittaker, 2006) are also reported in Table 5.5, along with the fit indices found in our fitted models.

Limitations

Although the utilization of SEM is appropriate and consistent with the goals of this study, we recognize that our results may be subject to sampling or selection effects with respect to at least three aspects: individuals, measures, and occasions. Thus, findings and generalizability of this study need to be carefully interpreted.

TABLE 5.2 Variables Included in the Study

Variable Name	Proxies	Range	Values
Academic Achievement (ACACH)	Total score on Stanford achievement math and reading tests	200 to 800	200 = Low academic achievement 800 = High academic achievement
Family SES (FSES)	Measured defined by variables that indexed family socioeconomic position, home ownership, and parents' occupation and educational achievement	−1.66 to 2.09	−1.66 = Lowest SES 2.09 = Highest SES
School SES (SCHSES)	% of students eligible for subsidized lunch	1 to 4	1 = High % of students eligible for subsidized lunch 4 = Low % of students eligible for subsidized lunch
Familism (FAM)	Should choose relative With serious problems, only relatives can help Job near parents most important	1 to 4	1 = Agree a lot 2 = Agree a little 3 = Disagree a little 4 = Disagree a lot
Bilingualism (BIL)	Knowledge of English (1995–1996) Knowledge of foreign language (1995–1996)	1 to 4	1 = Fluent bilingual 2 = English dominant 3 = Foreign language dominant 4 = Limited bilingual
Achievement Motivation (AMOT)	Highest level of education student expects to achieve Highest level of education student expects to attain	1 to 5	1 = Less than high school 2 = Finish high school 3 = Some college 4 = Finish college 5 = Finish a graduate degree

Findings

Descriptive Statistics

Table 5.3 presents the descriptive statistics of all the variables of interest in this study for the entire sample, as well as for each mode of adaptation. From looking at Table 5.3, we learned that the academic achievement of immigrant and second-generation students in the *integration* mode of adaptation is the lowest, compared to the one of students in other modes of adaptation. Furthermore, we learned that

TABLE 5.3 Descriptive Statistics of Study Variables

	All (N = 5,262) Mean (s.d.)	Integration (N = 1,133) Mean (s.d.)	Assimilation (N = 2,099) Mean (s.d.)	Separation (N = 898) Mean (s.d.)	Alienation (N = 1,132) Mean (s.d.)
Dependent Variables					
Academic Achievement					
Reading achievement	662.2 (61.5)	655.0 (68.0)	663.8 (52.7)	666.8 (56.4)	662.6 (72.1)
Math achievement	693.3 (61.9)	688.1 (67.1)	693.9 (54.0)	696.1 (63.9)	695.0 (68.2)
Independent Variables: Direct Effects					
Family SES	−0.06 (0.7)	−0.19 (0.7)	−0.08 (0.7)	0.00 (0.7)	0.00 (0.7)
School SES					
% students eligible for subsidized lunch	2.4 (1.0)	2.4 (1.0)	2.4 (1.0)	2.4 (1.0)	2.5 (1.0)
Independent Variables: Indirect Effects					
Familism					
Should choose relative	2.4 (0.9)	2.5 (0.9)	2.4 (0.9)	2.3 (0.9)	2.2 (0.9)
With serious problems, only relatives can help	1.6 (0.8)	1.8 (0.9)	1.6 (0.8)	1.5 (0.7)	1.4 (0.7)
Job near parents most important	1.6 (0.8)	1.8 (0.9)	1.6 (0.8)	1.5 (0.7)	1.4 (0.7)
Bilingualism	2.6 (1.0)	2.5 (1.0)	2.6 (1.0)	2.6 (1.0)	2.6 (1.0)
Achievement Motivation					
Highest level of education *r* wants to achieve	4.5 (0.8)	4.3 (0.9)	4.5 (0.8)	4.5 (0.7)	4.5 (0.7)
Level of education *r* expects to obtain	4.1 (0.9)	3.9 (1.0)	4.1 (0.9)	4.1 (0.9)	4.1 (1.9)

students in the *integration* mode of adaptation come, mostly, from low-income families. Also, students who are in the *integration* group exhibit a higher mean score for the familism scale, and a lower mean score for the achievement motivation scale, compared to their peers in other modes of adaptation. In addition, data show that students who choose *separation*, as a mode of school adaptation, show the highest mean scores for reading and math achievement, compared to their peers in other modes of adaptation. Another interesting statistic is that students included in the *separation* and *alienation* modes of adaptation tend to come from higher income families.

Statistics also indicate that, regardless of mode of adaptation strategy, immigrant and second-generation students attend schools with relatively high levels of poverty. Keep in mind that school SES ranges from 1 to 4, and that lower values indicate that the school is characterized by higher percentage of students eligible for free and reduced-price lunch. Similarly, the mean scores of students in all groups for the bilingualism scale are almost identical. Overall, although not fully bilingual, students in all groups seem to rate their language proficiency between the categories of English dominant and foreign-language dominant.

SEM Analyses

Five different structural equation models were estimated, one for the entire sample and one for students on each of the adaptation strategies. The standardized beta coefficients and fit indices from all the SEM analyses are presented in Tables 5.4 and 5.5. It is also important to notice that all the models explain a significant proportion of students' academic achievement. In fact, R-squares range from 8 percent to 27 percent. We found that the model that explains the most amount of variation in immigrant and second-generation students' academic achievement is for the group of students who have *assimilated* (R-squared = 27%). The model that explains the least amount of variation in academic achievement is for students who chose an *integration* strategy (R-squared = 8%) (see Table 5.4).

Furthermore, findings from the SEM analyses reveal that all signs of the estimated coefficients are as the theory would expect. That is, in four of the five models, we found that family SES is positively associated with students' academic achievement. The only case in which this finding does not hold true is for students in the *integration* strategy. For this particular group of students, family and school SES seemed not to have an impact on their academic achievement. Similarly, in four of the five models, higher levels of achievement motivation are strongly associated with higher levels of academic achievement. The only group that does not present this association is the one configured by students in the *separation* mode of adaptation. Furthermore, in all models, stronger family ties are associated with higher levels of academic achievement, holding other factors constant. Finally, we found a positive relationship between bilingualism and students' academic

TABLE 5.4 Standardized Coefficients

	All Sample		Integration		Assimilation		Separation		Alienation	
	ACACH	SE	ACACH	SE	ACACH	SE	ACACH	SE	ACACH	SE
FSES	0.13	—	0.06 (n.s)	—	0.14	—	0.16	—	0.12	—
SCHSES	0.16	—	0.08	—	0.19	—	0.17	—	0.15	—
FAM	-0.05	-0.16	-0.18	-0.21	0.32	-0.13	-0.26	-0.15	-0.09	-0.15
BIL	0.07	0.24	0.18	0.25	0.13	0.23	0.14	0.29	0.02 (n.s)	0.07
AMOT	0.15	0.35	0.09	0.06	0.12	0.14	0.03 (n.s)	0.16	0.23	0.12
R-squared	0.17		0.08		0.27		0.21		0.14	

** p-value < .001; n.s. = not statistically significant; all BETA coefficients are expressed in standard deviation units.

TABLE 5.5 Structural Equation Model Fit Indices

Fit Indices	Cutoff Points[1]	All	Assimilated	Integrated	Separated	Alienated
Root Mean Square Error of Approximation (RMSEA)	Below 0.06 is recommended	0.049	0.009	0.036	0.050	0.025 (0.01; 0.04)
Incremental Fit Index (IFI)	Above 0.95 is recommended	0.981	0.999	0.988	0.975	0.993
Root Mean Square Residual (RMR)	Below 0.10 is recommended	0.036	0.0130	0.026	0.044	0.019
Comparative Fit Index (CFI)	Above 0.95 is recommended	0.981	0.999	0.988	0.975	0.993
Non-Normed Fit Index (NNFI)	Above 0.95 is recommended	0.957	0.998	0.977	0.958	0.986
Parsimony Normed Fit Index (PNFI)	No threshold level (close to 0.50 is recommended)	0.435	0.363	0.432	0.579	0.415
Chi-Square	p-value > 0.05	0.001	0.265	0.001	0.001	0.018

[1]Fit indices taken from Bentler and Bonett (1980), Hu and Bentler (1999), Bentler and Chou (1987), Worthington and Whittaker (2006).

achievement. That is, the higher the value of the scale (i.e., when students tend to be limited bilinguals), the higher the academic achievement.

Findings also indicate that the coefficients vary in their magnitude. For instance, it is interesting to note that for the *integration* mode of adaptation, the strongest predictors of students' academic achievement are familism, achievement motivation, and limited bilingualism (see Table 5.4). Family SES is *not* a statistically significant predictor of academic achievement for those immigrant and second-generation students who have followed the *integration* path of adaptation. For the *assimilation* strategy, all the coefficients are statistically significant. Indeed, this is the group that, on average, represents the best structural outcomes in terms of their academic achievement. For students who adopt the *separation* path, we found that academic motivation is the weakest predictor of school achievement. Moreover, the other predictors were very important in predicting academic achievement—mirroring the coefficient estimates of students in the assimilation group. Finally, for students in the *alienation* strategy, the beta coefficients show that the most important predictor of academic achievement was achievement motivation. Next are school and family SES. Interestingly, bilingualism is not a statistically significant predictor of immigrant and second-generation students' academic achievement in this particular mode of adaptation.

To summarize our findings, the most important predictor of students' academic achievement for all groups, except for those students who alienate, is familism. The closer students feel to their families, the higher their academic achievement. For those students who *alienate*, the stronger predictor is their level of achievement motivation, meaning that the higher their educational aspirations are, the higher their academic achievement. Bilingualism and school and family SES play different roles in the diverse paths of adaptation. In some, like is the case of *separation*, bilingualism plays a more prominent role. In the case of *alienation*, bilingualism plays no role in determining students' academic achievement. Lastly, family and school SES are demonstrated to be important predictors of students' academic achievement, except for the *integration* strategy.

Discussion and Implications

Although some scholars argue that more recent children of immigrant face unique challenges and difficulties that set them apart from earlier generations of European immigrants, others remain more optimistic in seeing their gradual assimilation into the American mainstream as not being significantly different (Greenman & Xie, 2008). Our study found that immigrant and second-generation children vary significantly in how they adapt and are "being adapted" in terms of how each sub-sample represents four adaptation modes. By examining the strategies or modes in ways that allow us to see how key predictors are configured and lead to different levels of educational success, we can better understand diverse academic and occupational trajectories.

From the SEM analyses, we learned that all fit indices are within acceptable ranges, thus indicating that the CILS data do fit the proposed model of school adaptation for the entire sample, as well as for each of the four different adaptation strategies of interest that were tested. Three questions help in understanding our findings:

1. How do the main predictors of school success vary once the overall sample is divided into four modes of adaptation suggested by current conceptual frameworks?
2. Of the four modes or subsamples, which ones account for more variance than the combined undifferentiated total sample?
3. Which of the four modes produce the highest level of academic success?

The models that explained the most amount of variation in immigrant and second-generation students' academic achievement are the assimilation and separation models; both modes were above the variance accounted for in general. According to the existing theoretical frameworks (Berry, 1997; A. Portes & Zhou, 1993), this particular mode of adaptation is characterized by a relatively strong identification with the mainstream American culture (or high U.S. pull). It is important to remember that students in this particular group come from families with relatively higher income; therefore, they may have more resources (material and nonmaterial) valued by schools that help them succeed academically. The model that explains the least amount of variation in students' academic outcomes is that for those students who chose integration (Berry, 1997) or what some consider selective acculturation (A. Portes & Zhou, 1993) strategy. It is possible to think that this particular group of students is struggling with finding ways to remain close to their families and communities, while trying to negotiate their identities also in school and the multicultural marketplace it represents for these adolescents. We think is important to include the role of identity developmental processes in understanding the relative advantages and disadvantages that underlie divergent modes of adaptation. Thus, we need to refine existing theories to better capture how students' lived experiences in affective, motivational, and intellectual terms interface with divergent paths (see Portes & Salas, 2011).

The findings also reveal that school SES is a stronger predictor than family SES for students who assimilated, separate, and alienate. This finding underscores the importance of clearly grasping how social and economic capital work and interact in immigrant contexts. Our findings also show that familism is the strongest predictor of academic achievement, except for students who choose alienation as an adaptation strategy. This finding is consistent with existing research (A. Portes & Zhou, 1993, P. R. Portes, 1999; C. Suárez-Orozco & M. Suárez-Orozco, 2001) that suggests strong family lived experiences, or *vivencias*, are critical in determining school achievement among immigrant and second-generation students. Indeed, most recent evidence indicates that it is the complex combination of love, affection, appreciation, gratitude, responsibility, and sense of duty that characterized students' relationships with their families and influenced their academic and behavioral choices. Surprisingly, our findings show that achievement motivation (as measured by students' educational aspirations and expectations) is the most important predictor of students' who alienate. Furthermore, we found that this particular psychosocial factor is not a statistically significant predictor of academic achievement among students who adopt a separation strategy. The latter actually do better in school as a group and may be associated with greater individual agency in terms of adaptation. The existing literature (e.g., Feliciano & Rumbaut, 2005; Goyette & Xie, 1999; Kao & Tienda, 1995; A. Portes & Rumbaut, 2001) has suggested that most immigrant and second-generation adolescents hold very high ambitions and hopes for the future. Thus, our findings seem to qualify existing research in this particular area and, again, bring back the role of identity development in model development that includes adolescents and youth (Portes, Zady, & del Castillo, 1997).

Our SEM analyses reveal the existence of divergent paths of adaptation among immigrant and second-generation children and youth. Although this finding is critical, it is also necessary to understand the extent to which existing conceptual frameworks are useful in explaining these divergent paths. Do these theories predict the expected outcomes? According to Berry's conceptual framework, integration would lead to better school outcomes. Remember that integration occurs when there is an interest in maintaining one's culture and in participating in the culture of other groups in the larger society. The descriptive statistics presented earlier indicate that students who attempt to integrate may be less stable and have the lowest levels of academic achievement, compared to students who choose their own authentic paths of adaptation. This finding clearly contradicts Berry's model and the views of A. Portes and Zhou (1993) who likewise have also argued that selective acculturation, whereby students adopt aspects of mainstream U.S. norms while preserving aspects of their native language and norms have better educational outcomes. As noted earlier, students who chose this adaptation strategy exhibit lower levels of academic achievement, compared to students who separate sufficiently from each culture as a mode of adaptation. In addition to the descriptive findings, SEM analyses show that the model that explains the least amount of variation in students' academic outcomes is that for the integration strategy. This particular finding suggests the need to question the relative advantages (and disadvantages) of deliberately limiting assimilation and maintaining strong ethnic social ties. In other words, the argument that maintaining the culture of origin alone has a unilateral and protective effect on children is questionable, at least for school success, after taking into account key predictors as we have here.

Existing research and our findings do not explain the mechanisms that lead to divergent paths of school adaptation. We are aware that our coefficients do not explain the complexities embedded in the process of school adaptation among immigrant and second-generation children and youth. Future research must make an effort to explain how varying kinds of supports that families provide to their children are (or are not) translated into higher academic achievement. Similarly, future research must look into better understanding how the different uses of English and of their native language in school and in other informal social situations affect students' school adaptation process. Recent evidence (see Carhill et al., 2008) suggests that these informal contexts are crucial in understanding students' academic outcomes. From a developmental lens, it then seems that those who maintain a "standing quarrel" with both cultures in defining themselves could be forging the skills necessary in negotiating school and adolescent subcultural group demands.

Policy Recommendations

Although educational researchers need to continue to work to better the divergent paths of school adaptation among immigrant and second-generation students, policy makers and educators must work to address the diverse needs of these students. To meet the needs of immigrant students, educators should be aware of their specific circumstances and locations within U.S. educational system. The following are recommendations for policy and practice that grow out of this research study. First, educators and policy makers need to be aware of the fact that immigrant and second-generation students do not adapt to school uniformly. Indeed, the implications of shortsighted policies such as English only or, at the community level, L1 only maintenance by parents (willfully or not) are clear. Students' school adaptation process depends on a number of factors, including but not limited to their SES and lived experiences at home and school. Second, this study found that, for the most part, family relationships are the most important determinant of students' academic achievement. Thus, educators must find ways to validate students' lived experiences at home with their parents. One way of doing this is to provide bilingual language support at school for students and their families. Bilingualism may open additional opportunities for students' educational and professional development and can also improve their chances in the job market and indirectly those of the nation's global economy. Maintaining students' native language may also increase their social capital by helping to preserve and intensify their social ties with family and community members and with residents in their countries of origin. Another way of contributing to recognize the importance of family networks is to encourage educators and school administrators to incorporate the knowledge already embedded in students' daily lives—funds of knowledge (Moll, Amanti, Neff, & González, 1992)—into the school curriculum. Validating students' and families' experiences may yield better academic outcomes, as has been suggested by existing research (Rios-Aguilar, 2010).

References

Alba, R., Douglas M., & Ruben G. R. (1999). *The immigration experience for families and children.* Washington, DC: American Sociological Association.

Alba, R., Massey, D. & Rumbaut, R. (1999). *The immigration experience for families and children.* Washington, DC: American Sociological Association.

Bentler, P. M., & Bonett, D. G. (1980). Significance tests and goodness of fit in the analysis of covariance structures. *Psychological Bulletin, 88*(3), 588–606.

Bentler, P. M., & Chou, C. P. (1987). Practical issues in structural modeling. *Sociological Methods & Research, 16,* 78–117.

Berry, J., & Sam, D. (1997). Acculturation and adaptation. *Applied Psychology: An International Review, 46,* 5–68.

Berry, J. W. (1997). Immigration, acculturation, and adaptation. *Applied Psychology, 46,* 5–34.

Bradley, R. H., & Corwyn, R. F. (2002). Socioeconomic status and child development. *Annual Review of Psychology, 53,* 371–399.

Callahan, R. M., Wilkinson, L., & Muller, C. (2008). School context and the effect of ESL placement on Mexican-origin adolescents' achievement. *Social Science Quarterly 89*(1), 177–198.

Capps, R., Fix, M. E., Ost, J., Reardon-Anderson, J., & Passel, J. S. (2005). *The health and well-being of young children of immigrants.* Washington, DC: The Urban Institute.

Carhill, A., Suárez-Orozco, M., & Páez, M. (2008). Explaining English language proficiency among adolescent immigrant students. *American Educational Research Journal, 45*(4), 1155–1179.

Conway, K. (2009). Exploring persistence of immigrant and native students in an urban community college. *Review of Higher Education, 32*(3), 321–352.

Dougherty, K. (1994). *The contradictory college: The conflicting origins, impacts, and futures of the community college.* Albany, NY: State University of New York Press.

Feliciano, C. (2006). Beyond the family: The influence of premigration group status on the educational expectations of immigrants' children. *Sociology of Education, 79*(4), 281–303.

Feliciano, C., & Rumbaut, R. (2005). Gendered paths: Educational and occupational expectations and outcomes among adult children of immigrants. *Ethnic and Racial Studies, 28*(6), 1087–1118.

Fuligni, A. (1997). The academic achievement of adolescents from immigrant families: The roles of family background, attitudes, and behavior. *Child development, 68*(2), 351–363.

Gándara, P., & Hopkins, M. (2010). *Forbidden language: English learners and restrictive language policies.* New York: Teachers College Press.

Gibson, M. (2001). Immigrant adaptation and patterns of acculturation. *Human Development, 44,* 19–23.

Gibson, M., Gándara, P., & Koyama, J. (2004). *School connections: U.S. Mexican youth, peers, and school achievement.* New York: Teachers College Press.

Goldenberg, C. (1996). The education of language-minority students: Where are we, and where do we need to go? *Elementary School Journal, 93,* 353–361.

Goyette, K., & Xie, Y. (1999). Educational expectations of Asian American youths: Determinants and ethnic differences. *Sociology of Education, 72*(1), 22–36.

Greenman, E., & Xie, Y. (2008). Is assimilation theory dead? The effect of assimilation on adolescent well-being. *Social Science Research, 37*(1), 109–137.

Haveman, R. H., & Wolfe, B. L. (1994). *Succeeding generations: On the effects of investments in children.* New York: Russell Sage.

Hu, L., & Bentler, P. M. (1999). Cutoff criteria for fit indexes in covariance structure analysis: Conventional criteria versus new alternatives. *Structural Equation Modeling: A Multidisciplinary Journal, 6*(1), 1–55.

Ibañez, G. E., Kuperminc, G. P., Jurkovic, G., & Perilla, J. (2004). Cultural attributes and adaptations linked to achievement motivation among Latino adolescents. *Journal of Youth and Adolescence, 33,* 559–568.

Kao, G. (2004). Parental influences on the educational outcomes of immigrant youth. *International Migration Review, 38*(2), 427–449.

Kao, G., & Thompson, J. S. (2003). Racial and ethnic stratification in educational achievement and attainment. *Annual Review of Sociology, 29,* 417–442.

Kao, G., & Tienda, M. (1995). Optimism and achievement the educational performance of immigrant youth. *Social Science Quarterly, 76*(1), 1–19.

Kleyman, K., & McVean, A. (2008). Structural equation modeling. Center for Research Design and Analysis and the Interdisciplinary PhD Program in Social Psychology. Reno, NV: University of Nevada, Reno.

Lee, V. E., & Bryk, A. (1989). A multilevel model of the social distribution of educational achievement. *Sociology of Education, 62,* 172–192.

Linton, A. (2004). A critical mass model of bilingualism among U.S.-born Hispanics. *Social Forces, 83*(1), 279–314.

Moll, L. C., Amanti, C., Neff, D., & González, N. (1992). Funds of knowledge for teaching: Using a qualitative approach to connect homes and classrooms. *Theory into Practice, 31*(2), 132–141.

Ogbu, J. U. (1989). The individual in collective adaptation: A framework for focusing on academic underperformance and dropping out among involuntary minorities. In L. Weis, E. Farraf, & H. Petrie (Eds.), *Issues, dilemmas, and solutions* (pp. 181–204), Albany, NY: State University of New York Press.

Ogbu, J. U. (1992). Understanding cultural diversity and learning. *Educational Researcher, 21*(8), 5–14.

Padilla, A., & Gonzalez, R. (2001). Academic performance of immigrant and U.S. born Mexican heritage students: Effects of schooling in Mexico and bilingual English language instruction. *American Educational Research Journal, 38,* 727–742.

Portes, A. (2000). The two meanings of social capital. *Sociological Forum, 15*(1), 1–12.

Portes, A., & Fernández-Kelly, P. (2008). No margin of error: Educational and occupational achievement among disadvantaged children of immigrants. *Annals of the American Academy of Political and Social Science, 620,* 12–36.

Portes, A., & Hao, L. (2002). The price of uniformity: Language, family and personality adjustment in the immigrant second generation. *Ethnic and Racial Studies, 25*(6), 889–912.

Portes, A., & Hao, L. (2004) The schooling of children of immigrants: Contextual effects on the educational attainment of the second generation. *Proceedings of the National Academy of Sciences of the United States of America, 101,* 11920–11927.

Portes, A., & MacLeod, D. (1996). Educational progress of children of immigrants: The roles of class, ethnicity, and school context. *Sociology of Education, 69,* 255–275.

Portes, A., & Rumbaut, R. (2001). *Legacies: The story of the immigrant second generation.* Berkeley, CA: University of California Press and Russell Sage Foundation.

Portes, A., & Rumbaut, R. (2006). *Immigrant America: A portrait* (3rd ed.). Berkeley, CA: University of California Press.

Portes, A., & Schauffler, R. (1995). Language and the second generation: Bilingualism yesterday and today. *International Migration Review, 28*(4), 640–661.

Portes, A., & Zhou, M. (1993). The new second generation: Segmented assimilation and its variants. *Annals of the American Academy of Political and Social Science, 530,* 74–96.

Portes, P. R. (1999). Social and psychological factors in academic achievement of children of immigrants: A cultural history puzzle. *American Educational Research Journal, 36,* 489–507.

Portes, P. R., Smith, T. L., Zady, M. F., & Del Castillo, K. (1997). Extending the double stimulation method in cultural-historical research: Parent–child interaction and cognitive change. *Mind, Culture and Activity, 4*(2), 108–123.

Portes, P. R., & Rumbaut, R. (2009a). *The Children of Immigrants Longitudinal Study (CILS).* Retrieved on from http://cmd.princeton.edu/data%20CILS.shtml

Portes, P. R., & Salas, S. (Eds.). (2011). *Vygotsky in 21st century society: Advances in cultural historical theory and praxis with non-dominant communities.* New York: Peter Lang.

Rios-Aguilar, C. (2010). Measuring funds of knowledge: Contributions to Latina/o students' academic and non-academic outcomes. *Teachers College Record, 112*(8), 2209–2257.

Rios-Aguilar, C., Gonzalez Canché, M. S., & Sabetghadam, S. (2012). Evaluating the impact of restrictive language policies: The Arizona 4-hour English language development block, *Language Policy, 11*(1), 47–80.

Royston, P. (2007). Multiple imputation of missing values: Further update of ice, with an emphasis on interval censoring. *Stata Journal, 7*(4), 445–464.

Royston, P. (2009). Multiple imputation of missing values: Further update of ice, with an emphasis on categorical variables. *Stata Journal, 9*(3), 466–477.

Rumbaut, R. (1994). The crucible within: Ethnic identity, self-esteem and segmented assimilation among children of immigrants. *International Migration Review, 18:*748–794.

Rumbaut, R. (1996). The crucible within: Ethnic identity, self-esteem, and segmented assimilation among children of immigrants. In A. Portes (Ed.), *The New Second Generation* (pp. 119–170). New York: Russell Sage.

Rumbaut, R. (2008). The coming of the second generation: Immigration and ethnic mobility in Southern California. *Annals of the Academy of Political and Social Science, 620,* 196–236.

Schmid, C. L. (2001). *The politics of language: Conflict, identity, and cultural pluralism in comparative perspective.* New York: Oxford University Press.

Schneider, B., & Stevenson, D. (1999). *The ambitious generation: America's teenagers, motivated but directionless.* New Haven, CT: Yale University Press.

Stanton-Salazar, R. D. (1997). A social capital framework for understanding the socialization of racial minority children and youth. *Harvard Educational Review, 67*(1), 1–40.

Suárez-Orozco, C., Pimentel, A., & Martin, M. (2009). The significance of relationships: Academic engagement and achievement among newcomer immigrant youth. *Teachers College Record, 111*(3), 712–749.

Suárez-Orozco, C., & Suárez-Orozco, M. (2001). *Children of immigration.* Cambridge, MA: Harvard University Press.

Tienda, M. (1980). Familism and structural assimilation of Mexican immigrants in the U.S. *International Migration Review, 14,* 338–403.

United Nations. (2006). *Trends in the total migrant stock: The 2005 revision* (OP/DB/MIG/Rev. 2005). New York: United Nations.

U.S. Census Bureau. (2007a). More than 300 counties now "majority-minority." Retrieved from www.census.gov/Press-Release/www/releases/archives/population/010482.html

U.S. Census Bureau. (2007b). 2006 American Community Survey. Retrieved from www.census.gov/acs/www/

Valadez, J. (2008). Shaping the educational decisions of Mexican immigrant high school students. *American Educational Research Journal, 45*(4), 834–860.

Valenzuela, A., & Dornbusch, S. M. (1994). Familism and social capital in the academic achievement of Mexican origin and Anglo adolescents. *Social Science Quarterly, 15,* 18–36.

Warikoo, N., & Carter, P. (2009). Cultural explanations for racial and ethnic stratification in academic achievement: A call for a new and improved theory. *Review of Educational Research, 79*(1), 366–394.

White, M. J., & Glick, J. E. (2000). Generation status, social capital, and the routes out of high school. *Sociological Forum, 15*(4), 671–691.

Wolf, D. L. (1997). Family secrets: Transnational struggles among children of Filipino immigrants. *Sociological Perspectives, 40*(3), 457–482.

Worthington, R. L, & Whittaker, T. A. (2006). Scale development research: A content analysis and recommendations for best practices. *Counseling Psychologist, 4*(6), 806–838.

Zhou, M. (1997). Social capital in Chinatown: The role of community-based organizations and families in the adaptation of the younger generation. In L. Weis and M. S. Seller (Eds.), *Beyond Black and White: New voices, new faces in the United States schools* (pp. 181–206). Albany, NY: State University of New York Press.

Zhou, M., & Bankston, C. L., III. (1994). Social capital and the adaptation of the second generation: The case of Vietnamese youth in New Orleans. *International Migration Review, 18*(4), 821–845.

Zhou, M., Lee, J., Agius Vallejo, J., Tafoya-Estrada, R., & Sao Xiong, Y. (2008). Success attained, detained, and denied: Divergent paths to social mobility in Los Angeles's new second generation. *Annals of the Academy of Political and Social Science, 620,* 37–61.

6

RECOMMENDATIONS FROM A COMPARATIVE ANALYSIS OF EDUCATIONAL POLICIES AND RESEARCH FOR THE ACHIEVEMENT OF LATINOS IN THE UNITED STATES AND LATIN AMERICANS IN SPAIN TOWARD SMARTER SOLUTIONS

Martha Montero-Sieburth and Lidia Cabrera Perez

Despite 50 years of academic research and policy recommendations at all levels of administration and government, educational outcomes for the majority of Latinos in the United States have been inconsistent, unequal, and lacking a long-term strategy. Compared to the mainstream population, educational structures and policies for Latinos remain shortsighted and ensure unfair disparities. In an attempt to identify and recommend research-based solutions for this dilemma, this chapter compares known policies and research explanations for U.S. Latinos with those of Latin American immigrant students in Spain and presents an overview of the ways these students' educational needs are being met in each country. During the past 20 years, Spain shifted from being an emigrant to immigrant country and with some immediacy has responded to the influx of immigrants or foreigners[1] arriving in the 1980s with national policies and educational laws implemented at the local autonomous community levels. Extensive studies by the federal government and research centers and institutes describe immigrant groups by nationality, their process of integration into Spanish society, and their linguistic and cultural adjustments. Among the groups most studied are Latin Americans who, because of the strong historical, linguistic, cultural, and social connections between Spain and Latin America, have emigrated in large numbers and constitute Spain's largest group of foreigners. Although on the surface their reception, insertion, and adaptation appears to be similar to that experienced by Latinos in the United States, premigration factors, contextual differences, educational backgrounds, and local-level practices account for significant differences whereby Latin Americans in Spain have been more integrated and suggest that Latin Americans achieve higher educational outcomes than Latinos in the United States. The comparisons between the two countries that we offer in this chapter are instructive and serve as the basis for a set of policies that we propose.

Research Focus

The following questions guide this chapter: (1) What similarities or differences can be found between the policies and research developed and used in the United States for Latinos and those in Spain for Latin Americans? (2) What have been the comparative outcomes of such polices and research in the United States, a traditional country of immigration, versus Spain, a country that in only 20 years has been transformed from a country of migration to a country of immigration? (3) Have these policies and research-based practices been conducive to reducing inequalities between Latin American immigrant students and native students in Spain, and between U.S.-born Latinos and Latino immigrants and their European White counterparts and other underrepresented groups? (4) What factors can be identified from comparing such policy and research-based explanations from both countries, and which can provide smarter and more effective solutions for improving educational levels of U.S. Latinos? To answer these questions, we draw on our body of work, which includes the following: (1) Montero-Sieburth's published synthesis of research and U.S. educational policies from 2001 to 2007 (Montero-Sieburth, 2005, 2007; Montero-Sieburth & Batt, 2001); (2) Montero-Sieburth's (1996) studies in U.S. high schools with Latino students and communities; and (3) a continued review of educational policies and research on Latino achievement in the United States and comparisons made by Montero-Sieburth, Cabrera Pérez, and Espínola Mesa (2010) of U.S. Latinos and Latin Americans in Spain. This is complemented by content analyses of databases and studies in the United States and Spain (Montero-Sieburth, Cabrera, & Carro, 2009) and with studies of achievement levels of Latin Americans in Spanish schools conducted by Cabrera Pérez (Cabrera Pérez, 2008, 2010, 2012). Several papers comparing policies developed for Latinos in the United States with those in the Netherlands at European Conference on Education Research (ECER) have been presented in 2011, and those comparing U.S. policies for Latinos with Dutch and Spanish policies/research at American Education Research Association (AERA) (2012). In addition, Cabrera Pérez has analyzed trends in policy and research for Spain covering the past 20 years using comprehensive social science databases such as Dialnet for journals and books complemented by her own research on schools in the Canary Islands.

The Post–No Child Left Behind (NCLB) Context for Immigrant Latinos in the United States

Despite the promises of the NCLB of 2002, educational and labor market gains for Latinos are still "up for grabs" as indicated by Jeanne Batalova and Michael Fix (2011). These authors point out that nationally the second generation of immigrants has numerically surpassed the first generation by 36 percent.

Second-generation Latinos have had substantial gains in high school attendance, postsecondary enrollment, and college degree attainment, but they still lag behind non-Latinos in obtaining college degrees. Beyond the difficulties in the implementation of policies based on empirical research, there are more reasons why Latinos are not making stronger gains in education. First, the idea that reforms and policies would "level the playing field" for all students has simply not been realized. Latinos continue to be recipients of segregated schooling and experience biased and discriminatory practices. As research by Montero-Sieburth et al. (2010) has shown, teachers normalize their expectations about Latinos "not making it" based on their second-language learner status or by simply being classified as Latinos. Second, many of the policies have been applied generically without being targeted to Latinos and thus have not addressed the particular needs of this student population. Others have followed color-blind policies not fitting the contexts of Latino students' experiences and thus ignoring racialization processes. Third, many of the policies also represent different interpretations of what needs to be done; some, like NCLB, use punitive accountability measures. Fourth, few of the blue-ribbon research reports that have been commissioned to remedy Latino educational disparities have been followed up on (see, e.g., Secada et al., 1998). Instead, policies have been reactive, rather than proactive, and have not used the knowledge, skills, and community resources of Latino communities. Schools have been dominated by a top-down business and management model based on accountability measures, professionalization of teachers, and empirically based "best practices." For economically stable school districts with available resources, adequate infrastructures, and qualified teachers and administrators, outcomes are positive, but for poorer school districts with limited resources, the outcomes are dim. In these schools, Latinos who lack the required human and cultural capital may actually be set up for failure because those unprepared to do well on tests may fail, continue to study to the test, or simply give up, perpetuating Latino dropout rates.

Beyond the use of surface "band-aid" solutions, not openly discussed or understood, is the fact that many of the policies adopted to dismantle inequality have not been grounded in the social, cultural, community, and historical contexts that profoundly affect the educational outcomes of Latinos (P. R. Portes, 2005). The inequalities that Latinos face with growing poverty rates, exacerbated by the current economic crisis, unemployment, and lack of strong welfare support (when needed) are insurmountable. According to Papademetriou, Somerville, and Sumption (2009), economic conditions at the point of arrival constitute one of the factors affecting first-generation immigrants' long-term social mobility. In contrast, urban concentration appears to influence policies for the second generation.

Just as Gunnar Myrdal in *An American Dilemma*, written 68 years ago, warned about the economic and social divisions between the "haves and have-nots," Joseph Stiglitz spells out in *The Price of Inequality: How Today's Divided Society Endangers our Future* (2012) how similar divisions exist today between the top and bottom echelons of society. Little income and wealth are generated at the bottom compared to the wealth being generated at the top. Yet the cost of living is higher than ever. Lacking any distributive power at the top, monies simply do not trickle down. Thus, economic disparities readily translate into diminished educational returns, particularly for Latinos whose youth are among the poorest in the United States. According to López and Velasco (2011) of the Pew Research Center, close to 6.1 million Latino children aged 17 and younger are living in poverty, becoming the single largest group of non-White poor children. Such disparities begin for Latinos in early childhood and, without resources or support, continue into adolescence contributing to what Hayes-Bautista, Schink, and Chapa (1988) identified as a Latino underclass.

Assimilation trends show that second-generation Latinos may experience upward economic and social mobility compared to the first generation, yet some of these advantages (A. Portes; Rumbaut, 2004; Telles & Ortíz 2008, Chapter 4, this volume) tend to dissipate by the third generation. Although this may not be a generalized phenomenon, such mobility negatively affects Latinos, and particularly Mexicans, who are highly discriminated against (A. Portes & Hao, 2004) and whose educational future appears bleak (Telles & Ortíz, 2008). From empirical data discussed in his chapter in the present volume, Alejandro Portes shows that the adaptation of the second generation and the determinant factors for their future not only stem from the human capital of parents of immigrant children, but also from the social context in which immigrants are received and the composition of the immigrant family. Thus, where Latinos start in their educational trajectories, their use of social class and cultural capital compared to mainstream White European counterparts become extremely significant. In this regard, the findings of Maurice Crul and John Mollenkopf (2012) for Mexicans in California, Dominicans in New York, and Turks throughout Western Europe prove useful. The entry level at which Dominicans and Mexicans in the United States start is highly differentiated by the availability of resources and provisions of welfare and social benefits that exist from that of Turks in Western Europe. Unlike Latinos who may live in ghettos, segregated neighborhoods, or poor housing, and with little medical support, Turks in Western Europe have access to higher living standards, guaranteed by benefits of the welfare state, which offers quality housing, education, health care, and employment. Similar advantages are much harder to obtain in the United States. Although the European educational system uses tracking and sorts students into high school programs that become holding areas and may lead to lower end jobs, the fact that educational quality is available and the cost of higher education is affordable reduces the starting point for Turks over that of Latinos in the United States. This is also the case when Latinos in the United States are compared with their Latin American counterparts in Spain where entry levels tend to be higher given the federal and local autonomous community support.

Spain: A Rapid Assimilation Approach

Spain (total population 47,150,819) is the country with the highest percentage of documented immigrants within the European Union (Fernández-Castillo, 2009). After Moroccans, Latin Americans account for the greatest percentage (12.2%) of the country's 5.7 million foreigners, or 36.2 percent of the total immigrant population. Ecuadorians (11.13%), Colombians (6.4%), Argentineans (3.63%), Bolivians (3.37%), Peruvians (2.31%), and Brazilians (1.75%) represent the largest groups of Latin Americans living in Spain, but the actual numbers vary according to where they are concentrated within each of Spain's 17 autonomous communities. The Canary Islands, where much of the research informing this chapter was carried out, has a population of 2,125,256, of which 306,307 (14.4%) are foreigners; 181,656 (59.3%) are Europeans, followed by Latin Americans who number 75,943 (24.7%) of the total foreign population (Colectivo IOE, 2002, 2003, 2008; Instituto Nacional de Estadística, 2009; Vasileva, 2011).

Over the past 20 years, Spain has enacted national policies that seek to integrate newcomers and provide schooling with the objective of diminishing the social, economic, and cultural disadvantages of immigrant students from Latin America (Garcia Castaño, Fernández Echeverría, Rubio Gómez, & Soto Paéz, 2007; Gómez Quintero, 2006). In all schools, integration drives assimilation. Article 27 of the Spanish constitution stipulates that "all minors below the age of 18 have a right to education and equality of educational opportunities," and such a right is not linked to nationality or the socioeconomic condition of families. Education is compulsory until the age of 16, and by law students must be enrolled in and attend school post age 18. Immigrants can either seek financial help provided by the local communities to continue to study or take advantage of the free professional courses (carpentry, management, etc.) available to them.

The Ley Orgánica (Organic Law of Foreigners, April 2000), its recent amendment in February 2009, and the royal decree of 2011 support the integration of immigrants by their intent to eradicate racism, xenophobia, and discrimination, which alone suggests that although there are policies to support the education of immigrants, there are also anti-immigrant sentiments toward them. Just as the amendment grants rights, it also obliges immigrants to attend school. Complementing this law is the Ley Orgánica de Ordenación General del Sistema Educativo (Organic Law for the General Organization of the Education System, January 1990; LOGSE) and the Ley Orgánica de Educación (Organic Law of Education, February 2009; LOE), which grants rights of education, unconditionally grants recognition to those with special educational needs or who are socially or culturally disadvantaged, and requires "respect for cultural differences and solidarity" (Fernández-Castillo, 2009, p. 185).

Although the intent of these federal laws is equity and inclusion, their implementation at the local autonomous level has been uneven and, in Spain's current economic recession, inconsistent. Despite such instability, some autonomous communities strive to meet the objectives of the laws. For example, in 2011, the Canary Islands instituted a decree entitled, the Policy for Specific Educational Support that requires services and special attention be given to meet the educational needs of immigrant, talented, or special needs students. Those relevant for immigrant students include the following: (1) ordinary (requiring teachers to use preventive, reinforcement, peer, and single grouping strategies in their activities) and (2) extraordinary (requiring teachers to develop individualized adaptations of the curriculum by cycle, course, or subject area).

Each of the 17 autonomous communities in Spain can decide on the educational programs and curriculum it implements at the local level based on demographic analysis and economic resources made available by the national/federal government. Documented and undocumented students between the ages of 3 and 16 are placed in appropriate grade levels and, irrespective of their place of origin or nationality, are provided with educational services. The curriculum for all students in Spain is the same, but once enrolled, immigrant students can receive the following: (1) individualized educational support for talented students, curricular support or instructional adaptations, including for culturally diverse students, and after-school programs such as pull-out classes in Spanish or Spanish as a second language; (2) compensatory programs with curricular diversification for students with limited educational levels, to at least complete high school; or (3) professional qualifications programs enabling 16-year-old students who have not finished secondary school to receive training to enter the labor market. In addition, funding from local governments provides "intercultural mediation" to sensitize students to new cultures and train teachers to use different modules that fulfill the school's intercultural educational commitment. Teachers not only advance their knowledge and professionalization in intercultural education, but also learn strategies on how to teach immigrants. Moreover, schools at the local level can opt for school-wide or reduced intercultural programs in accordance with European Union policies. In many schools "reception and citizenship coexistence" programs (Aguado, 2003, 2006, 2010) are established to transition incoming students through peer guidance. One of the innovations of this approach are the "cultural mediators" hired by local government as coaches who support the integration of students and their families into the community. They thus serve as a bridge to connect the school with immigrant students by conducting parent outreach, helping students negotiate learning issues, and supporting teachers with immigrant students.

These intercultural coexistence initiatives have been received quite well in schools and have not only contributed to the development of positive attitudinal and behavioral outcomes for students of different cultures (Cabrera Pérez, Montero-Sieburth, & Trujillo, in press), but also helped to identify highly committed teachers who, despite lack of pay, are willing to engage in intercultural activities and projects. Nonetheless, schools have also been criticized for not dealing concretely with the educational needs of immigrant students and for being inconsistent in the delivery of programs and implementation of services, thereby reducing opportunities established by federal legislation. In some schools, however, intercultural education programs are more window dressing than actual educationally driven opportunity programs (Cabrera Pérez et al., in press). A case in point is the temporal reception and language classes created for immigrants in Catalonia, which have been criticized for creating segregated and residual holding spaces. Critics such as Quintana (2003) warn that immigrant students leave such classrooms as soon as possible, and Carbonell, Simó, and Tort (2002) challenge the need to create such measures. In the current economic crisis, severe reductions or elimination of intercultural programs in the autonomous communities is also taking place.

Although much of the research and data is governmental, universities, institutes, nongovernmental organizations, or individuals interested in migration studies or integration carry out additional research (Santibáñez Gruber & Maiztegui Oñate, 2006a). Results are circulated or presented at regional conferences and often come to the attention of policy makers at local and national levels (Maiztegui-Oñate & Santibáñez-Gruber, 2010; Martinez-Alvarez, 2002; Navarro Sierra & Huguet, 2006). This has resulted in commissioned research from cities or regions with heavy immigrant saturation, such as Madrid and Barcelona, and Catalonia and Andalusia. Currently, the development of theoretical models such as comparative international education is a trend focused on Latin American national groups, rather than subgroups, and the data that inform these models represent general, rather than within-group, analysis (García Castaño, Rubio Gómez, & Bouachra, 2008). The Spanish Ministry of Education (Ministerio de Educación del Gobierno de España) not only publishes studies comparing native Spanish and immigrant grade attainment from elementary to higher education, but also reports on yearly achievement outcomes and commissions comparative research between Spaniards and other national immigrants such as Romanians or Chinese. Yet what is evident from this research is a tendency toward understanding the mechanisms by which Latin Americans do poorly in school, resulting in a focus on "failure." The within-group variation among second-generation Latin Americans has only recently begun to be studied because it is a young generation, but analysis of the academic achievement of Latin Americans compared to other ethnic groups such as Moroccans or Asians is also now emerging.

Much of the research on immigration trends has been quantitative, yet qualitative studies are on the rise. One such study was conducted by Trujillo González (2010) analyzing national-level studies based on educational indicators; foreign students show lower basic competencies compared to those born in Spain. Gibson and Carrasco (2010) as well as Gibson and Rios Rojas (2006) in their comparison of immigrant youth education in California (United States) and Catalonian schools indicate that through tokenistic practices, marginalization of students, teachers with meritocratic ideologies and inadequate curriculum materials, immigrant students in Spain do not always have a welcoming experience. Such research shows that immigrant students with poor schooling integration and little or no support from families tend to join gangs, drop out of school, and experience downward assimilation. Trujillo González's (2010) study shows that cliques are often formed: "The Colombians, Ecuadorians and Venezuelans form a separate group among themselves, unified by being Latinos, and identified with each other, making integration with the rest of the students in educational centers difficult" (p. 23). Aguado's (2010) research indicates that the education of Latin American parents, particularly mothers, positively influences the education of children. Cabrera Pérez (2012) indicates that age of arrival is another significant factor for Latin Americans, similar to Rumbaut's (2004) findings of Latinos in the United States. Those who arrive during their adolescent years as the 1.5 generation have a greater chance of dropping out of secondary school and not becoming integrated. Yet segmented assimilation theories, which demonstrate that there is not one single line of assimilation of Latinos in the United States, instead explain accommodation of either upward or downward mobility depending on socioeconomic status, peer networks, and coethnic support (Haller, A. Portes & Lynch, 2011; A. Portes & Hao, 2004; A. Portes & Rumbaut, 2001; Rumbaut & A. Portes, 2001). These theories have been widely studied in Spain (Aparicio, 2007) and the Netherlands (de Graff & van Zenderen, 2009; Vermeulen, 2012) for the second generation, although used and valued differently in the European context. Segmented assimilation does not fit national-level analyses in Europe given the variability of data and polarization factors (Crul and Doomernik, 2003); further, it has been noted that it presents a pessimistic picture of youth outcomes that is confused with the concept of the underclass (Vermeulen, 2012). Notwithstanding, segmented assimilation studies in Spain have shown some surprising results for Latin American immigrants compared to the results that have emerged for U.S. Latinos. Although issues of discrimination play a great role in creating downward assimilation for U.S. Latinos, Peruvians in Madrid, even though they are culturally and linguistically closer to Spaniards, do poorly in school compared to Moroccans and Dominicans who are both discriminated against (Aparicio, 2007).

Unlike the U.S. research and policy trends that have been based on the assumption that the cultural differences of Latinos are significant determinants of school success, in Spain, a focus on aspiration levels, motivation, and discrimination (rather than just cultural explanations) appear to be driving current research. Cabrera Pérez (2012), for example, argues that it is not the culture of origin or the lack of educational and social opportunities that stand in the way of Latin American students' educational achievement, but rather it is the educational level they arrive with, as well as the support of their family and peers, that counts in developing their academic expectations and motivations. In addition, comparative studies of Latin American students in their countries of origin and in Spain show that previous schooling and learning can be traced and understood for adaptation in new contexts (see, e.g., the research of Jordi Pamies [2006] on Yebala youth at the periphery of Barcelona, or Rolando Poblete Melis [2011] on Peruvians in Chile).

Research from the Spanish Ministry of Education (Ministerio de Educación del Gobierno de España, 2011) indicates that the academic achievement of first-generation Latin Americans tends to be lower than the native Spanish students, but higher than the achievement levels of other immigrants. However, only 2.2 percent have university diplomas, and 50 percent have engaged in studies leading to professional careers. Compared to the first generation, Latin Americans of the second generation fare better and continue to progress academically, even though they confront adjustments early on (Ministerio de Educación del Gobierno de España, 2010). A characteristic of the second generation is that their families have had higher socioeducational backgrounds in the country of origin (Serra, 2008; Trujillo González, 2010). But generalizations about upward mobility across and within groups cannot be made easily. Not all Latin American immigrants have poor educational trajectories in relation to other groups, and they are highly differentiated by regions as in the case of Catalonia, Granada, Madrid, and the Canary Islands (Serra, 2008). The issues of segregation may be more acute in cities like Barcelona where 15 percent of students in public schools are foreigners compared to 3 percent in private schools (Carrasco, 2006), but blending may be easier in the Canary Islands among Venezuelans and Canarians. Polarization of these experiences is also evident where some Latin American students despite the odds do well, whereas others do poorly. Yet despite entry-level difficulties in school, Latin Americans, especially in the second generation, bolstered with coethnic support, families, and peer groups, show upward mobility and advancement into higher education.

The United States and Spain: Similarities and Differences in Policies and Research

Key to understanding the impact of similarities and differences of U.S. and Spanish policies and research on educational needs of immigrant Latino students to the United States and Latin American immigrants to Spain is an initial grounding in the historical, social, and linguistic contexts of immigration. In terms of similarities, both Spain and the United States participated in the colonization of Latin America. Westward expansion of the United States in the 19th century, promoted by the notion of Manifest Destiny, culminating in the Mexican-American War and the Treaty of Guadalupe-Hidalgo of 1848, resulted in the United States acquiring Texas, California, and the territories comprising what are now New Mexico, Arizona, Nevada, Utah, and parts of Wyoming and Colorado. According to the treaty, Mexicans living in those annexed areas had the choice of relocating south of the Rio Grande, the new U.S./Mexico border or staying where they were, receiving American citizenship with full civil rights; more than 90 percent remained in the new U.S. territories. In the case of Spain, its domination and control of Latin America gave way to a caste system and racialization processes still embodied today in social class differences and the blending of Latino, Indian, Spanish, and African roots of *mestizaje*. Although Latinos in the United States have been part of the educational reform process for many years, they continue to live in poor neighborhoods and attend underfunded schools with poor teachers, resulting in limited opportunities for advancement. In contrast, given its historical connections and common language, Spain's response to Latin American immigrants has been one of relatively more acceptance, driven by economics (its construction boom, which went bust in 2008) and the future need for young workers given its growing aging population. Although compulsory and free education has been guaranteed as a right in the United States until the age of 18, with a growing second generation of Latin Americans and deepening economic crises, the educational deliverables promised by general and subsequent laws and policies in education are still in question. In this section, we examine the responses of the United States and Spain to immigration, in particular to the home language, the preparation of teachers, and high school completion rates.

Both the United States and Spain have policies engaging language issues of their immigrant populations. During the U.S. expansion into the southern border, English predominated as the official language of government, commerce, and in most regions, education. Speaking Spanish or other languages was not only discouraged, but often considered being disloyal to America. The incorporation of other Latino groups such as Puerto Ricans and Cubans, for example, further complicates the use of the home language vis-à-vis the official status of English. As Alba (2005) argues, even though bilingualism persists in America, English still dominates, with the real risk that by the third generation, Spanish is lost. Much also depends on programs that prevent the loss of Spanish as the home language and of the (still little researched) support of community and family to retain it. This is so in spite of the acknowledgement that bilingualism extends cognitive development. Thus, in the United States, there have been efforts to simultaneously suppress the use of Spanish and promote bilingualism. The teaching of English as a second language (ESL) has supplanted bilingual education in most cases, but the training of teachers in ESL has not been part of leadership development as is amply demonstrated. The use of Castilian Spanish, the language of colonization in Latin America, facilitates today the education and assimilation of Latin American immigrants in Spain despite the multiple geographic and dialectical variations. Latin American immigrants adapt to Castilian Spanish even though many immigrants from the Caribbean may be required to take Spanish as a second language. Immigrants living in semiautonomous regions where languages such as Catalan/Valencian, Galician, Basque, and Aragonese have constitutional protection are placed in bilingual programs.

The training of teachers is strongly equated with providing learning opportunities for students. Teachers in the United States receive pre- or in-service training in dealing with immigrant populations, English Language Learners (ELL) students, or bilingual students. In Spain, such training is made available to regional areas for teachers who need to upgrade their knowledge in specific areas. Although the professionalization of teachers in the United States is based on standards-based performance with testing and accountability measures, including teachers being "highly qualified," the evaluation of teachers in Spain is tied to meeting the needs of immigrant students like other native students based on available local resources.

In terms of high school completion rates and tracking, school districts in the United States measure such progress based on school reports and rankings of their schools in meeting standards, whereas the Spanish Ministry of Education draws the progress of students from local and regional statistics to present its records and federal statistics. Whereas in the United States both schools and teachers are held accountable for the learning of students, in Spain, it is the student with local school support who is enrolled and completes school and is then held accountable for learning.

The main differences between the two countries appear in the distinctions made in terms of the following: (1) the selective effect of geographic location and social proximity of countries; (2) national groups and ethnic groups; (3) the use of culture; (4) available schooling resources; and (5) the concept of race and its use, discrimination, and stigmatization. In their cross-national quantitative study of economic outcomes for Latin Americans who migrate to Spain versus Latino immigrants to the United States, Connor and Massey (2010) argue that selection effects based on geographic location and social proximity of each country affect each group differently. As they describe, Latin Americans immigrating to Spain are mostly from South America and from middle-class backgrounds, whereas Latinos who cross the border to the United States are largely Mexicans and Central Americans of lower-class origins. For immigrants to the United States, the cost of migration is low, but social costs are high; whereas for Latin Americans going to Spain, the social costs are lower because of fewer cultural and linguistic barriers, but the costs of migration are high. For many U.S. Latinos, being undocumented or having overstayed visas places them in a kind of marginalized twilight zone with limited legal status and employment options. On the other hand, many Latinos in Spain have either already undergone the legalization process or have received amnesty. And as reported by Connor and Massey (2010) female Latin Americans in Spain, they also have greater employment opportunities among undocumented migrants than those in the United States.

Latin Americans in Spain are seen as a collectivized group identified by nationalities with hardly any discussion of cultural differences as significant attributes. The very idea that failure might be explained by cultural differences between teachers and Latin American students is not apparent because of the emphasis placed on the commonalities that facilitate blending into Spanish society (Carabaña, 2006), whereas the concept of cultural attributes in the United States highlights differences among and between ethnic groups. In the Spanish context, Latino cultures are often explained in relation to success or failure, disadvantages stemming from parental influences on language, or position on the socioeconomic ladder. Latinos are thus "ethnicized and essentialized" and considered monocultural, despite national and subgroup variations. Mexicans, Peruvians, Argentines, Hondurans, and so forth are lumped together as "Latinos." This has led to "one-size-fits-all" policies at the national level and teachers in local schools not being aware of individual students' subtle particularities and differences based on their countries of origin.

Another difference lies in the ways in which the concept of race is used in U.S. schooling to profile students, but it appears to be less of a focus in Spanish schools where many South Americans are viewed as Europeans, with the exception of Afro-Caribbean Blacks who are stereotyped when they first arrive. In the United States, even though Latinos can be of any race, they are attributed phenotype characteristics based the lightness or darkness of skin color. Being identified as part of an ethnic group is of paramount importance in U.S. schools, and establishing allegiance to and identity within such peer groups offers young Latinos opportunities for asserting themselves and for expressing oppositional behaviors (Ogbu, 1991). Thus, U.S. explanations of Latino schooling failures are closely linked to ethnic, racial, and cultural differences. Schools' adoption of multicultural education practices in the United States is oriented toward reducing racism and discrimination among and between ethnic groups by promoting respect for cultural differences. Diversity of student populations has not been a focus in Spanish schools until recently, but the influx of Latin American immigrants has raised concerns about respect for cultures based on aggregate national groups rather than ethnic groups. To remedy discrimination, Spain uses an "intercultural education" approach, which is also intended to integrate Latin Americans into schools. However, the scope of incorporation and support for such programs in schools is contingent on available funds.

The sources and distribution of funding for public schooling are quite different for U.S. Latinos and Latin Americans in Spain, and this has a considerable effect on access to education. In the United States, because public school costs are largely paid for by the income generated from local property taxes, and because students must generally attend the school closest to where they live, the value of the homes in the school district has a direct impact on the amount of money available to local schools and therefore the type and quality of schooling students receive. Thus, urban (and often rural) schools, particularly, may be stratified on the basis of the family income levels in the communities they serve, which in turn determine the funding available from the local property tax base. In Spain, school funding is made available at the national level and allocated to the various local autonomous government offices based on demographic analysis of the local community needs, estimates of the numbers of students to be enrolled, and numbers of individual student services including innovative intercultural education programs. In this way, "slots" for students are created. Urban schools serve the majority of Latin Americans living in Spain who, drawn by work opportunities, settled in the cheap housing erected in large Spanish cities during Spain's massive construction boom. However, the large concentration of immigrants is leading to a shortage of slots and "White flight," in which Spaniards leave the urban areas and their schools seeking schools with little or no immigrant students. The result is segregated urban schools, ghettoization, and as in the United States, problems of social polarization in large Spanish cities (Serrano & Moreno Fuentes, 2007). In the United States, Latinos experience discrimination based on the perception of color and class, which can be strong and decisive detriments to successful schooling. In Spain, discrimination is greater for immigrants from North Africa and Morocco than it is for Latin American students (Trujillo González, 2010). Such discrimination tends to take place at the beginning of the school year and is not considered a cause of school failure. Latin Americans, however, encounter cultural shock regarding the customs used in Spain and suffer low self-esteem and discrimination based on poverty and ignorance. Poverty also plays a role in extending discrimination. For some Spaniards, Latin Americans are viewed as the poor relatives, a process that impedes the establishment of social and legally equal relationships (Abizanda & Pinos, 2002), and for U.S. Latinos, low socioeconomic indexes are often used to characterize students without recognizing the rising numbers of middle-class Latinos and their historically established permanent settlement throughout the United States.

The stigmatization of student identity is also a source of difference between the two contexts. In the United States, stigmatization may be the result of normative behavior and teachers' preconceived expectations of Latino students, or it may be the result of the way students' chances for success are viewed in terms of their color and language. In Spain, being a "new" and Black immigrant presents obstacles for some Latin Americans, such as Black Dominicans, although such students report that they try to ignore stigmatization and being stereotyped, and that over time they overcome such barriers (Horcas Lopez & López Martín, 2009). However, in the current economic crisis, stigmatization and discrimination feed into the strong anti-immigrant sentiment being expressed by natives who view Latin Americans as consuming the already limited public services including health care, social services, and education provided by the state at a cost to native Spaniards.

Results from this research on Latinos in the United States and Latin Americans in Spain show that both countries share the view of students/immigrants as "problems." This view is dispelled by the cases of students who succeed, versus those who fail, but in such polarization, explanations identifying premigration educational factors as well as settlement adaptation are needed. Research results on Latinos in the United States identify the need to work closely with Latino families, peers, and community arenas in order to overcome the odds students face with segregation and discrimination (A. Portes & Hao, 2004). Teachers must be trained to use identifiable learning strategies that engage Latino students. Moreover, as Fernández-Kelly (2008) suggests, the transferability of social class and cultural capital are assets that need to be capitalized on for second-generation immigrants. A problem that concerns policy is the fact that the United States has neglected to adopt solid research results but has made unsystematic and reductionist recommendations or has processed findings in isolation, targeting outcomes that do not include Latinos. In Spain, prevalent explanations of Latin American academic achievement identify cultural deficiency, linguistic, and curricular differences as blocks to educational advancement. The solution sought out is preparing teachers to work with immigrant students using intercultural education methods for academic improvement. Compared to many who arrive with low education in the United States, Gratius (2005) points out that Latin Americans arrive in Spain with a higher educational background than those who go to the United States: "Latin American immigration to Spain is not the exportation of poverty but a migration of workers specialized in the middle sector" (p. 22) whose cultural, idiomatic, and religious affinity facilitates rapid integration compared to those of immigrants from North Africa and Asia.

It is clear that both countries confront similar issues with regard to the schooling of students of Latin American origin and on how to best provide quality education to reduce disadvantages and inequalities. In the United States, parity in education is based on availability of sustained resources and support from schools, teachers, parents, and community members toward learning opportunities. In Spain, mobility is provided to Latin Americans by an educational system that, irrespective of their nationality, offers schooling supported with cultural mediators, language classes, and intercultural education. To the extent that resources are available, programs can continue to provide an education.

Recommendations for Smart Solutions

The comparisons and analysis of the similarities and differences of U.S. and Spanish educational policies and research explanations discussed in this chapter offer opportunities to advance policies and smart solutions. We discuss some of these possibilities subsequently.

Decolonization of Policy Paradigms and Research Explanations through Historical Agency: The decolonization of policy paradigms, research explanations, and practices is necessary for providing smart solutions. In this regard, it is important to confront color-blind policies and practices on issues that U.S. Latinos face in their everyday lives. In the case of Spain, incorporating aspects of Latin American and Spanish cultures is critical; otherwise, we risk creating new colonization spaces by imposing one-size-fits-all approaches. Discussions of race in the United States, linked to historical contexts and applied to racial and biological inferiority explanations, or to cultural differences, need to be critically examined and questioned within proposed policies. Likewise, given their social, economic, and social disadvantages, Latin Americans in Spain are presumed to need remediation, but this remediation needs to be implemented in terms of the additive rather than subtractive resources it provides. A critical examination of the underlying social and economic discriminatory practices that may arise

from projected policies is needed in order to uncover persistent racism and its consequences.

The Development of Comprehensive Policy Initiatives at Required Levels:
There is a critical need for comprehensive, national programs and policies of education that target the needs of Latinos in the United States and Latin Americans in Spain in school, without assuming the "one-size-fits-all" ideology. The intricacies of learning and the ways that Latinos or Latin Americans navigate schools need to be understood at their core, instead of using interventions based on cultural deficit, cultural deprivation, and "at-risk" factors. Comprehensive policies that focus on schooling in relation to health, social housing, and labor opportunities need to be developed and expanded rather than reduced. Instead of reproducing top-down policies, more grassroots and local community policies are required, which are linked to educational outcomes that integrate socioeconomic and political structures including education, work, legal services, housing, language learning, work orientation, and health care (see also Pajares, 2005).

The Development of Problem-Solving Practical Research Initiatives: Research that emanates from community levels needs to be longitudinal so that practical solutions can be examined beyond their publication impact. Working research into policy, even in short-term political terms, requires forethought about outcomes. Past research points to usable knowledge that can be derived from comparative studies and which can help change stagnant educational structures.

The Expansion and Internalization of Multicultural/Intercultural Training:
In the United States, teacher expectations for Latinos are often low and are based on normative judgments regarding the use of Spanish and their abilities to learn English and do well in school. These preconceptions are also found in some of the explanations identified for teachers in Spain. Multicultural thinking that goes beyond essentializing cultures needs to be developed within an understanding of ecologically and historically grounded schools. Teachers can generate arenas for multicultural interactions that allow for communication inside and beyond the classroom (e.g., La Clase Mágica). Furthermore, teacher training in diversity, intercultural education, and specific strategies for teaching Latin American students as well as Spaniards has to be fostered throughout schools in Spain. How normalization works its way into everyday teaching needs to be deconstructed—by institutionalizing intercultural education with cultural mediators within schools in Spain and by creating similar liaisons and relationships in U.S. schools.

The Reinvention of the Use of Culture: Culture matters, not because cultural differences and linguistic differences are identified, but rather because situational contexts in which processes of interaction and engagement take place can be situated and explained. As Lindo (2000) remarks, "Culture specificity is not an explanation; it demands explanation" (p. 218). Cultural explanations of differences are highly valued in the United States, under the assumption that changing the culture of the child changes his/her opportunity structure, which implies that culture is considered to be a commodity. Instead, culture needs to be viewed as a historical lens through which socioeconomic adaptation, curricular differences, and peer groups and parents play a significant role. There is a need to understand culture in a more grounded fashion with explanations that incorporate other psychological factors, engagement in school issues, teacher expectations, and institutional and structural issues. Just as Latinos/Latin Americans are products of their culture, they too are producing culture, and that interplay that needs to be understood. How culture becomes incorporated and to what degree significant discussions about such processes are taking place are essential steps in this process.

Reevaluation of the Significance of Language and Literacy Learning: In the United States and even in Spain, language learning needs to be viewed beyond remediation practices and as a process of enhancing communication. Although Latin Americans share a common language and culture with Spaniards, language difficulties arise and become an obstacle to learning, often requiring the use of Spanish as a second language. This can be used as a positive transition for learning. The same could be the case in the United States where Spanish or bilingual education or ESL can be taught. Thus, instead of viewing Spanish-language use in the classroom as a problem, home-language use can be a scaffold for second-language development within an additive model that includes strategies for adequate language development. Such a model could incorporate examples from the Spanish-language varieties spoken in the students' countries of origin and could be housed within developmental and content support programs rather than as a general subject area.

The Development of Community Agency through Social Organizing: Community agency fostered by the use of community "funds of knowledge" (Moll, 1992) is an important way to become an active force linking parents, students, and community members. Using community-based networks, such as National Latino Education Research Agenda Project (NLERAP), to promote school and home agency of Latinos is a step in the development of social organizing. Latin American associations in Spain are used for remedying problems of adaptation, yet they tend to be reactive and may need to become more proactive in providing greater support toward integration and solidarity for Latin Americans in Spain. In the United States, many community agency associations serve as testing grounds for leadership training and development.

The Enhancement of Parental Engagement and Intergenerational Learning: In both the United States and Spain, the relationship of parents to education and the schooling of their children requires that schools organize parents in timely ways, when they are not at work, through leadership training and centered around the lives of students by providing intergenerational language-learning opportunities. Parental engagement linked to schools such as those discussed in this book needs to be institutionalized because the prevention results indicate that Latinos whose families embrace biculturalism rather than acculturation are not only happier and healthier, but also benefit from protective factors that lead to increases in educational achievement, quality of life, and sociocognitive functioning (Bacallao & Smokowski, 2005). In the United States, models of bicultural parental engagement have been recognized; however, outreach to parents beyond cultural celebrations and language classes need to be more fully developed in Spain.

The Adaptation of "Smart" Curriculum: Parallels can be found in the curriculum adaptations and the development of instructional materials, especially in language, multicultural/intercultural education, and bilingual education. The drive for Common Core Standards in the United States and the Programme for International Student Assessment in Spain demands an examination of trends that seek the expansion of knowledge, skills, and dispositions out of context. We argue that such expansion needs to occur within the social and political contexts in which learning takes place. If curriculum is diversified, it cannot be at a lower level that closes out opportunities for future advancement of students. Thus, what is needed are structurally sound programs that have been well thought out and tested before being implemented. In both cases, transitional programs (afterschool programs, peer support groups, and mentoring programs) for Latino/Latin American students that advance them into higher education and activate their cultural capital are needed.

The Deconstruction of Structural Differences: We need to expand on comparative studies to analyze different opportunity points of the educational ladder, such as age on entering school, number of contact hours, or early childhood education exposure. Furthermore, we need to understand the long-term impacts of an education subsidized by the welfare state on educational outcomes. Latinos in the United States do not start at the same level as Latin Americans do in Spain, partly because of lack of generalized state support. Moreover, the schooling trajectories of Latinos in the United States may take longer depending on the curricular programs in which they are enrolled. But how a nation responds to those most in need of educational advancement will determine the outcome of future generations.

In summary, the research-based policies in both countries may have some general parallels, in that many begin with compensatory policies and remediation and move toward assimilation and integration. Further, these policies share the desired outcome goal of producing law-abiding and responsible citizens. Although Latinos have experienced a great deal of experimentation and variation in programs and projects promoted by policy and research outcomes, this has often been without regard to lived realities. The contexts in which Latinos and Latin Americans find themselves require reinvention within political and social discourse arenas.

Conclusion

The discussion of policies and educational practices used in the United States and in Spain illustrate the ways in which these explorations not only can contribute to new conceptual and theoretical knowledge about how the explanation of achievement is constructed, but also can show how students' identities are being socially and culturally constructed. Although policies may differ in their intent and produce other outcomes that ignore significant local research stemming from Latino communities in the case of the United States, and limited within-group research in the case of Spain, the fact is that they are both trying to find solutions to educate immigrant students. Much can be learned from each country's educational policy trajectories, which are directly committed to equalizing the inequalities that Latinos in the United States and Latin Americans in Spain experience so that they can realize their full potential as productive citizens, to the benefit of the future of both countries. In Henry Trueba's (2004) call to action for the NLERAP, he reminds us that researchers, because of their reach and scope in working with diverse groups, can be a powerful force in education reform. Further, it is critical that we strive to understand the diversity and heterogeneity of Latinos not as monolithic and fixed and replicating existing norms, but within a long-term agenda that meets the needs of local communities.

Note

1. Research using cross-national comparisons has been conducted recently in Europe. (1) The TIES project involving eight countries of Europe in studies of the second generation has published several country reports, articles, and a book with Maurice Crul and John Mollenkopf entitled *The Changing Face of World Cities: Young Adult Children of Immigrants in Europe and the United States* (2012). (2) The Children of Immigrants in Schools study directed by Richard Alba compares education in the United States and in Europe through five component projects: (a) "The transition to the labor market in France and the United States," with Richard Alba and Roxane Silberman; (b) "School funding and tracking in New York and Amsterdam," with Jennifer Holdaway and Maurice Crul; (c) "Post-secondary education: The impact of timing, differentiation, and second chances in Great Britain and the United States," with Mary Waters and Anthony Heath; (d) "Innovative, promising practice schools for children of immigrants," with Carola Suárez-Orozco and Mikael Alexandersson; and (e) "Navigating borders in schools and communities: Moroccan and Mexican immigrant youth in Catalonia and California," with Margaret Gibson and Silvia Carrasco (Alba & Waters, 2011; Crul & Mollenkopf, 2012.)

References

Abizanda, F., & Pinos, M. (2002). *La inmigración en Aragón.* Seminario de investigación para la paz. Zaragoza.

Aguado T. (2003). *Pedagogía intercultural.* Madrid: McGraw-Hill.

Aguado T. (2006). *Educación intercultural: Necesidades de formación del profesorado desde una perspectiva europea.* Madrid: UNED.

Aguado, T. (2010). Diversidad cultural y logros de los estudiantes en educación obligatoria. *Lo que sucede en las escuelas.* Estudios Creade.

Alba, R. (2005). Bilingualism persists, but English still dominates. *Migration Information Source.* Retrieved from www.migrationinformation.org/USfocus/print.cfm?ID=282

Alba, R. & Waters, M. (Eds.) (2011). *The Next Generation: Immigrant Youth in a Comparative Perspective.* New York: New York University Press.

Aparicio, R. (2007). The integration of the second and 1.5 generations of Moroccan, Dominican and Peruvian origin in Madrid and Barcelona. *Journal of Ethnic and Migration Studies, 33*(7), 1167–1193.

Bacallao, M. L., & Smokowski, P. R. (2005). "Entre dos mundos" (between two worlds): Bicultural skills training with Latino immigrant families. *Journal of Primary Prevention, 26*(6), 485–509.

Batalova, J., & Fix, M. (2011). *Up for grabs: The gains and prospects of first and second generation youth adults.* Washington, DC: Migration Policy Institute.

Cabrera Pérez, L. (2008). *La integración cultural y social de inmigrantes latinoamericanos. Inquietudes y sugerencias para políticas de cambio.* Madrid: Universitas.

Cabrera Pérez, L. (2010). La integración cultural y social de inmigrantes latinoamericanos en España. *Revista Estudios,* (23). Escuela de estudios generales de la Universidad de Costa Rica. Retrieved from www.estudiosgenerales.ucr.ac.cr/estudios/index.html

Cabrera Pérez, L. (2012). *Igualdad de oportunidades y diferentes resultados educativos entre Dominicanos y Venezolanos en Islas Canarias.* (Monograph, La Laguna University, Canary Islands, Spain)

Cabrera Pérez, L., Montero-Sieburth, M., & Trujillo, E. (2012). Window dressing or transformation? Intercultural education influenced by globalization and neoliberalism in a secondary school in the Canary Islands, Spain. *Multicultural Perspectives, 14*(3), 144–151.

Carabaña, J. (2006). Los alumnos inmigrantes en la escuela español. In E. Aja y J. Arango (Eds.), *Veinte años de inmigración en españa. Perspectiva juridical y sociológica (1985–2004)* (pp. 275–299). Barcelona: Fundación CIDOB.

Carbonell, J., Simó, N., & Tort, A. (2002). L' escolarizació del infants immigrants. In Carbonell et al. (Eds.) *Magribins a les aules: El model de Vic a debat* (pp. 37–44). Barcelona, Spain. Eumo Press.

Carrasco, S. (2006). *The poverty of children in migrated families or analyzing the well-being of children in migrant families: Lessons from the Barcelona reports.* Paper presented at the WELLCHI Network Conference 2, "Well-Being of Children and Labour Markets in Europe: Different Kinds of Risks Resulting from Various Structures and Changes in the Labour Markets," Centre for Globalization and Governance, University of Hamburg, Hamburg, Germany.

Colectivo IOE. (2002). *Inmigración, escuela y Mercado de trabajo: una radiografía actualizada.* Barcelona, Spain: Caixa Foundation.

Colectivo IOE. (2003). Alumnos y alumnas de origen extranjero: Distribución y trayectorias escolares diferentes. *Cuadernos de Pedagogía, 326,* 63–68.

Colectivo IOE. (2008). Dimensiones de la inmigración en España. Impactos y desafios. *Papeles de relaciones ecosociales y cambio global, 13,* 95–104.

Connor, P., & Massey, D. S. (2010). Economic outcomes among Latino migrants to Spain and the United States: Differences by source region and legal status. *International Migration Review, 44*(4), 802–829.

Crul, M., & Doomernik, J. (2003). The Turkish and Moroccan second generation in the Netherlands: Divergent trends between polarization within the two groups. *International Migration Review, 37*(4), 1039–1064.

Crul, M. & Mollenkopf, J. (2012). entitled *The Changing Face of World Cities. The Second Generation in Europe and the U.S.* New York: Russell Sage Foundation

Crul, M., & Mollenkopf, J. (Eds.). (2012). *The changing face of world cities: Young adult children of immigrants in Europe and the United States.* New York: Russell Sage Foundation.

de Graff, W., & van Zenderen, K. (2009). Segmented assimilation in the Netherlands? Young migrants and early school leaving. *Ethnic and Racial Studies, 32*(8), 1470–1488.

Fernández-Castillo, A. (2009). Psycho-educative and socio-political framework for intercultural education in Spanish schools, its limitations and possibilities. *International Journal of Intercultural Relations, 33,* 183–195.

Fernández-Kelly, P. (2008). The back pocket map: Social class and cultural capital as transferable assets in the advancement of second-generation immigrants. *Annals of the American Academy of Political and Social Science, 620*(1), 116–137.

García Castaño, F. J., Rubio Gómez, M., & Bouachra, O. (2008). Población inmigrante y escuela: Un balance de investigación. *Revista de Educación, 345,* 23–60.

García Castaño, J., Fernández Echeverría, J., Rubio Gómez, M., & Soto Páez, L. (2007). Inmigración extranjera y educación en España: Algunas reflexiones sobre el alumnado nueva incorporación. In M. A. Alegre & J. Subirats (Eds.) *Educación e Inmigración: nuevos retos para España en una perspectiva comparada.* Madrid, Spain: Centro de investigaciones sociológicas.

Gibson, M., & Carrasco, S. (2010). The education of immigrant youth: Some lessons from the U.S. and Spain. *Theory into Practice, 48*(4), 249–257.

Gibson, M., & Ríos Rojas, A. (2006). Globalization, immigration and the education of "new" immigrants in the 21st century. *Current Issues in Comparative Education, 9*(1), 69–76.

Gómez Quintero, J. D. (2006). La emigración latinoamericana. *Contexto global y asentamiento en España, 21,* 157–194.

Gratius, S. (2005). El factor hispano: El efecto de la inmigración latinoamericana a Estados Unidos y a España. Real Instituto el Cano de estudios internacionales y estratégicos. Retrieved from www.realinstitutoelcano.org/wps/portal/rielcano/contenido?WCM_GLOBAL_CONTEXT=/elcano/elcano_es/zonas_es/dt49-2005

Haller, W., Portes, A., & Lynch, S. M. (2011). Dreams fulfilled, dreams shattered: Determinants of segmented assimilation in the second generation. *Social Forces, 89*(3), 733–762.

Hayes-Bautista, D., Schink, W. O., & Chapa, J. (1988). *The burden of support: Young Latinos in an aging society.* Palo Alto, CA: Stanford University Press.

Horcas Lopez, V., & López Martín, R. (2009). *El papel de la educación en la integración social de las segundas generaciones de inmigrantes: Oportunidades y amenazas para desarrollar un contexto escolar inclusivo.* Valencia, Spain: Editorial Tirant Lo Blanch, S.L.

Instituto Nacional de Estadística. (2009, June). El número de extranjeros empadronados se sitúa en 5,6 millones de los cuales 2,3 millones son ciudadanos de la UE. Notas de Prensa. Retrieved from www.ine.es/prensa/prensa.htm

Ley Orgánica. (1990, January). De Ordenación General del Sistema Educativo LOGSE. *BOE, 238,* October 4, 1990.

Ley Orgánica. (2000, April). De 11 de Enero, sobre derechos y libertades de los extranjeros en España y su integración social. *BOE, 10,* January 11, 2000.

Ley Orgánica. (2009, February). De 11 de Diciembre de reforma de la Ley Orgánica, 4/2000, de 11 de enero, sobre derechos y libertades de los extranjeros en España y su integración social. *BOE, 299,* December 12, 2009.

Ley Orgánica. (2011, October). De 27 de Julio de modificación de los artículos 31 bis y 59 bis de la ley orgánica (4/2000). De 11 de enero, sobre derechos y libertades de los extranjeros en España y su integración social. *BOE, 180,* July 28, 2011.

Lindo, F. (2000). Does culture explain? Understanding differences in school attainment between Iberian and Turkish Youth in the Netherlands. In H. Vermeulen and J. Perlmann (Eds.), *Immigrants, schooling and social mobility? Does culture make a difference?* (pp. 206–224). London: MacMillan Press; St. Martin's Press.

Lopez, M. H., & Velasco, G. (2011, September). The toll of the great recession: Childhood poverty among Hispanics sets records, leads nation. Washington DC: Pew Hispanic Center.

Maiztegui-Oñate, C., & Santibáñez-Gruber, C. (2010). Migration and education: An overview of the Spanish case. Retrieved from http://migrationeducation.org/48.1.html?&rid=163&cHash=9d6f60e57eb65e106fdd8b0e5ae6d3ee

Martinez-Alvarez, M. C. (2002). *La escolarizacion de los hijos de los inmigrantes en Espana II.* Madrid: Confederacion Sindical de Comisiones Obreras.

Ministry of Education of Spain. (2010). El rendimiento educativo del alumnado inmigrante analizado a través de Pisa 2006. Madrid, Spain: Ministry of Education.

Ministry of Education of Spain. (2011). *Sistema estatal de indicadores de la Educación.* Madrid, Spain: Ministry of Education.

Moll, L. (1992). Funds of knowledge for teaching: Using a qualitative approach to connect homes and classrooms. *Theory into Practice, 31*(2), 132–141.

Montero-Sieburth, M. (1996). Teachers', administrators' and staff's implicit thinking about "at risk" urban high school Latino students. In F. Rios (Ed.), *Teacher thinking in cultural contexts* (pp. 55–84). Albany, NY: State University of New York.

Montero-Sieburth, M. (2005). Explanatory models of Latino/a education during the reform movement of the 1980s. In P. Pedraza and M. Rivera (Eds.), *Latino education: An agenda for community action research* (pp. 99–153). Mahwah, NJ: Lawrence Erlbaum.

Montero-Sieburth, M. (2007). *Academic models: Explaining achievement.* In L. Díaz Soto (Ed.), *Praeger handbook of Latino education in the United States* (Vol. 1, pp. 8–23). Santa Barbara, CA: Praeger.

Montero-Sieburth, M., & Batt, M. C. (2001). An overview of the educational models used to explain the academic achievement of Latino students: Implications for research and policies into the new millennium. In R. Slavin & M. Calderón (Eds.), *Effective programs for Latino students* (pp. 331–368). Mahwah, NJ: Lawrence Erlbaum.

Montero-Sieburth, M., Cabrera, L., & Carro, L. (2009). Multidisciplinary analysis of gender, education, and transnational households influenced by globalization: Narratives of Dominican women in the Canary Islands, Spain. Presentation at AERA Annual Meeting, "Disciplined Inquiry: Educational Research in the Circle of Knowledge," San Diego, CA.

Montero-Sieburth, M., Cabrera Pérez, L., & Espínola Mesa, C. (2010). The effects of globalization and transnationalism on policies and practices in the education of Latinos in the U.S. and Latin Americans in Spain. In E. Murillo, S. A. Villenas, R. Trinidad Galván, J. Sánchez Muñoz, C. Martínez, & M. Machado Casas (Eds.), *Handbook of Latinos and education* (pp. 135–156). New York: Routledge.

Myrdal, G. (1996). *An American dilemma: The Negro problem and modern democracy.* Piscataway, NJ: Transaction.

Navarro Sierra, J. L., & Huguet, A. (2006). Inmigración y resultados escolares. *Cultura y Educación, 18*(2), 117–126.

Ogbu, J. (1991). Immigrant and involuntary minorities in comparative perspective. In M. A. Gibson & J. Ogbu (Eds.), *Minority status and schooling: A comparative study of immigrant and involuntary minorities* (pp. 3–36). New York: Garland.

Pajares, M. (2005). *La integración ciudadana. Una perspectiva para la inmigración*. Barcelona, Spain: Icaria.

Pamies, J. (2006). *Dinámicas escolares y comunitarias de los jóvenes de la Yebala en la periferia de Barcelona* (Doctoral dissertation, Departamento de Antropología Social y Cultural, UAB). Retrieved from wwwub.es/~xcol/311

Papademetriou, D. G., Somerville, W., & Sumption, M. (2009, June). *The social mobility of immigrants and their children.* Washington, DC: TransAtlantic Council on Migration, Migration Policy Institute.

Poblete Melis, R. (2011). *Intercultural education, theories, politics and practices, Peruvian migration in today's Chile: New situations and challenges for integration* (Doctoral dissertation, Autonomous University of Barcelona).

Portes, A., & Hao, L. (2004). The schooling of children of immigrants: Contextual effects on the educational attainment of the second generation. *Proceedings of the National Academy of Sciences of the United States of America, 101*(33), 11920-11927.

Portes, A., & Rumbaut, R. G. (2001). *Legacies: The story of the immigrant second generation.* Berkeley, CA: University of California Press and Russell Sage Foundation.

Portes, P. R. (2005). *Dismantling educational inequality: A cultural-historical approach to closing the achievement gap.* New York: Peter Lang.

Quintana, A. (2003). Estrategias de acogida y acompañamiento en ESO: Una propuesta de itinerario con alumnado de incorporación tardía. *Aula de Innovación Educativa, 126,* 53–57.

Rumbaut, R. (2004). Ages, life stages, and generational cohorts: Decomposing the immigrant first and second generations in the United States. *International Migration Review, 38*(Fall 2004), 1160–1205.

Rumbaut, R., & Portes, A. (2001). *Ethnicities: Children of immigrants in America.* Berkeley, CA: University of California Press and Russell Sage Foundation.

Santibáñez Gruber, R., & Maiztegui Oñate, C. (Ed.). (2006a). *Inmigración: Miradas y reflejos. Historias, identidades y claves de intervención social.* Bilbao, Spain: Universidad de Deusto.

Santibáñez Gruber, R., & Maiztegui Oñate, C. (2006b). La escuela, puente de integración de jóvenes inmigrantes: Animando al éxito. In Santibáñez Gruber, R. & Maizteguí Oñate, C. (Eds.), *Inmigración: Miradas y Reflejos. Historias, Identidades y Claves de Intervención Social* (pp. 199–219). Bilbao, Spain: Deusto University Press.

Secada, W. G., Chavez-Chavez, R., Gracia, E., Munoz, C., Oakes, J., Santiago-Santiago, I., & Slavin, R. (1998). *No more excuses: The final report of the Hispanic dropout project.* Washington, DC: Department of Education.

Serra, C. (2008). El alumnado extranjero en Cataluña: La continuidad de los estudios después de la etapa obligatoria. In A. Madaro (Ed.) *Experiencias de Acogida e Integración Educativa del Alumnado Inmigrante Iberoamericano* (pp. 103–119). Madrid, Spain: Organization of Ibero-American States for Education, Science and Culture/Ministry of Work and Immigration.

Serrano, J. F. J., & Moreno Fuentes, F. J. (2007). *La sostenibilidad económica y social del modelo migratorio español.* Madrid, Spain: Centro de Estudios Políticos y Constitucionales.

Stiglitz, J. (2012). *The price of inequality: How today's divided society endangers our future.* New York: W. W. Norton.

Telles, E., & Ortíz, V. (2008). *Generations of exclusion: Mexican Americans, assimilation, and race.* New York: Russell Sage Foundation.

Trueba, E.H.T. (2004). *The new Americans: Immigrants and transnationals at work.* New York: Rowman & Littlefield.

Trujillo González, E. (2010). *Conflictos interculturales en la escuela: Una experiencia de investigación etnográfica en un instituto de enseñanza secundaria de la isla de Tenerife.* (Monograph, La Laguna University, Canary Islands, Spain).

Vasileva, K. (2011). 6.5% of the EU population are foreigners and 9.4% are born abroad. *Eurostat: Statistics in Focus, 34,* 2011. Retrieved from http://epp.eurostat.ec.europa.eu/cache/ITY_OFFPUB/KS-SF-11-034/EN/KS-SF-11-034-EN.PDF

Vermeulen, H. (2012). Segmented assimilation and cross-national comparative research on the integration of immigrants and their children. In J. Schneider & M. Crul (Eds.), *Theorizing integration and assimilation* (pp. 71–87). New York: Routledge.

Zolberg, A. R., & Woon, L. L. (1999). Why Islam is like Spanish: Cultural incorporation in Europe and the United States. *Politics and Society, 27*(1), 5–38.

7

DEVELOPMENT AND ITS SOCIAL, ECONOMIC, AND EDUCATIONAL CONSEQUENCES

The Case of the Zimapán Hydroelectric Project

Sergio Quesada Aldana

In recent decades, Mexico, as is the case in many other countries in Latin America, has been forced to enact very specific development policies as set forth by the World Bank. The Mexican government, in order to obtain much-needed loans, has been required to put forth projects that are particularly linked to large-scale development, and one of the preferred types of projects promoted by the World Bank has been the construction of hydroelectric dams. In the early and mid-1990s, the World Bank and the Mexican Federal Commission of Electricity (CFE) jointly financed several large hydroelectric works. When construction of the Zimapán Hydroelectric Project, located in the central region of Mexico, commenced in August 1990, an additional recommendation of the World Bank was that the CFE hire a multidisciplinary team to study the pre- and posttraumatic effects of the possible social, economic, and psychological impacts related to the large-scale relocation of families affected by the hydroelectric project's construction.

The multidisciplinary team, composed of two anthropologists, an agronomist, a geographer, and a sociologist, hired by the CFE, conducted field study from 1990 until 1994, the year the Zimapán Hydroelectric Project was inaugurated. The principle investigator (myself, Quesada Aldana) participated in and led the CFE team up until 1993. Afterward, I continued independent follow-up fieldwork in an ongoing ethnographic study with a team of Universidad Autónoma de Querétaro (UAQ) graduate students in anthropology of the extended area surveyed, utilizing the cultural and sociological practice of participant observation and structured questionnaires applied to approximately 5 percent of the families affected. Both quantitative and qualitative analyses were conducted. The work has continued through the production of this chapter. Here, I report on the results of both the earlier team research and the follow-up work. Both efforts found that the social, cultural, and economic impact of this development have been far-reaching, both temporally and geographically, because large portions of the original population from the region have migrated both within Mexico and to the United States, including to the state of Georgia.

Millions of dollars are invested each year by international aid agencies based in the developed world (e.g., the World Bank, the International Monetary Fund, and U.S. Agency for International Development (USAID)), such as in development projects ostensibly designed to raise the economic and social well-being of their target communities in the developing world. These projects are often designed to ensure that the countries receiving the aid can build the infrastructure necessary to accommodate the economic and industrial growth that international aid agencies identify as necessary to development. However, often when the projects are drafted, little attention is paid to the ripple effects these projects can have and the larger social and political repercussions that they can cause. Such is the case of the Mexican Zimapán Hydroelectric Project funded by the World Bank in the early 1990s. This dam fulfilled its intended goal of increasing the energy-generating capacity of the Mexican state, but it precipitated countless unintended consequences including social and economic instability in the communities surrounding the dam, widespread immigration from rural Mexico to the United States, and eventually, social and economic pressure on the communities and schools in the United States where these migrants landed.

Mexican presidents have historically solicited loans from the World Bank and other international development agencies as parts of larger economic and societal development strategies. Securing such loans is often motivated by political and economic self-preservation (Andere & Kessel, 1992; Balán, Browning, & Jelin, 1973). During his 1988–1994 administration, Salinas de Gortari successfully sought one such loan from the World Bank. The funds were granted, not surprisingly, with a number of conditions including budgeting for the construction of two hydroelectric dams. For the World Bank, the dams were an assurance, the idea being that the Mexican state would be better able to generate the energy needed for the related projected industrial development to succeed. The World Bank's stipulations were intended, among other things, to ensure that the Mexican government officials would not direct the funds elsewhere—on perhaps more whimsical projects—and the project was viewed as a good use of somewhat neglected resources in the generation of electricity. This chapter centers on the human costs that the Zimapán and Aguamilpa Dam projects extracted on the Mexican peasant communities they displaced. My analysis suggests that policy conversations about Latinos in U.S. education, at minimum, be aware of the national and international consequences of development policy—especially in Mexican contexts.

Studying the Zimapán Hydroelectric Project

In 1989, the World Bank and the federal government of Mexico initiated the Zimapán Hydroelectric Project in the Mexican central regional states of Querétaro and Hidalgo. The two institutions had each agreed to finance 50 percent of the total cost of the project. However, the World Bank requested that the Mexican government have an independent specialist team to monitor and advise the latter in matters related to the relocation of the affected populations, especially in regard to economic, ecological, social, and cultural issues. The purpose of this monitoring was to assure minimum impact on the relocated people. The team consisted of UAQ researchers hired through the Instituto Nacional Indigenista (INI), the institution that assessed and monitored the CFE, the federal agency in charge of the project. Initially, the INI team functioned as a critical body with the main objectives of assessing and monitoring the relocation process. However, by the project's second year, high-level authorities within the organization had been co-opted by the interests of the CFE. By early 1992, the research on which this chapter was based was initiated independently of the INI.

The total area affected by the reservoir of the Zimapán Hydroelectric Project covered approximately 2,350 hectares, 1,617 hectares located in the state of Hidalgo and the remaining 733 hectares in Queretaro. Although Hidalgo counted more hectares, Queretaro had more residential communities affected by the dam. In Hidalgo, 400 people reported losing their homes; in Queretaro, the number was 2,152. The communities affected by the loss of their dwellings were relocated to four new localities, one in the state of Queretaro: Bella Vista del Rio part of the *ejido* (a plot of communal land that was formerly owned by the state and worked by the peasants). However, with the implementation of the North American Free Trade Agreement (NAFTA), these once-communal lands were privatized where Vista Hermosa, La Vega, and Rancho Nuevo intersect. Bella Vista del Rio was completely new in terms of its design and construction and neighbored the historic Mesa de Leon.

The negative impacts of the Zimapán Hydroelectric Project were not limited to the loss of homes. Rather, various kinds of property were subsumed by the project including cultivated lands for grains, vegetables, fruit trees, palm trees, common reed grasses (used for handicrafts), and maguey (a species of cactus), as well as structures related to agricultural infrastructure, such as silos, corrals, fences, dirt reservoirs, irrigation canals, and so forth (Quesada Aldana, 1991, 1994, 1997). The affected peasants were either compensated for or reimbursed for all of these goods by the CFE. Yet, some loses were impossible to compensate, such as irreparable damage to several species of flora particular to the area including the equino cactus rescued by a team of Universidad Nacional Autónoma de México biologists. The species no longer reproduces in its natural form and with its original characteristics.

One of the tasks to be carried out by the monitoring team included extensive and continuous surveys of the entire affected region. Contrary to the CFE assessment that only five communities would be affected by the future reservoir, the team's surveys revealed that at least 38 communities were impacted in some way by the construction of the Zimapán Hydroelectric Project. In the area of the reservoir alone, 17 *ejidos*, in addition to some private property, were affected. This was due, in part, to the numerous subprojects involved: the construction of roads, the installation of electrical lines, the construction of windows and ducts for the tunnels, and the establishment of camps for the workers, as well as depots for construction materials. Moreover, resettlement influenced communities both materially and culturally, However, CFE demonstrated little interest in researching or preserving the latter.

Global Free Trade, Local Development

Few talked about the NAFTA when the project began; however, it quickly became obvious that this dam project was designed and approved precisely because of the dynamics of NAFTA. At the time, the state of Queretaro did not require the amount of energy this dam would produce. Nonetheless, Queretaro and the surrounding region were earmarked to take an integral role in the Mexico's development were the treaty approved. In other words, the hydroelectric plant was the means, or at least a necessary condition, to facilitate the approval of NAFTA by the U.S. government in that the Mexican state was committed to providing a modern highway system to facilitate the transportation of merchandise, an inexpensive labor force, and sufficient natural resources. Most importantly, Mexico needed to demonstrate that it could provide independent and abundant sources of energy with its hydroelectric plants to support a growing industrial infrastructure supported by international investment

The World Bank's dam-building projects in developing countries have not always had positive results for the communities involved (Derman, 1998; Donahue & Johnston, 1998; Hansen & Smith, 1982; Loker, 1998). In the context of Mexico, dam building is full of bitter memories of populations (often rural, impoverished subsistence farmers) having been forcibly evacuated by the army or police or of having to witness the water level rise over their properties as the reservoir filled (Aguirre Beltrán, 1958; Bartolomé & Barabas, 1990; McMahon, 1989; Poleman, 1964; Villa Rojas, 1948; Winnie, 1958). In the case of the Zimapán Project, the World Bank wanted to do things differently. Forced relocation would have to take place. However, the CFE wanted to change communities' attitudes with the strong message that the sacrifices needed would ultimately benefit Mexico and Mexicans. In addition, and even more importantly, CFE made provisions to improve the resettlement process by providing displaced residents with better living conditions than they had previously experienced. Resettlement guidelines included generous monetary compensation for land, houses, and other valuables lost and relocation to a visibly new and therefore "better" town. On paper, this seemed a good idea. In fact, the peasants involved in the relocation saw the move as an opportunity to make money; and, in many cases, they seized the opportunity. News of the compensation program led to quick home additions and even the construction of new houses, knowing that the entire community would soon be covered by water, and knowing that the government would pay for every building in the flooded zone. Payment included monies for each tree on their land (both fruit and timber) as well as for food and medicinal plants, such as agaves and other cacti, and reed grasses used for crafts. Additionally, the owners would be given at least two hectares of land for every hectare flooded. Finally, the compensation program dealt with the issue of relocated housing: the resettlement of all these people into an entirely newly developed town.

One of the most relevant aspects of the affected population's social organization was the appearance of representative committees organized to negotiate with the CFE usually composed of the *ejido* and municipal authorities. Nevertheless, the population later modified the constitutions of some of these committees with the idea of ensuring greater representation of the affected people. Some of the committees in question tried to reinforce their strategies of negotiation by depending on external assessors such as the National Peasant Confederation (CNC in Spanish), regional governments, universities, and the federal government and private assessors.

A Culture of Migration

Even before the Zimapán Dam, a culture of migration had already existed in the communities in question. Peasant agriculture was supported by a subtropical climate and an abundant, although polluted, water source. These ecological conditions allowed farmers to harvest up to three crops per year; however, the size of the farms was too small to sustain entire families, forcing them to find complementary sources of income. As a result, most of the male population also worked as construction workers. A third of the female population of working age worked as household domestics in the nearby cities of Queretaro, San Juan del Rio, and Mexico City. Patterns of migration, mostly to the United States, began in the 1940s, motivated by curiosity and as a desire to supplement their families' incomes (Chayanov, 1925/1985).

More recently, Basaldúa (1994) established that the patterns of migration to the United States were carried out in large part among peasant migrants who worked their own parcels of land (or who had done so prior to the hydroelectric project). In fact, there was a markedly greater incidence of migration among the landholders than among the simple laborers and the joint holders of tenured lands. In addition, during the 1990s, based on a long-standing agreement with the U.S. government, the Mexican secretary of the government (the secretary of state) issued permission for migrants to work in the United States. The municipality of Cadereyta sent more workers than any other municipality in the state of Queretaro. However, from 1971 forward, certain Texan and Californian ranchers broke the agreement between the two countries, paying lower wages to their migrant workers. Although the Mexican government protested, the flow of migrants searching for work in the United States did not slow (Basaldúa, 1994).

Notably, migrant workers from the *pueblos ribereños*, or "riverbank towns," worked not only in agriculture but also in various service sectors such as cleaning, cooking, plumbing, and so forth, and in construction work. Migrating to the United States, workers learned new skills such as auto mechanics, electrical technology, refrigeration, heating, and so forth. In many cases, workers returned to teach their family members and friends what they learned in the United States, so that others would have the possibility of going to the United States with a knowledge base that which would facilitate their finding work.

Ribereños (the self-styled name of the people of Bella Vista del Rio) seasonally in the United States returned to Zimapán with a new *norteña* (Northern Mexico) or *bracera* (illegal migrant worker) culture, different from their original *ribereña* culture. In this sense, but within the sociocultural organization of the *ribereños*, Basaldúa (1994) remarks (my translation):

> With constant migration, they have succeeded in establishing labor routes and in acquiring knowledge of the laws and regulations of the North-Americans. We also find the influence of habits of conduct and the management of money because of migration. With a base in the comparison of other populations, the peasants of Vista Hermosa had reinforced the structure of the *ejido* organization. It can also be inferred that the influence of this migrating factor has helped the peasants in their orientation towards negotiating mechanisms during the adjustment period of the resettlement. Their management of public relations, their experience in matters of economic negotiation and the search for better benefits in their labor actions has all been taken advantage of during this adjustment. (p. 161)

Leaders of the local committees organized to negotiate with the CFE claim were not migrants. Yet, the influence of migration on the sorts of demands presented to the governmental agencies was undeniable, and *ribereño* negotiators clearly benefited from the experiences of the *norteños* or *braceros* in their meetings with the *ejidos*, friends, and families.

In the stores of the former communities (and including in those of the current Bella Vista del Rio), it was (and still is) very common to hear of the "adventures" of the migrants in the United States, where they tell of the existence and the functions of the farm workers' unions and how the workers are compensated when something out of the ordinary happens. One informant pointed out:

> Over there, everyone works the same . . . you end up really tired, but you earn good money. And if there is any accident, or they don't honor the contract, well, there are dollars to compensate for that . . . that way you learn to defend yourself and they almost always respect you for that . . . according to the contract . . . The same with the houses, if you buy one and you have problems, well, you can sue them and it's expensive for them, but

well, sometimes they even pay you too much . . . and that's the way it is in the stores, if you buy something in the stores and it turns out bad, well, you complain and they give you another one, a new one or you get your money back, in that way you learn to defend yourself. And then you come back here and you've forgotten how it is, and we start to complain and most of the times there isn't anything we can do but put up with it . . . this has to change.

Finally, our informants emphasized that migrating seasonally to the north was status related. Before the population received their compensation payments from the CFE, only a small minority could go to the United States. However, with the compensation payments, practically all of the heads of household went to the United States for at least short periods of time and were therefore able to say that they too had been "on the other side."

The Aftermath of Relocation

In November 1994, the Zimapán Hydroelectric Project was inaugurated with a great deal of "pomp and circumstance" by the president of Mexico, Carlos Salinas. The final cost was more than 2 billion pesos (approximately US$60 million). Although the officials were thrilled with the "modernity," of the new Bella Vista del Rio community, nostalgia and uncertainty ran high among relocated residents.

Compared to the subtropical land that they used to have, their new arid settlement was less than the "Promised Land." Moreover, despite the fact that the affected people, as we have mentioned, were subsistence farmers with knowledge of construction, the Mexican government denied them the right or means to design or build their own houses with a peasant architectural pattern. Instead, the CFE hired a professional construction firm, and the design of the new town was more a modern urban complex than a peasant village. In fact, it remains the most modern settlement of its kind in the whole central region of Mexico, with an auditorium (and other buildings that the community members seldom use) and wide, illuminated streets, sewage, and drainage. The construction firm, rather than designing a peasant-style community laid out in a semidispersed settlement pattern, where fruit trees surround the houses and there is enough land for gardens and farm animals, the new houses were built city style, or wall to wall, where privacy was no longer possible. With the loss of their accustomed privacy, various dilemmas ensued including fights over one neighbor watching another's wife. The new settlers, nevertheless, adapted their modern yards, incorporating animal corrals and small kitchen gardens. When the engineers and architects from the project suggested that a communal corral be constructed at the town's edge, the villagers insisted that they required their own corrals to house their livestock, asking such questions as the following: How would they know whose eggs were whose? To whom would the corral belong? Or, who was going to take care of or feed the animals? And so forth. The idea of a common corral far from their own homes seemed ludicrous to them.

Although the design of the houses was a tremendously contentious issue, the economic situation was even more serious. For the first time in their lives, the new settlers had a lot of cash but no one from the Mexican government or the World Bank to advise them on how to best invest the funds, and, indeed, not a single investment project was created for these relocated peasants. Furthermore, no plan for developing the area was drafted. Moreover, although the CFE offered the peasants new farmland with irrigation services, these lands were located more than 70 kilometers away from Bella Vista. The offer was, consequently, rejected. Living in a modern, urban town and commuting 140 kilometers daily to tend between four and eight hectares did not seem practical or profitable to most of the affected peasants. The peasants preferred to receive compensation in cash, rather than in land. In the end, the peasants lost the only good land that they had, in some cases keeping plots of land without irrigation in the middle of the desert. Therefore, one result of the Zimapán Hydroelectric Project was a community of subsistence farmers with no land.

Landless peasants are not rare in Mexico; peasants with a lot of cash are uncommon in any part of the world. Although one might assume that these peasants were happy with their newfound monetary wealth, the same families were very unhappy with their situation. They were compensated with a great deal of money, but they found themselves adrift without bearings because they could no longer farm and interact as they had for generations. They had been given little direction as to how to put their newly gained "fortune" to practical use to sustain themselves and improve their impoverished lives. As a result, they spent their money on unproductive and fruitless projects and soon were as penniless as before.

Lacking significant investment in Bella Vista del Rio, the money the peasants received in compensation was spent on furniture, cars, and trucks. Although some bought tractors, they bought them for status and to buy something they could never buy before; the tractors found little practical use because the farmland was not apt for agriculture. Others spent their money on guns and liquor. Others opted to invest their money in migrating to the United States. The *ribereños'* wealth facilitated their migration north. No longer did they have to walk for eight days eating only dried tortillas, corn, and water (Basaldúa, 1994). Now the population could migrate to the United States in their own vehicles, by bus, and in some cases, by air. The residents of Bella Vista, for the first time in their history, had the resources to pay on average US$1,000 to the *pollero*, or "coyote," to help them cross the border. Others opted for buying an airline ticket in order to bypass many of the difficulties involved in crossing the U.S.-Mexican border. The residents of Bella Vista del Rio had not only sizable bank accounts, but also the support of the CFE. Passports and visas were easily obtained.

The combination of unbridled spending habits with no investment advice, the global economic crisis, and constant peso devaluation was such that these once "wealthy" peasants were as poor as they were before, despite the generous compensation they received, and without fertile, irrigated lands of their own. Migration, previously a supplement to their incomes, became the only option for survival.

Before the hydroelectric project, approximately 25 percent of the economically active population immigrated to the United States temporarily. Today, between 60 and 75 percent of the population has migrated north. Before the dam project, migration to the United States had been an exclusively masculine activity, with women seeking work inside Mexico in San Juan del Rio, Querétaro, or even Mexico City. Today, women too have joined men in international migration. Alcohol-related crimes resulted in many families losing a loved one. Often, the perpetrator fled north.

Escaping Violence

During the government of Vicente Fox (2000–2006), the immigrant population from Mexico to the United States grew markedly, increasing by 25 percent per year compared to the previous administration of Ernesto Zedillo (1994–2000). Fox's political discourse on immigration revealed his support for the phenomenon, and immigrant remittances, long considered one of the most vital contributors to the Mexican economy, were surpassed only by the petroleum industry (PEMEX) and tourism. It was said that Vicente Fox, as governor of Guanajuato, believed that Mexican universities and other institutions of higher education should dedicate their time to educating peasants, teaching them English as well as providing them with some technical training, so that they could earn better salaries in the United States and bring more dollars to home (personal communication).

During the administration of Felipe Calderon (2006–2012), the number of immigrants leaving Bella Vista del Rio and many other small towns literally emptied parts of the region, with very young children and their elderly caretakers left behind. Campaigning in Querétaro, Calderon often urged the population to immigrate to the United States—that they shouldn't pay attention to the "Gringos" threatening to build a wall along the entire border. He urged them not to worry— reassuring them that he would help them jump over any wall. Many immigrated because of economic reasons. Today, the number has increased dramatically mainly because of the violence in Mexico from the drug cartel wars. As I write this chapter, the drug-related violence has claimed more than 45,000 lives.

Policy and Its Consequences

The case of the Zimapán Hydroelectric Project illustrates how Mexican peasants sacrificed their homes, their lands, their communities, indeed, their very way of life, for the benefit of Mexican industrial development. Temporary or seasonal migration to the United States has become a way of life for these peasants of the present Bella Vista del Rio community. However, this forced "way of life" could have been avoided, without a doubt, if the government had provided other options for productive work in their own land. In conclusion, the Zimapán Dam Project was an attempt to *descampesinizar* (depeasantize) the Mexican countryside so as to remove obstacles in the way of the development for big business, both national and international. The cost for the peasant classes has been great indeed. Its impact, as well as that of other international development projects, has been seen on both sides of the border. Many of the children of Querétaro are now growing up in the shadows in the United States. Educational policy in the United States for Latino children cannot, perhaps, influence the larger forces of economic globalization at play in the Western Hemisphere. However, at minimum, educators and policy makers can take note of and perhaps collectively work to bring attention to the sorts of regional development policies taking place and, even more importantly, the toll that such policies take on families and communities.

References

Aguirre Beltrán, G. (1958). Viejo y nuevo Ixcatlán. *La Palabra y el Hombre, Universidad Veracruzana, Xalapa,* 7(July–September), 241–266.

Andere, E., & Kessel, G. (Eds.). (1992). *México y el tratado trilateral de libre comercio: Impacto sectorial.* Mexico, DF: McGraw-Hill.

Balán, J., Browning, H. L., & Jelin, E. (1973). *Men in a developing society: Geographical and social mobility in Monterrey, Mexico.* Austin, TX: University of Texas Press.

Bartolomé, M. A., & Barabas, A. M. (1990). *La presa Cerro de Oro y El Ingeniero El Gran Dios* (Vol. 2). Mexico, DF: Dirección General de Publicaciones del Conaculta/Instituto Nacional Indigenista.

Basaldúa, M. (1994). *La respuesta política de la población de Vista Hermosa al proyecto hidroeléctrico de Zimapán* (Master's thesis). Universidad Autónoma de Querétaro, Querétaro.

Chayanov, A. V. (1925/1985). *La organización de la unidad económica campesina.* Buenos Aires, Argentina: Ediciones Nueva Visión.

Derman, B. (1998). Balancing the waters: Development and hydropolitics in contemporary Zimbabwe. In J. Donahue & B. R. Johnston (Eds.), *Water, culture, and power: Local struggles in a global context* (pp. 73–93). Washington, DC: Island Press.

Donahue, J., & Johnston, B. R. (Eds.). (1998). *Water, culture, and power: Local struggles in a global context.* Washington, DC: Island Press.

Hansen, A., & Smith, O. (1982). *Involuntary migration and resettlement: The problems and responses of dislocated people.* Boulder, CO: Westview Press.

Loker, W. M. (1998). Water, rights, and the El Cajón Dam, Honduras. In J. Donahue & B. R. Johnston (Eds.), *Water, culture, and power: Local struggles in a global context* (pp. 95–119). Washington, DC: Island Press.

McMahon, D. F. (1989). *Antropología de una presa. Los mazatecos y el proyecto del Papaloapan.* Mexico, DF: Dirección General de Publicaciones del Conaculta/Instituto Nacional Indigenista.

Poleman, T. (1964). *The Papaloapan Project.* Stanford, CA: Stanford University Press.

Quesada Aldana, S. (1991). La asesoría y monitoreo en un reacomodo involuntario: Proyecto hidroeléctrico Zimapán. *Avances, 10,* 12–16.

Quesada Aldana, S. (1994). La interdisciplina como un caso de la antropología del desarrollo: Implicaciones teórico-metodológicas en torno a la presa de Zimapán. *Auriga, 10,* 101–112.

Quesada Aldana, S. (1997). La antropología del desarrollo y los campesinos: Reubicación involuntaria en la presa de Zimapán. In G. Real Cabello (Ed.), *El Campo Queretano en transición: Transformation of rural Mexico* (Vol. 9). San Diego, CA: Center for U.S.-Mexican Studies, University of California.

Villa Rojas, A. (1948). A short note respecting the anthropological investigation in the Papaloapan Valley. *Boletín Indigenista, 8*(2), 130–134.

Winnie, W.W.J. (1958). The Papaloapan Project: An experiment in tropical development. *Economic Geography, 3*(July), 227–248.

8

TRANSNATIONAL MOBILITY, EDUCATION, AND SUBJECTIVITY

Two Case Examples from Puerto Rico

Sandra L. Soto-Santiago and Luis C. Moll

In this chapter, we address educational policy issues stemming from research with children who are experiencing transnational mobility. We do so primarily through case examples of the educational "repositioning" of two such students, concentrating on what Aranda (2007) calls, "the subjectivity of incorporation" (p. 225). This focus of study, as she explains, is on how immigrants "interpret their own experiences of mobility and integration," and how existing social and institutional structures "shape experiences of incorporation and immigrants' subjectivity generally" (pp. 199–200). In both examples, how these students engage the practices of schooling, including the social, emotional, and intellectual processes involved, and how the students confront said practices, are the objects of study. We also illustrate how resilience emerges in the children confronting the challenges of new school systems and spotlight issues of language and identity, which are often present. The latter vary in intensity depending on the children's lived experiences (*vivencias*) and on the social and economic resources they, and their families, have at hand (see Moll, 2011).

Although transnational perspectives, by which we mean the dynamics of migrants who maintain social ties or movement between home and host countries, have achieved prominence in immigration literature, especially in the writings of sociologists (e.g., Glick Schiller, Basch, & Szanton Blanc, 1995; A. Portes, Guarnizo, & Landolt, 1999), issues or practices of education are not often the object of analysis. However, whenever families move between countries, children experience significant social and cultural changes, if not traumatic upheavals, of which the primary site of action is often the school, with its demands for cultural adjustments, the learning of a new language, and the formation of new identities (Olsen, 2008; Sánchez & Machado-Casas, 2009).

Children who are part of these households "on the move" often have no say regarding the transnational resettlements of their families, but they do have to face the struggles that come in conjunction with leaving their homeland and adapting to a new setting, or subsequently returning to their country of origin which, for them, may now be a "foreign" land. Language learning and confronting the exigencies of school life, which includes not only classroom work but also negotiating peer relations in the new environment, are two of the main issues these students face.

The transnational movement of students is an important educational policy issue in countries with strong ties to the United States, such as Mexico (Hamann, Zúñiga, & Sánchez García, 2006; Martínez-León & Smith, 2003), which is currently experiencing a growing return migration, motivated partly by the draconian immigration laws in the United States. The most recent estimates, based in part on the 2010 Mexican census, indicate that since 2005, 1.4 million Mexicans have returned to Mexico from the United States, including more than 300,000 U.S.-born children (thus American citizens), providing a new twist to well-established transnational trends (Passel, Cohn, & González Barrera, 2012).

The focus of the present chapter is Puerto Rico, which represents a very different picture of transnational relations, as we discuss below, particularly because Puerto Ricans' U.S. citizen status greatly facilitates the unimpeded bidirectional "to and fro" (*el vaivén*, in Spanish) between the island and the United States. However, as Aranda (2008) points out, unlike other U.S.–born minorities, to whom they are often compared, Puerto Ricans cross cultural, racial, and language borders upon migration, "making their U.S. minority experience akin to the immigrant experience" (p. 427). When students return to schools, in the United States or Puerto Rico, they quickly have to establish new peer relations as they learn the language and its academic registers within an entirely different teaching structure, and seldom do they have a formal support system that aids them with these difficult processes (Moll & Soto-Santiago, 2010).

In the discussion that follows, we detail two case examples of this transnational movement. We start with a brief outline of the political relations between Puerto Rico and the United States, which creates the fundamental context for the dynamics discussed. We then present the examples, based on interview data collected by the first author with the students and their parents. We emphasize in these examples the different "transnational subjectivities" of these students (Dahinden, 2009), and how these subjectivities are mediated by structural factors, namely, the schools, and by the social, class, and educational positioning of the students. In the final section, we offer several policy recommendations to mitigate the current impacts of shortsighted policies on these transnational students' education today.

The Puerto Rican Context

Puerto Rico has had a complex sociopolitical relationship with the United States since 1898, when, as a result of the Spanish-American War, Spain ceded Puerto Rico to the United States. In 1901, Puerto Rico became, and still is, an "unincorporated territory" of the United States (to use the U.S. legal term). In 1917, one month before the United States formally entered World War I, the U.S. Congress granted U.S. citizenship (and the "right" to be conscripted into the U.S. armed forces) to all Puerto Ricans. From that point on, movement from the island to the mainland, and back, became part of Puerto Ricans' everyday reality (Duany, 2002, 2007). The flow of Puerto Ricans between the island and mainland has remained constant, and according to U.S. Census Bureau (2010) data, there are currently approximately 3.7 million Puerto Ricans on the island, whereas more than 4 million live on the mainland. The proximity of the island to the mainland, which facilitates transnational movement, the long-standing historical relationship of the United States and Puerto Rico, and the unique legal status of Puerto Ricans as both Puerto Rican nationals and U.S. citizens have created a space for Puerto Ricans to move within and between cultures and countries in ways that are difficult or impossible for other immigrant groups.

Transnational mobility has become a defining characteristic of Puerto Rican society, and, as such, we would argue that no issue in Puerto Rico, including, and perhaps especially, education, can be understood apart from this transnational reality. Puerto Rico has indeed become what Duany (2002) calls a "nation on the move," in which transnationalism permeates all aspects of island life. As noted in the chapter by Quesada Aldana in this volume (Chapter 7), this is a most critical global issue that remains alien for mostly monocultural, if not ethnocentric, dominant-group policy makers in the United States.

As an example, in 2010, more than 31,000 individuals reported having moved to Puerto Rico from the United States (U.S. Census Bureau, 2010). Certainly, among these were families with children and youth who had attended schools in the United States and who upon moving to Puerto Rico are now enrolled in schools on the island. When such fluid mobilization is viewed from an educational standpoint, one can easily imagine the many possible ways in which moving affects students. Transnational lifestyles can be harsh for students who are involved in these movements (Prewitt-Díaz, 1994). They disrupt schooling for students by interrupting their academic year. Further, one of the problems that these students must face is how others perceive them in each location and how their identities and language use change accordingly (Lorenzo-Hernández, 1999; Reyes, 2000).

Language, as always, is a pivotal factor in negotiating schooling, not only academically, but also for social and historical reasons. Because English is a "minority" language on the island and is often perceived as the language of the colonizer, its use by newcomers or returning students (and these students themselves) might not sit well with peers in schools (Pousada, 1999). Although all students in Puerto Rican public schools are required to take English courses for the 12 years of their primary and secondary schooling, most students never become fluent in the language. English is not necessary for everyday life on the island; Spanish clearly predominates in all social domains, so that students may not sense a need to learn English. At the same time, as a U.S. colony, with all the dependent economic and political relations that status involves, everyone recognizes the instrumental importance of learning English, and it is found everywhere in the Puerto Rican cultural landscape, with Anglicisms well integrated into the local Spanish vernacular. However, political ideologies come attached to the use of English, such as the favoring of American ways (see Rios-Aguilar et al., Chapter 5, in this volume) or the desire for Puerto Rican statehood, and these political and social alignments have consequences for the general social acceptance of the language. The reality for students, then, is that many of them move to the United States not knowing sufficient English to participate fully in American schools and return with weakened Spanish-language and literacy skills that do not serve them well in schools on the island.

Another challenge relates to the identities of these students. In the United States, they are expected to assimilate to American culture in schools, but their parents and family members often encourage them to maintain their Puerto Rican culture and identity (Prewitt-Díaz, 1994). These students are raised with a sense of pride in their Puerto Rican roots, and they identify themselves as Puerto Rican, but they also become immersed in American youth culture. This acculturation, which may be manifest in attire, choice of music, popular culture, use of language, and so on, becomes problematic once students return to the island where such behaviors are rejected by many local Puerto Ricans (Lorenzo-Hernández, 1999; Vega de Jesús & Sayers, 2007).

Consequently, students who have undergone these processes of acculturation in the United States, but whose families decide to return to the island, must undergo a similar process of acculturation in a different language and cultural environment. These students need to become once again accustomed to the Puerto Rican educational system and to the use of Spanish as the language of instruction and peer interaction. Reyes (2000) explains that whereas these students perceive themselves as Puerto Rican, they soon "discover that they are viewed as outsiders and excluded from participation unless they reverse the [U.S.] acculturation process" (p. 44). Their language, often a mix of English and Spanish ("Spanglish"), and their American ways are the main reasons why peers reject them. After struggling for acceptance in the U.S. environment, they now have to reverse these newly created identities if they want to gain acceptance in Puerto Rico once again.

The examples summarized below featuring two students, each with particular life circumstances, elaborate on some of the points made previously. We highlight issues of language and identity, which are central to the students' schooling experiences whether in the United States or in Puerto Rico, and underscore the emotional dynamics in the students' transnational movements and in their formation of new subjectivities. All the interviews used for these cases were conducted by the first author in the language preferred by the participant. The interviews with Héctor's and Jesús's mothers were in Spanish and translated into English by the author. The interview with Jesús was in English.

The Case of Jesús

Jesús was interviewed in 2010 when he was 14 years old. He lives in a small town in New Jersey with his mother and three younger siblings. He was born in Puerto Rico, and soon thereafter, his parents moved to the United States seeking better job opportunities. When he was two years old, his mother, Nelly, returned to Puerto Rico with him and his U.S.-born younger brother. After a couple of months on the island, however, she decided to go back to the United States. The family was still living there when Jesús started school. He had never attended school in Puerto Rico until, when he was nine years old, his mother returned again to the island, with her now four children. The family moved to a rural town in the island's interior because they had relatives living there who would facilitate the transition and provide shelter and support as they reestablished themselves. During our interview, Jesús shared that he had been excited about moving back to Puerto Rico because although he could not remember his native country, he was raised with a strong sense of pride for Puerto Rico; the family's sole ethnic and cultural identity was Puerto Rican. Unfortunately, his experiences on the island, specifically in schools, were not as pleasant as he had hoped. Soon after starting school, Jesús realized that, contrary to his own sense of self, his peers did not perceive him as Puerto Rican, and there were other challenges he had to face in schools.

Upon starting school, Jesús realized that to his new peers he was an outsider. As such, he was not accepted among the other children's social groups.

> Some of the kids made me mad because they wouldn't let me play basketball with the kids that were there. 'Cause I was an *Americanito* they would call me. It got me pretty mad. . . . Actually over here (in the U.S.) I feel really Puerto Rican, over there (in Puerto Rico) I feel like a white boy.

There is a clear distinction between how Jesús identifies himself and how his peers perceive him. He also makes a strong statement about his different identities in Puerto Rico and the United States. Although he was in Puerto Rico when the previous event took place, he felt more Puerto Rican in New Jersey because no other Puerto Ricans were judging his identity. In Puerto Rico, he stood out as different among all the other native students.

As a consequence of the rejection by his peers, Jesús was isolated in school. Making friends was a difficult process that lasted about a month after he had arrived. He could not understand the social practices at the school but knew he was not welcomed in them.

> If you weren't one of those in a group like playing basketball in the court or going to hang out with the kids then you had to go to lunch after everybody else did. I don't know, it feels like a group thing where people went together and if you weren't part of the group you couldn't go.

Because he did not belong to any groups, Jesús was not invited to play sports, which he enjoyed (he had played on several sports teams in New Jersey). He even had to eat his lunch by himself. Understandably, this rejection was particularly painful, as Jesús was only nine years old.

When asked about his teachers, Jesús recalled a specific teacher who did not help him and instead made the situation worse. Although he is fluent in both Spanish and English, he was used to English as the medium of instruction and communication in his school setting in the United States, and, therefore, it took him some time to become accustomed to Spanish as the language of instruction.

> There was this teacher that didn't really understand anything that was happening. She would always tell me, "Why didn't you finish?" I could not finish as fast as everybody else and she would yell at me, take my paper away, rip it or something. If she would have, like, at least helped me with something I would have probably done a lot better. This was social studies.

Instead of being a source of support for Jesús, this teacher resorted to humiliation by questioning his competence and even ripping his schoolwork. As Jesús says, had she understood his situation, his outcomes in her classes would have been different. She made him feel as though he was unable to handle the material in her class instead of trying to help him cope with the new situation.

When speaking about teacher support in the United States, Jesús states that he felt he had all he needed; however, in Puerto Rico it was lacking:

> They [U.S. teachers] give help on things that you need. They actually sit down and actually help you find it instead of well "look for it yourself, go ahead and do it."

Having attended U.S. schools since kindergarten, Jesús had become accustomed to receiving support from all the school staff. He felt unaided while he studied in Puerto Rico and that his teachers expected him to learn and do everything on his own without their providing any assistance.

Interestingly, when asked about what he liked or enjoyed about schools in Puerto Rico, he did not refer to teachers or classes but to other elements of the school system.

> The food was good. The food over here [in the U.S.] is all packaged and it's so nasty. . . . [Wearing uniforms] felt kind of weird but nobody was making fun of the clothes I was wearing because everybody was wearing the same clothes.

Public schools in Puerto Rico offer fresh food that is prepared daily by employees of the school cafeteria. Instead of the pizzas, hamburgers, and chips that he was used to eating in U.S. schools, in Puerto Rico Jesús was eating food he considered to be tastier and more nutritious. Although uniforms tend to be uncomfortable and disliked by returning students, Jesús liked them. Based on how he talks about uniforms, it appears that Jesús felt that wearing a uniform made it possible for him to blend in because he resembled the rest of the student population.

His Mother's Perspective

There were many valuable experiences that Jesús shared during his interview. However, there were other aspects of his school adaptation process that his mother, Nelly, shared with me and that Jesús did not address. Through her interview, she shared accounts of her son's experiences at the school and her own struggles to get Jesús moved from the class he was placed in upon his arrival into the class in which she felt he belonged.

When Nelly moved back to Puerto Rico, Jesús was enrolled in a school that had two groups of fourth graders. Jesús was placed in the group that, according to his mother, was less challenging academically and included the students who did not care about school.

> I opposed to them putting him in that group. They didn't consider my opinion; it was worth nothing to them. I know my child has the ability to read and write in Spanish and they did not listen to me.

The school staff did not think that Jesús was competent enough in Spanish to be placed in the higher-level group because he came from the United States, and they doubted that he could handle the demands of a more academically challenging group.

As a result of the placement in the lower group and his association with the other students in that class, Jesús's behavior started to change. He began to disengage from school and started adopting the disruptive and disobedient conduct typical of his classmates.

> He got used to being with the troublemakers and when they moved him to the other group he was not interested anymore. Placing my child in that group only harmed him. He had already lost interest and he would skip class and go to the river [a gathering place near the school]. Now, he supposedly has a learning disability and problems focusing.

Although some months later Jesús was transferred to the higher-level fourth grade group, it was already too late because he had lost interest in school. He would skip class and continued to follow the behavioral patterns of the peers in his first classroom.

Nelly shared how helpless she felt because the school staff did not listen to her, and she worries their decision has impacted Jesús, perhaps for the rest of his life.

Thinking that he might never be the same child, Nelly decided to return to the United States for the sake of her four children. She did not want to see Jesús's siblings *in the same situation* and regrets having moved to the island because of what her oldest child experienced in school.

> Had it not been for the school issues I would still be in Puerto Rico. When I came back [to the U.S.] it was because there was nothing else I could do with him. I realized that if I did not return to the U.S. I was going to lose my children. I think I actually hurt them by moving to Puerto Rico.

Despite Nelly's decision to move back, Jesús continued to portray the same behavior upon returning to New Jersey, and as a consequence, he was diagnosed with a learning disability when in the United States. Nelly is convinced he does not have the condition and attributes this situation to his initial placement in the lower group. He has now been labeled as a Special Education student with a learning disability, and Nelly believes that his behavior will never be the same as it was before they moved to Puerto Rico.

The Case of Héctor

Héctor, interviewed in 2008, is a Puerto Rican student who moved to California with his family after this state had implemented Proposition 227 (the English-only law). He returned to Puerto Rico three years later. The experiences and struggles that Héctor had as a migrant student in California, and consequently as a return migrant in Puerto Rico, shaped and changed his ideologies regarding language learning and usage and his academic identity formation.

At the time of the interview, Héctor was a first-year college student in Puerto Rico. He was enrolled in an intermediate-level English course designed for students who demonstrate high proficiency in English, according to scores from college entrance exams. Qualifying for this course should not be surprising for a student like Héctor because of the English-language skills he had acquired previously.

The son of an electrical engineer, Héctor's middle-class family was financially able to send him, and his older and younger sisters, to private schools in Puerto Rico. These schools usually offer strong academics and an English-language curriculum. However, Héctor has a varied educational background; as a student on the island, he attended both public and private schools. Although in Puerto Rico it is customary for middle-class families to send their children to private school, their decision to do so often depends on where the family lives. In areas where the schools are considered to be safe and academically rigorous, families such as Héctor's might opt to send their children to public school. Héctor was enrolled in public schools during his elementary school years, when the family lived in smaller, more rural towns, but his parents moved him to private schools for his high school years, when they lived in a metropolitan area.

Moving to California was a significant event in Héctor's life. This move represented not only a definite change in school and social environment but also a change in language use. Although prior to moving Héctor had a fair knowledge of English, given his schooling history, he soon realized that his fluency was not good enough to perform well in school or to interact with many of his peers. As a consequence, Héctor soon became frustrated and wanted to return to Puerto Rico. There were, however, several factors that influenced his adaptation process as well as his English-language development that enabled him to feel more comfortable in California.

The language policy context in California is relevant to understanding this example; in a sense, it helped define the school as a receiving community for him. In June of 1998, a new law was passed in the state of California, via popular vote on a referendum known as Proposition 227. This law severely curtailed bilingual education in favor on English-only instruction. This restrictive policy has become the status quo in California. Although the law proposes a one-year immersion program, language acquisition experts generally agree that academic English cannot be learned in such a short time (Hakuta, 2011). Results from a study based on a survey administered to California school principals (Basurto, Wise, & Unruh, 2006) show that after years of implementing the English-only policy, principals still favor bilingual education. This was the language environment in California schools when Héctor moved to that state.

Héctor's parents moved the family to California because his father was offered a good position. His father was an engineer, and his mother was a stay-at-home mom. Héctor's case is representative of a current worldwide brain-drain phenomenon (Aranda, 2007; Patterson, 2006). Although a high proportion of working- and lower-class Puerto Ricans still decide to migrate seeking a better life, many others holding professional degrees migrate to the United States seeking job opportunities that are not available in Puerto Rico. Oftentimes, they migrate already having arranged positions that they have attained through job fairs or other means. As Hector states:

> We moved because of my dad's job. They offered him a position over there in California and we decided to move there. I was there for two and a half years. We came back for the same reason, they offered him a position here in Puerto Rico and we came back.

The opportunity of a steady, high-paying job, led this family to move to California. Yet, less than three years later, they returned to Puerto Rico for the same reason. Thus, regardless of the class and economic standing of the family, the reason Puerto Ricans migrate is still often job related.

Héctor's family moved to Kolber (pseudonym), California, where the Latino population comprised 4.7 percent of the town's population and where the median household income at the time was $114,064 (U.S. Census Bureau, 2010). Héctor and his sister went to a middle school were only around 1 percent of the school population qualified for free or reduced-price lunch (Education Data Partnership, 2010). This is clearly an affluent town were most of the population hold professional degrees and schools have abundant resources. Given his family's human and social capital, one could anticipate that Héctor's experiences as a migrant student would be considerably different from those of working-class students moving to the United States. Yet, in spite of the opportunities available to him because of his family's social status, he still reports experiences similar to those of any newly arrived migrant who is struggling with English and new school environments.

> At the beginning I felt isolated. I was always in a little corner, alone, quiet, I used to cry; practically the first entire month I would cry. Every time I would go home and I would say, [. . .] "I want to go back to Puerto Rico."

As any other newcomer, Héctor had to deal with the emotional stress of performing in English, negotiating peer relations and identities, and making sense of classroom demands, all as part of his subjective process of incorporation.

Using English at Home

Prior to moving to California, Héctor's use of English was limited to 50 minutes a day of English class in school and occasional entertainment activities such as playing videogames and watching English-language movies. This is a common pattern among public school students in Puerto Rico.

> I did not have cable television, I just had the local channels, did not have Internet either. I used to watch the movies they would show on the local channels and Dad would help me translate them, because he knew English. The movies I would watch in English but with Spanish subtitles and that is how I practically started to learn from the movies. Every now and then I would sit down to read a book in English.

Although English is one of the official languages of Puerto Rico, it is rarely spoken outside the classroom, and students often see no reason to learn it other than for academic or recreational purposes. Nevertheless, it is easy for a dedicated student to get good grades in English; this was the case of Héctor, who also had the help of his bilingual father. His grades and performance in English class led him to feel superior to the rest of his classmates.

> I can say that when I was in elementary school (in Puerto Rico). I was somewhat above the rest of the students in terms of English, I learned, I really did learn. I always had an A in the class. . . . I could say that I was always among the top 10 to 5 students in the class. Compared to other students, I knew

more English, like I could understand the teacher better than the other students and in analyzing sentences and what those meant I had a better a idea of what they were referring to than other students.

Héctor perceived himself as superior when it came to knowing English and he was also interested in learning it because his family encouraged him to do so. The middle-class families' various forms of capital may have a strong influence on how students perceive the importance of learning English.

I have seen it in my family, dad, my uncles, my cousins, all of them are professionals and have told me that English has a great influence in their jobs because most of the interviews that [recruiting] companies do are in English and well, being bilingual has more . . . how do I put this, is better, it has more advantages.

In his case, Héctor's main influence appears to have been his father. Having learned the importance of English himself, he made sure to transmit this to Héctor by teaching him that English would lead to a better lifestyle and better job opportunities.

He learned it here in this university. He graduated from here and learned it here. . . . He told me that he had to learn English in his classes; he said that he would pay a lot of attention because he knew that for the job fairs and the interviews and to get a job, he needed English.

Based on the advice provided by his family, especially his father, Héctor's main reason for learning English was strictly instrumental: to find a good job in the future. Hence, as an eighth grader, he did not have many other purposes for it.

Nevertheless, in spite of excellent grades and a sense of accomplishment as an English-speaker, Héctor's uses of English were limited before moving to California. It is thus understandable that Héctor's first and primary struggle as migrant student in California was becoming fluent in English to succeed in school and for any other activity or interaction.

Learning English while Making Friends

When Héctor moved to California, one of the most significant elements in his adaptation process was his peers, who for the most part were also in the English immersion program. Through them he realized that learning English was a laborious process that other students were also struggling with.

I met a German boy, he got to the U.S. at the same time I did and the English he knew was similar to mine and we used to communicate that way. When he moved, they placed him in the same classroom I was in and that is how we met. I could understand everything he would say and he could understand everything I said. Since we spoke the same way he knew what I was referring to and with him I used to talk a lot on the phone and though messenger. There was another one from Sweden who also was like us, he spoke very little English and since he practically spoke the same gibberish I did, I could understand him. I woke up with them. I spent the first six months of my first year here [in the U.S.] with them. We used to go everywhere together, to the movies, to eat ice cream, playing, everything, the three of us.

Meeting these boys, who were going through a similar situation, was a relief for Héctor. He made friends who understood him and that sympathized with his feelings, helping him cope with the isolation he experienced. As he says himself, he "woke up," or realized that he was going to be fine.

Language Support through Sports

There were also significant events related to other peers in which Héctor's desire to continue his normal routines from Puerto Rico led him to expand his language use. As a baseball player, he soon joined a team and found an interesting strategy that allowed him to play without having to rely much on English.

No one spoke Spanish in the team. I was the only Puerto Rican on the team and at school. There were many Mexicans and two Colombians and if I am not mistaken a Panamanian but they rarely spoke Spanish with me. I would stay quiet and whatever they told me to do, I would do. I would not speak at all because the sport is the same so they would tell me do this and would point. What I used to do was that if they were going to do an activity I would stay in the middle of the group so that I could see some people do it first and then I would repeat what they were doing and that is how I would do it.

Héctor's desire to play his favorite sport led him to find ways of interacting with the team and playing the game without having to use English. He was successful with his strategy and managed to be part of both a baseball and a soccer team.

A Teacher Who Made a Difference

Although Héctor's parents were able to afford tutoring sessions to help him learn the language, this was a minimal component in his language-learning journey. In turn, his peers were pivotal to his gaining access to social groups, increasing his confidence, and learning English. Yet, he still had to deal with his limited English interfering with his performance in school. However, there was one person that contributed to his academic development and helped him become the student he had been in Puerto Rico. Héctor's English Language Arts teacher became his mentor.

> Since I was in elementary school, up until I moved to the United States, I always got As, I never got a B, always As. Seeing that change of getting Fs and Ds and Fs and Ds, one after the other, I got frustrated. I would cry, "I want to go (to Puerto Rico) because this is going to ruin the good grades that I have always had," but that was until this teacher, Mrs. A, got there.

Mrs. A developed an informal bilingual strategy that allowed her to teach her class while also helping Héctor. She not only helped him with her class, but would also help Héctor outside of school by translating assignments and exams into Spanish because he felt that the immersion program was not helping him.

> She would teach the [English] class and explain to everyone and then she would come to me individually and explain it all again. She helped me a lot because I got better grades. Every time I had doubts about something, any material, I would always go to her and she would translate and explain it to me. She would explain it in English and Spanish, even if it was for another class. She helped me because it came to a point in which I did not know what to do and well, since I did not have any help, I did not have anyone to ask for help and well, I would go to her and she would explain everything. She was like, a helping guide. Anything that I needed, I would go to her.

Mrs. A became a primary source of support for Héctor. She helped him gain his confidence as a student as and a learner of English. Although she was teaching under the restrictions of Proposition 227 and was restricted in her use of Spanish in the classroom, her decision to use Spanish changed Héctor's life. Because of her help, Héctor was able to finish that school year with a B grade point average, and to learn he was capable of meeting his schoolwork's demands.

The Challenge of Return Migration

Héctor progressed in school, and his social life also improved as he became more proficient in English and made new friends. His use of English also changed as he became more fluent. An example of this improvement is that he became a language broker for his mother, who did not speak English, so whenever she had to run an errand he would accompany her to help her communicate with others. Children of migrant parents often assume this role, assisting relatives and family friends in their interactions with English-speaking individuals (Faulstich Orellana, 2009). Yet, after being in California for almost three years, Héctor's father received a new and attractive job offer in Puerto Rico, and the family went back to their homeland. Now Héctor's challenge was not learning English but rather being able to recall the schooling practices in Puerto Rico and getting reacclimated to using Spanish instead of English on a daily basis.

When Héctor returned to Puerto Rico, he was in the middle of eighth grade. His parents enrolled him in a public school where he soon realized that he had to negotiate his language use carefully in order to gain acceptance from his peers. He also learned that as a bilingual student he had responsibilities that he needed to accept. One of his first challenges at that school was deciding which social groups to join and which to avoid. Although there was a group of students who were bilingual like him, he chose not to establish a friendship with them because the rest of the school rejected them.

> I remember that there were three [students], two boys and a girl, they always spoke English in all the classes, everything, everything and they would even forget how to speak Spanish. . . . That was in the eighth grade. My friends would always say, "Oh, these *Gringos*, don't hang out with them, man, no one likes them," and this was because they were always trying to let people know that they knew more, more English. Sometimes they would make fun of [other people's] mistakes because they would correct not with the intention of helping but rather as a way of laughing at them. That is why I never socialized with them; they were always apart. I never hung out with them, not even a single day.

Héctor was aware that the behaviors of this group of nonmigrant bilingual students were unacceptable because they used English as a weapon, as a means to establish superiority. He did not agree with their using English to ridicule other students, and thus he preferred to stay away from the group.

Reducing His English to Help Friends

In terms of language negotiation, there is one specific event in which Héctor decided to use his skills in English in an unexpected way. In California, Héctor became aware of the importance of having strong support when one is learning a language and decided to provide that support for a group of peers.

> Sometimes there would be occasions in the eighth grade in which I did not want the other kids to feel bad and sometimes I would lower my English level to their level. I remember that we had a group assignment in which we had to speak in front of the class. The thing is that in my group there were three kids who basically knew no English and so they would speak and only a little bit of what they were saying could be understood. I had an idea of what they were saying but when it was my turn to speak I did not want to speak with the English that I know, because I did not want to overshadow

them. I did not want my English to affect their grade because they were my friends and so I lowered my English and made mistakes on purpose. I pronounced some words incorrectly so that their grade would not be affected. [. . .] Our teacher noticed but she did not say anything.

Héctor had gained the confidence he once lost in California, and although he could have used his skills to outperform his classmates, he decided to do the opposite. By lowering his language skills, he sought to sound in a way similar to his peers so they would not feel inept.

A Challenging Teacher

In Puerto Rico, Héctor had a difficult time finding an English course that was challenging. His English-language use stagnated, and he felt that he did not advance in his learning. However, upon entering high school, he met an English teacher who, like him, was a return migrant. Héctor felt that this teacher pushed him, and he learned new language skills: those necessary for college.

She had lived in the U.S. and studied her high school and college over there. I use to tell her that I wanted to study in the U.S. and she used to tell me about how it was, how she got there. Sometimes we would talk about the difference between Spanish and English and her process when she went to high school. There was a moment where we did have that relationship of sharing our experiences. . . . She would make you speak English. She worked a lot with essays, analysis and critical thinking. There was always something to work on. I always thought she was an excellent teacher. She helped me a lot to search for scholarships for schools in the U.S. she even called one of her universities for me once. So, I have a lot of appreciation for her. I liked her a lot.

Héctor's affection for this teacher not only derives from her having lived and studied in the United States, but also her ways of teaching. He seems to appreciate that she pushed him into areas that he needed to improve in preparation for his college years. She also helped with other aspects, like searching for scholarships for college, and showed an authentic caring and desire to help. As a return migrant, this teacher became someone that Héctor could identify with in Puerto Rico.

Influence of Circular Migration on Academic Perceptions

Héctor's overall experience related to English, both in California and in Puerto Rico, has provided him with a sense of what are effective ways of teaching and learning English. That he learned English in California under Proposition 227, in an English-only environment, seems to have influenced his perceptions on the effectiveness of his teachers upon returning to the island. His experiences with teachers in California became the basis for comparing his English teachers in Puerto Rico and the efficacy of their teaching techniques.

The first English teacher Héctor had when he returned to Puerto Rico used a technique commonly employed in English classrooms throughout the public schools in the island. She used Spanish as the main medium of instruction for her English class. Having returned from California, Héctor thought of this as an ineffective way of teaching because students were not asked to use English in class.

> She used to jump from English to Spanish constantly. On many occasions, students spoke more Spanish than English. Sometimes, she gave the instructions in English, if she saw that some students were not following her, she would then say them in Spanish. Sometimes she would teach the entire class in Spanish, but the material was in English . . . and she would explain it all in Spanish so that they could understand. It has its good side so that students know what they have to do, but if you want to learn English, well you are not going to learn English like that, and so it could be said that it was the only bad side of that English class.

Although he seemed to like the teacher, Héctor considered it a significant flaw that she relied on Spanish for most of her instruction and allowed students to use that language while their supposed goal was to learn to speak English.

A year after having class with that teacher, Héctor started at a new school, and, in this new setting, his English teacher did not allow her students to use Spanish while they were in the classroom. She attempted to create a full immersion environment where students were not only surrounded by the language but also forced to use it.

> The English teacher, she was Puerto Rican, she studied in Río Piedras (The University of Puerto Rico); she studied English there. She specialized in that language and she knew a lot of English but she would not help her students, for her entire English class, if you did not understand it, you did not understand it, that was your problem and you had to find someone to help you understand [the material]. And I believe that this way she forced students to stay focused in the class and to look for a way to learn English so that they could do well in the class. . . . You would see everyone always working with the class, "man, I have to do well in the English class, help me with this, how do I pronounce it" because she used to take points off for [incorrect] pronunciation. If you said a word in the wrong way, she would stop the class to tell you, "Look, you say it like this." It made students speak correctly. That is a method that I found interesting.

Héctor saw this teacher as more effective in her teaching practice because she was pushing students to use English. She used the same technique used in California, which probably contributed to Héctor approving of her teaching style more than the style of his previous teacher who used Spanish to teach the English class. Ironically, he did not perceive that the strategic switching to Spanish that he criticized in his first Puerto Rican teacher's instruction was the same strategy that helped him survive initially in the California school.

Challenging and Nonchallenging Courses

At the time of our interviews, Héctor reflected on his life experiences but also on his present situation. He seems to feel that the education he received in the United States was of good quality and that it prepared him for his future goals.

> In Puerto Rico, it became very easy and I did very well, 4.0 in everything. Because the education I was given in the U.S. was more advanced than the one in Puerto Rico and when I came back to Puerto Rico they were giving me material I had already taken in the U.S. so all I had to do was translate what I had learned from English to Spanish.

Going to school in Puerto Rico was in many ways easier than going to school in California because the school that Héctor attended in California was, according to him, more academically advanced. He also found that translating what he had learned already from English to Spanish sufficed to help him perform well. When Héctor spoke of his current college English course, he seemed to have found a balance in his language-learning process. He expressed that he was finally in a class where he felt confident enough but also where he still had much to learn.

> I feel comfortable because in this English class there are many students, well almost all of them know English, that the English they know is good. Some are superior to others but there are a couple of us who are at the same level. I also compare the readings to the ones from high school because it is the same format, read this, and analyze it using these questions. Besides that, I see that the teaching system that my instructor uses is very good, very different, I had never seen it and yes, I feel that I am where I need to be. It is not too challenging but it is not too easy either. I am right there.

At this point in his academic life, Héctor could appreciate the teaching style of his high school teacher who pushed him and prepared him for college. He felt that he still had more to learn but that he was at the right level, where he belonged. He also seemed to like that most of his classmates in this course were at the same level he was, which was different from many of his previous classes, in which he felt superior or even lowered his skills to make his classmates feel at ease.

Discussion

We have presented two exploratory cases of the lived experiences of two transnational students. The examples highlight how their experiences of schooling in both Puerto Rico and the United States help shape their emergent subjectivities, especially when dealing with issues of language, identity formation, and peer relations as they face divergent realities of schooling. Although the examples do not provide much detail about topics broadly associated with immigration, such as social network formation, changing family practices, the nature of assimilation, economic factors, racist resistance to the presence of transnational students, and the like, they do highlight emotional dynamics, which are central to any form of transnational movement (Zembylas, 2012). They also serve to inform and reframe a more intelligent construction of policy-driven practices and alternatives in education.

Jesús is perhaps a clearer example of how emotionally laden experiences shape student subjectivity. His peers ostracized him, denying him opportunities to play sports, which seemed central to his evolving sense of self, and he struggled for acceptance in his new school setting in Puerto Rico. Even his identity as a Puerto Rican, which was clear and uncontested in New Jersey, became a source of contention on the island. He reflects on what to him is a peculiar and troubling displacement when he comments that he is Puerto Rican in New Jersey, but a "white boy" (meaning American) in Puerto Rico. He eventually achieves some form of peer integration, but, much to his mother's dismay, with those students who were most academically disengaged, and starts cutting classes to be with them at the river, a hangout of sorts for the students with little interest in school.

This chain of events and peer relations seem to have led to Jesús's being defined as a dysfunctional learner. The teachers' attitudes toward him did not help; Jesús perceives the teachers as offering little empathy or understanding of his plight. It may be that in the rural town where his family settled, teachers were simply not prepared to deal with returning students, their apparent limitations with Spanish, and their lack of understanding of Puerto Rican instructional practices. In any case, his relations with teachers marked him as problematic, and Jesús was eventually diagnosed as having a learning disability, a conclusion with which his mother clearly disagrees. These negative experiences in school motivated his mother to return the family to the United States for the third time, a frequency that is not at all unusual among Puerto Rican transmigrants.

Héctor presents a different example. His family appears more affluent, as evidenced by his father's profession and the neighborhood into which they settled in California. This middle-class migration from Puerto Rico has become more common in recent years and contrasts with the long-standing movement to the United States of the working class, characterized by return moves to the island (Aranda, 2007). However, Héctor's class advantages did not necessarily shelter him from the deep emotional upheaval accompanying the resettlement process; he reports that initially he cried every day, wanting to return to the island. His discovery that his English was far from adequate to deal with social and academic issues at school was also unsettling to him. He relied on the friendship of other immigrant students, mostly from European countries, to start feeling a bit more comfortable, as they shared the burden of not knowing English well and adapting to unfamiliar school routines.

California's English-only language policies also became an issue in Héctor's acclimatization. However, a caring teacher implemented personalized, bilingual instructional practice with him, strategically translating content and instructions into Spanish so that he could better comprehend the academic tasks and assignments required of him; she also became a confidante during that initial year of adjustment, greatly facilitating his transition. Notice that no one assumed Héctor had learning difficulties, as they did in Jesús's case, but simply that he faced a language barrier that could be managed with some reasonable bilingual support. Héctor also found a welcoming context in sports. By joining the school baseball and soccer teams, he was able to engage with native English-speaking peers and cultivate social relationships.

Héctor's return to Puerto Rico, motivated by a job offer for his father, seemed to be rather unproblematic, except that he discovered he had to moderate his English fluency in school or risk damaging friendships with other local students. He would even deliberately make mistakes in English, pronouncing words incorrectly, and avoid English-speaking classmates, so as not to stand out too much in class and risk being ostracized by peers, in ways reminiscent of Jesús's situation. Jesús was rejected because of his lack of fluency in Spanish; Héctor feared rejection because of his fluency in English. Ironically, Héctor seems to have internalized the restrictive language ideology of California and does not take into account that he was able to succeed as a student in California because his teacher used Spanish to scaffold his English schoolwork. Given his favorable circumstances, his Spanish was never threatened.

It is clear from the examples that migration, as Zembylas (2012) suggests, always produces intense emotional dynamics and mediates notions of self and one's sense of belonging. Both examples illustrate that migration can cause, at least in some ways, a sense of personal trauma for the students involved. In the case of Jesús, this trauma impacted his family as well, prompting his mother to return the family to the United States. Given the growing incidence of transnational movement of families and students, it behooves administrators and teachers to become better prepared to work with this population of students. Indeed, the educational systems in Puerto Rico, the United States, and elsewhere should take certain steps to address these students' needs, such as developing consistent systems for handling student enrollment, actively acknowledging these students in the school and the curriculum, and creating venues for student support. However, a first step could be to make educators aware of the phenomenon of transnational migration and the emotional toll it can take on students.

Even if Puerto Rico, the focus of study here, never develops a full program that takes into consideration returning migrants, preparing Puerto Rican teachers to work with returning and transnational students could ameliorate the challenges students face. Teachers are the most important school staff because they have direct and daily contact with students and are in charge of instruction. Teachers have the power to either further contribute to the invisibility of these students or help them become noticed by other school staff and peers in order to assist them with the process of incorporating fruitfully into a new social, linguistic, and academic environment.

References

Aranda, E. (2007). Struggles of incorporation among the Puerto Rican middle class. *Sociological Quarterly, 48*, 199–228.

Aranda, E. (2008). Class backgrounds, modes of incorporation, and Puerto Ricans' pathways into the transnational professional workforce. *American Behavioral Scientist, 52*, 426–456.

Basurto, I., Wise, D., & Unruh, R. (2006). California school principals: Perceptions of the effect of Proposition 227. *Educational Leadership and Administration, 18*, 99–108.

Dahinden, J. (2009). Are we all transnationals now? Network transnationalism and transnational subjectivity: The differing impacts of globalization on the inhabitants of a small Swiss city. *Ethnic and Racial Studies, 32*(8), 1365–1386.

Duany, J. (2002). The Puerto Rican nation on the move: Identities on the island and in the United States. Chapel Hill, NC: University of North Carolina Press.

Duany, J. (2007). Nación, migración, identidad: Reflexiones sobre el transnacionalismo a propósito del caso de Puerto Rico. In S. Báez Hernández, A. Bencomo, & M. Zimmerman (Eds.), *Ir y venir: Procesos Transnacionales entre América Latina y el norte* (pp. 223–234). Houston, TX: La Casa.

Education Data Partnership. (2010). Fiscal, demographic and performance data on California K-12 schools [Special Programs Table for 2000–01]. Retrieved from www.ed-data.k12.ca.us/Navigation/fsTwoPanel.asp?bottom=/indexDB.asp

Faulstich Orellana, M. (2009). *Translating childhoods: Immigrant youth, language, and culture.* New Brunswick, NJ: Rutgers University Press.

Glick Schiller, N., Basch, L., & Szanton Blanc, C. (1995). From immigrant to transmigrant: Theorizing transnational migration. *Anthropological Quarterly, 68*(1), 48–63.

Hakuta, K. (2011). Educating language minority students and affirming their equal rights: Research and practical perspectives. *Educational Researcher, 40*(4), 163–174.

Hamann, E. T., Zúñiga, V., & Sánchez García, J. (2006). Pensando en Cynthia y su hermana: Educational implications of United States–Mexico transnationalism for children. *Journal of Latinos and Education, 5*(4), 253–274.

Lorenzo-Hernández, J. (1999). The Nuyorican's dilemma: Categorization of returning migrants in Puerto Rico. *International Migration Review, 33*(4), 988–1013.

Martínez-León, N., & Smith, P. H. (2003). Educating bilingualism in Mexican transnational communities. *NABE Journal of Research and Practice,* Winter, 141–152.

Moll, L. C. (2011). Only life educates: Immigrant families, the cultivation of biliteracy, and the mobility of knowledge. In P. R. Portes & S. Salas (Eds.), *Vygotsky in 21st century society: Advances in cultural historical theory and praxis with non-dominant communities.* New York: Peter Lang.

Moll, L. C., & Soto-Santiago, S. (2010, October). *El vaivén: Return migration and education in Puerto Rico and Mexico.* Paper presented at the On New Shores Conference, University of Guelph, Guelph, Ontario, Canada.

Olsen, L. (2008). *Made in America* (10th ed.). New York: The New Press.

Passel, J., Cohn, D., & González Barrera, A. (2012). *Net migration from Mexico falls to zero— and perhaps less.* Washington, DC: Pew Hispanic Center.

Patterson, R. (2006). Transnationalism: Diaspora-homeland development. *Social Forces, 84*(4), 1891–1907.

Portes, A., Guarnizo, L. E., & Landolt, P. (1999). The study of transnationalism: Pitfalls and promise of an emergent research field. *Ethnic and Racial Studies, 22*(2), 217–237.

Pousada, A. (1999). The singularly strange story of the English language in Puerto Rico. *Milenio, 3,* 33–60.

Prewitt-Diaz, J. O. (1994). *The Psychology of Puerto Rican migration.* Lancaster, Pennsylvania: U.S. Department of Education.

Reyes, X. A. (2000). Yankee go home? In S. Nieto (Ed.), *Puerto Rican students in US schools* (pp. 39–67). Mahwah, NJ: Lawrence Erlbaum.

Sánchez, P., & Machado-Casas, M. (2009). At the intersection of transnationalism, Latina/o immigrants and education. *High School Journal,* April/May, 3–15.

Vega de Jesús, A., & Sayers, D. (2007). Voices: Bilingual youth constructing and defending their identities, across borders: A binational study of Puerto Rican circular migrant students. *Multicultural Education, 14*(4), 16–19.

U.S. Census Bureau. (2010). State and country quick facts [Tables with general demographics data]. Retrieved from http://quickfacts.census.gov/qfd/states/06000.html

Zembylas, M. (2012). Transnationalism, migration and emotions: Implications for education. *Globalisation, Societies and Education, 1*(1), 1–17.

A Closer Look at Families, Classroom Learning, and Identity Development

9

FINDING A PLACE

Migration and Education in Mixed-Status Families

Ariana Mangual Figueroa

The 2010 census has confirmed the significance of two trends that began in the last decade—first, the internal migration of Latinos from traditional receiving states such as California, Florida, and New York to new settlement areas in the South and Midwest; second, the growing number of children born in the United States to at least one undocumented parent (Passel, Cohn, & Lopez, 2011; Passel & Taylor, 2010).[1] Of the 5.1 million children of undocumented migrants living in the U.S., 1.1 million are undocumented migrants like their parents, and 4 million are U.S.-born citizens (Passel & Taylor, 2010). In emerging Latino communities, undocumented children tend to be older siblings who migrated with their parents, whereas younger children are usually U.S.-born citizens (Passel & Cohn, 2009). Scholars refer to such families as mixed-status families, and they are composed of undocumented migrant and U.S.-born members, as well as members in various stages of applying for citizenship (Fix & Zimmerman, 2001). As of 2009, 6.8 percent of U.S. public school students lived in mixed-status families (Passel & Cohn, 2009).

Although mainstream perceptions of Spanish-speaking migrants suggest that they are resistant to learning English and that their enrollment in bilingual education programs hinders assimilation (Cummins, 2000; Wiley & de Klerk, 2010), empirical research shows that language loss is more normative than achieving bilingualism (Wong-Fillmore, 2000). Secondary analyses of the 2000 census provide evidence that linguistic assimilation among Latinos occurs within just three generations of arrival to the United States (Alba, 2004). Longitudinal studies of Spanish-speaking communities across the country show that the vast majority of children of immigrants become English speakers at the expense of retaining Spanish (López & Stanton-Salazar, 2001; Rumbaut & A. Portes, 2001) and that school language policies increase the pressure placed on students to learn English and shed Spanish (A. Portes & Hao, 1998). The most recent longitudinal study of immigrants shows that although the children of immigrants have a strong desire to learn English and do acquire conversational English rapidly, the schools that they attend often deny them much-needed opportunities to learn the academic English that they need to master in order to succeed by traditional schooling measures (C. Suárez-Orozco, M. M. Suárez-Orozco, & Todorova, 2008).

This chapter hopes to contribute to a growing body of research that documents migrant families' language use in order to understand which practices foster learning in home and school settings (Bhimji, 2005; Delgado-Gaitan, 1992; Valdés, 1996; Vásquez, Pease-Alvarez, & Shannon, 1994). I draw from a 23-month ethnographic study of an emerging community located in the Rust Belt region of the United States, part of the new Latino diaspora, in order to analyze the ways in which members of one mixed-status family talk about their migration and educational experiences. I address the following questions: First, how do educational programs foster or constrain migrant parents' opportunities to be involved in their children's schooling? Second, how do undocumented parents and children demonstrate their perceptions of the relative value of Spanish and English? In the following section, I provide an overview of the language socialization framework that frames this study. I then describe the city of Millvalley where this study took place and introduce the Marinero-Chavez family, which is the focus of this chapter.[2] After presenting the findings, I discuss the implications for educators and researchers and consider three areas for policy change at the national level.

Diversity within the Family

Language socialization is an interdisciplinary paradigm that focuses on interrelated processes of language acquisition and socialization (Ochs, 1986). Empirical research has shown that becoming proficient in the grammatical conventions of a linguistic code and competent in the social norms for interacting with others is a concurrent process that transpires throughout an individual's life span and across settings (Garrett & Baquedano-López, 2002). Sociocultural perspectives on learning underscore the way in which a group's identity is both shaped by historical conditions and renegotiated during ongoing culturally organized activities that are shaped by institutions such as schools (Lave & Wenger, 1991; Rogoff, 1990; Vadeboncoeur & P. R. Portes, 2002). Children are agentive social actors who participate in the negotiation of cultural practices as they are taught and as they learn (Ochs & Schieffelin, 2008; Whiting, 1980). The use of multiple communicative resources allows interlocutors who occupy different social roles (e.g., family members of multiple ages with different migratory statuses) to achieve common ground during routine interactions (Hanks, 2006).

Although language is the primary medium by which interlocutors arrive at shared understandings about themselves and the world, it is also the way in which individuals convey their unique perspectives and positions. Focusing on the heterogeneous experiences of members of a nuclear family helps to counter-act tendencies to essentialize or homogenize the shared practices of the cultural group (Ochs, 2002). Locally situated perspectives on socialization that highlight the dynamism and diversity inherent in learning and development can debunk deterministic views of culture that lead to deficit models of historically mar-ginalized groups (Gutiérrez & Rogoff, 2003; Ovando, Collier, & Combs, 2003; Valencia, 2002). Ethnographic studies of language use in Latino families point to the various linguistic and cultural resources employed in multilingual families and suggest important implications for redefining power relations in home and school interactions (González, 2001; Mercado, 2005; Valdés, 1996; Zentella, 2001). This chapter identifies the multiple perspectives that parents and children have about language and learning and explores how these beliefs are shaped by migration and education experiences.

By viewing the language and cultural practices in Latino families as sites for learning, this research highlights the ways in which individuals and community members' participation in culturally specific activity systems shapes their "funds of knowledge" (Moll, Amanti, Neff, & González, 1992, p. 133). In keeping with this approach, this chapter focuses on the social networks in which learning occurs. Elsewhere I have shown that funds of knowledge in mixed-status communities are saturated with concerns about citizenship status that are transmitted to children (Mangual Figueroa, 2012); in this chapter, I demonstrate how parents and children talk about the ways in which language education policies (Shohamy, 2003) and migration processes shape the social networks that they can access. The findings show that migration and education practices, historically seen as distinct spheres of policy and behavior, converge in the everyday lives of mixed-status families. Closely examining parents' and children's language use during everyday interactions advances our goal of helping educators to develop classroom practices and school policies responsive to the experiences of the mixed-status families that they serve.

Mixed-Status Families Living in Millvalley, Pennsylvania

This 23-month, multisited ethnographic study (Marcus, 1995) took place in Mill-valley, Pennsylvania, a postindustrial city located in the Rust Belt region of the United States, part of the new Latino diaspora (Wortham, Murillo, & Hamman, 2002). During the period in question, there were ongoing efforts to clarify how many Latinos belonged to the emerging community. The 2006 American Com-munity Survey reported that Latinos totaled 1.8 percent of Millvalley's population and that Mexicans comprised 1,537 of the 5,466 Latino residents. A local pedia-trician, and founder of the first bilingual health clinic in Millvalley, estimated that there were between 10,000 and 15,000 Latino residents. He attributed the rapid growth of the Latino community to high fertility rates (D. Correa, personal com-munication)[3] that were consistent with national trends (Durand, Telles, & Flashman, 2006).

In the spring of 2009, local leaders began encouraging Latino residents to participate in the 2010 census. Sister Elise, a Catholic nun and trusted advocate of many members of the Latino community, conducted outreach in order to assuage undocumented migrants' fear of being reported to Immigration and Customs Enforcement (ICE) by explaining that their responses to the questionnaire would be anonymous (E. Smith, personal communication). This mirrored a national phenomenon in which church leaders of Spanish-speaking congregations worked to encourage undocumented migrants' participation in the census (Preston, 2009). The 2010 census reports indicate that Latinos are the fastest growing group in the county where Millvalley is located; within the past decade, respondents who identified as Hispanic grew by 71 percent.

These demographic changes have led to the implementation of a range of formal and informal educational reforms within Millvalley. According to a local Millvalley newspaper, in 2004–2005 there were 273 English-as-a-second-language (ESL) students enrolled in the Millvalley Public School District (MPSD); in 2007–2008 the number rose to 485, and it was projected to reach 1,085 students by 2010–2011. By 2007, the ESL services being provided by itinerant teachers proved insufficient, and the MPSD was legally mandated to expand its ESL programs. According to Ned Tieran, the director of ESL for MPSD, after a year of contentious debate between community members and district leadership, it was decided that the two ESL programs for Spanish-speaking students would be housed in the kindergarten through twelfth-grade feeder schools located in the Brickyard neighborhood of Millvalley (N. Tieran, personal communication). Students were placed in the ESL program based on their responses to a home-language survey administered upon enrollment and their scores on a statewide standardized assessment; they were assigned one or more periods of ESL classes depending on their English proficiency. During the summer of 2009, Tieran recruited a Spanish-speaking ESL teacher to work at Ridge Elementary School. Although there was no formal policy in place to hire school staff who spoke the same home languages as their students, he did so in order to facilitate communication among ESL students, parents, and teachers (N. Tieran, personal communication; see also Mangual Figueroa, 2013).

I recruited four mixed-status families to participate in this study through the "snowball method" of asking one person to introduce me to a family that in turn recommended other families (Ritchie, Lewis, & Elam, 2003). The parents had all lived in other parts of the United States before migrating to Millvalley, where they settled in the Brickyard neighborhood. The children in all four families attended the Brickyard public schools described previously. The eldest children in the focal families were undocumented migrants like their parents, whereas the younger children were U.S.-born citizens. In two of the families, the undocumented youth were enrolled in middle and high school; in the other two families, the undocumented children attended elementary school. My weekly visits to the families' homes would begin when the children arrived home from school and would last until dinner. I did not predetermine which activities I would observe; I documented the families' participation in routine after school activities.

I recorded more than 45 hours of interaction in the families' homes, collected artifacts such as school correspondence and children's drawings, and wrote field notes for each visit. I also conducted interviews with school district employees and wrote field notes for parent/teacher conferences and community forums on immigration policy. I coded all of the field notes and video logs, focusing on the multiple ways in which families referred to their migratory status during everyday interactions. I developed a series of theoretical constructs about how citizenship was understood and enacted in everyday life. I triangulated these constructs with other data sources (Goetze & LeCompte, 1981) including the interviews and artifacts. Conversation analysis transcription methods highlighted the complex communicative resources that interlocutors used to convey their stances and identities during interaction (Ochs, 2002; Schegloff, 2007).

The Marinero-Chavez family that is the focus of this chapter is represented in Figure 9.1. In addition to traditional genealogical notations denoting marriage and descent (O'Neil, 2008), the shading indicates the family members' migratory status. The shaded symbols indicate U.S.-born children, and unshaded symbols denote undocumented migrant family members born in Mexico.

In 2004, Inés, Ignacio, and Pedro migrated from a coastal city in Southwestern Mexico to the city of Orange Grove, Florida, where Inés's father lived. Two years later, they moved to Millvalley where Ignacio's family offered the couple housing help and assistance finding work. The Marinero-Chavez family lived in a one-bedroom apartment on the third floor of a house that was owned by Ignacio's uncle. Ignacio's father, along with his wife and three children, occupied the first and second stories of the house. Pedro was in third grade at the time of this study and had recently been reclassified as English proficient and exited from Ridge Elementary School's ESL program. Fani and Junior were four and two years old, respectively; when I first met the family, they attended a neighborhood Head Start program. Although all of the focal families knew a family member or friend who was deported during the course of this study, the Marinero-Chavez family was the only one in which a parent was deported.

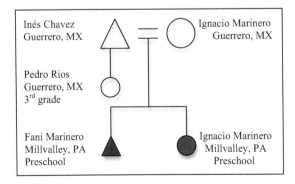

FIGURE 9.1 The Marinero-Chavez Family

Ignacio was deported in December 2009, after failing to produce state-issued identification when stopped during a routine stop for a traffic violation.[4] Within a month and a half of his deportation, Ignacio crossed the border from Mexico to the United States for a second time in order to rejoin his family. The interactions presented in the following section took place about a month after Ignacio returned to Millvalley.

Findings

The following three examples are excerpts from a conversation that I recorded in the Marinero-Chavez home on March 31, 2009. The family had just begun to readjust to school and work schedules after Ignacio's deportation and return migration; the exchanges that took place on this day were embedded within typical after-school routines. At around 4:00 p.m. Inés arrived home after having picked up Fani and Junior from day care, and by 4:30 p.m. Pedro was dropped off by the school bus. I spent my afternoon visits with the family in the common room of the apartment where the living room, dining room, and kitchen were located. Once Ignacio arrived from work, he joined us in the common room while Inés prepared dinner. Both parents and children participated in the conversations and activities that transpired throughout the afternoon.

Example One: From Bilingual to English-Only Schooling[5]

This exchange followed a conversation about the siblings' language use in which Inés explained that her children tended to speak only in English with their cousins and peers (see Table 9.1 for transcription conventions). She then recounted Pedro's experience learning English as a recent migrant to the United States and compared the language education programs of the schools that he attended in Orange Grove and Millvalley.

1 Inés: *Él no hablaba nada de inglés cuando llegamos (.5) Yo dije como le voy hacer*
    He didn't speak any English when we arrived. I said how am I going to do it

2 *ahora que vaya a la escuela*
    now so that he can go to school

3 Ariana: Yah

4 Inés: *Pero en Orange Grove? esa escuela(.)yo creo que me ayudó basta::nte porque*
    But in Orange Grove? that school. I think it helped me a lot because

5 *allá el sistema es muy difer[ente°=*
    there the system is very different

6 ((gestures as if weighing an object in each hand))

7 Ariana: [*Sí*
           Yes

8 Inés: =*allá hablan el inglé?- te hablan en español? y te van metie:::ndo* ↑
          there they speak English- they speak to you in Spanish and they add

9   *el inglés poco a poco.* ((signals forward and up with right hand)) *Y aquí no* ↑.
          English little by little. And here no.

10   *Aquí tienes que aprender el inglés* ((snaps and crosses hands))
          Here you have to learn English

11 Ariana: *Eso se llama el mode::lo de inmersión. Es como sumergir al niño en un*
            That is called an immersion model It's like submerging a child in

12   *baño de [agua=* ((gestures with two hands as if dunking an object in water))
            a bath of water

13 Pedro: [*SÍ YO SABÍA* ↑ *EL INGLÉS* ↑
             YES I KNEW ENGLISH

14 Ariana: =*a ver si aprende a nadar, y si no?* ((wipes one hand with the other))
            to see if they learn to swim, and if not?

15 Pedro: *sabÍA* ↑ *un poquito de ingLÉS* ↑ *porque saqué um high SCORE*
            I knew a little bit of English because I got um high score

16 Ariana: *en ESL?*
            in ESL?

17 Pedro: I was the highest [score um

Inés described the anxiety that she felt as a recent migrant who wondered about how she would help Pedro make the transition to U.S. schools when neither of them spoke English (line 1). She found support in the bilingual school that Pedro attended because Spanish was spoken and English was introduced gradually (line 9). This model contrasted sharply with the English-only school-ing that Pedro received in Millvalley; Inés stated that *"el sistema es muy diferente"* / the system is very different (line 5). Although the bilingual programming was a significant source of help for her (line 4), the same kind of language support did not exist in Millvalley schools (*"y aquí no"*/ and here no, line 9). Notably, Inés talked about Pedro's language learning by describing the way that bilin-gual schooling fostered her ability to support his development. She highlighted the benefits of bilingual education not only for Pedro as a learner—in other moments she claimed that Pedro most certainly would have been retained a grade if he hadn't attended a bilingual school—but also for her own ability to partici-pate in his schooling.

As I began to characterize the Millvalley ESL program as a "sink or swim" (Villanueva, 2000; Wiley & Wright, 2004) approach to teaching English with-out native language support, Pedro interrupted me and asserted that he did in fact know how to speak English. He rejected Inés's claim that he could not speak English when they first migrated to the United States and shouted that he *did* know English (line 13). He explained that the proof of his English-language ability was the fact that he received a high score (line 15), probably referring to the standardized assessment of language ability that he had taken in the previ-ous spring when he was reclassified as English proficient. I confirmed that he was referring to his score in ESL, and his excitement about having the "highest score" (line 17) demonstrated his uptake of the local school language policy that valued language acquisition reflected in students' performance on standardized exams.

Example Two: Demographic Changes in Millvalley Schools

As Inés prepared dinner, we continued talking about Ridge Elementary School. I mentioned that I had recently spoken with the head of ESL for the MPSD about the increasing number of children enrolling in the school's ESL program. Inés offered her perspective on recent changes that she had noticed in Millvalley's growing Latino community.

18 Ariana: *Y me dijo que::: en el último mes? Me dijo que ha:::n matricula:::do casí quince*
           And he told me that in the last month. He told me almost fifteen have enrolled

19   *niños nuevos en el programa de ESL. Así que va creciendo la población*
           new children in the ESL program. So therefore the population keeps growing

20   *de no solo [Latinos-*
           of not only Latinos-

21 Inés: *[Sí he notado basta::::nte Lati:::nos (.) sí::::*
               Yes I've noticed a lot of Latinos yes

22 Ariana: *Sí? De Latinos han llegado mucho?*
           Yes? A lot of Latinos have come recently?

23 Pedro: >*Mami, mami, mami< no le heches mole:::°*
           ((glancing at the food on the table))
           Mommy, mommy, mommy don't add mole

24 Inés: *Por lo regular (.) en la misma familia? por ejemplo nosotros que vinimos*
           Usually in the same family for example we came

25 *de Orange Grove? Que a veces no sa::::ben como esta:: (.)*
           from Orange Grove. Sometimes they don't know what it's like

26 *Y luego te preguntan pues qué tal es allá? no pues que aquí*
           And then they ask you well what's it like over there? no well here it's

27 *es muy diferente (.) estamos bien=*
           very different. we're fine

28 ((gestures as if she was weighing two objects in her hands))

29 Pedro: *Hola, I'm Pedro*
           Hi, I'm Pedro
           ((teeters and waves at the camera, making a clownish face))

30 Inés: *=que sé yo (.) O hay más trabajo.*
           or whatever. Or there's more work.

31 *Por lo regular↑ >el Latino viene<*
           Usually Latinos come

32 *siguiendo::: el trabajo*
           following the work

33 Ariana: *el traba[jo=*
           work

34 Inés: [*y el tipo de pago de trabajo°*
           and the working wages

35 Ariana: =yah

36 Inés: *Y entonces >allí también vienen los niños↑< y ya se establecen.*
           And then the children come there too and they establish themselves.

37 *Y es↑ chistoso porque >la mayoría de los Latinos que estamos aquí< en*
           And it's funny because the majority of the Latinos that are here in

38 *Millvalley? nos conocemos* ((makes several circles with her index finger))
           Millvalley know one another

Inés chronicled the economic circumstances that drove Latinos to engage in secondary migration from traditional settlement states in the United States to emerging diasporic communities like Millvalley. She detailed the phone conversations typical among family members trying to determine the best place to live and raise a family (lines 25 and 26), and her words and gestures once again underscored the fact that Millvalley was very different from Orange Grove (lines 26 and 27). As Inés described the migratory experience that she and others shared, Pedro enacted his own representation of a migrant living in Millvalley. Speaking in a mock Spanish (Hill, 1997) characterized by elongating the closed Spanish vowel sounds of *hola* (pronouncing the 'o' like the [ɔ] sound in the word 'open' and the 'a' like the [?] in 'laugh') and pronouncing *Pedro* like *Pay-dro* (elongating the 'a' and 'o' sounds), he teetered toward the camera and waved while making a clownish expression. Pedro's caricature is particularly interesting because of his use of mock Spanish—it was as if he was imitating an English speaker parodying a migrant. Inés painted a portrait of Latino migrants seeking work and enrolling their children in school (line 36), while Pedro provided insight into local perceptions of migrants that he and others may have encountered upon their arrival in Millvalley.

Example Three: Establishing and Dismantling Social Networks

In this final example, Inés talked about her experience participating in educational events held at the Head Start center that Fani and Junior attended at the beginning of this study. As in her previous accounts, Inés's descriptions of schooling experiences in the United States were linked to migration and, in this case, Ignacio's deportation. She described the support she received from the director of the Head Start program—an educator who was learning Spanish and established relationships of trust with many of the Latino families whose children were enrolled there.

38 Inés: *Sí, y cuando tuve el problema* ((gestures toward Ignacio)) *ella me ayudó bastante,*
Yes when I had that problem she helped me a lot, she

39 *me dio una prórroga de un mes*↑ *para que la niña estuviera ause:nte*↑*, pero pues*
gave me a window of one month in which the girl could be absent, but well

40 >*ya no pudo*< *regresa:::r. De hecho*↑ *ya era muy complicado por los*
Horarios
she couldn't return. In fact it was already too complicated because of the schedule

41 ((gestures with hands as though she was weighing one object in each hand))

42 *Pero SÍ me dolió mucho*↑ *que ella saliera de allí° porque era una*
buena↑
But yes it hurt me very much that she had to leave there because it was a good

43 *escuela*↑ *(.) conocí a más pa::dres de fami::lia*↑ *(.) convivíamos cada mes*↑
school.   I met more parents and   we came together every month

44 Ariana: *Sí eso cuenta mu::cho verdad? poder ver:::se y poder habla:::r*=
Yes that matters a lot right? To be able to see one another and to be able to talk

45 Inés: *Sí::::::*
Yes

46 Ariana: =*compartir comi::::da*
share food

47 Inés: *Sí::::::y plati:::cas (.) con más ge::::nte*
yes and you talk   to more people

48 Ariana: *y Marta me dijo que también ponen como temas =*
          and Marta told me that they also propose topics

49 Inés: *Sí::::::*
          Yes

50 Ariana: *=de inmigración::::n, educación::::n*
          like immigration,   education

51 Inés: *Sí(.) entonces ella es muy abierta (.) te ayuda bastante. La última ↑ vez fue::: la*
          Yes. So she was very open   she helps you a lot. The last time was the

52   *reunión de noviembre, no ↑ de diciembre. Y puso Santa Clo:s, y*
          November meeting, no the December one. And she put up Santa Claus and

53   *le dieron regalos a todos ↑ los niños, hasta los >que no iban allí<.*
          they gave gifts to all of the children, even those that didn't go there.

54 Ariana: *ah ha*
          um hmm

55 Inés: *Entonces este, dio jugue:::tes, luego el día de Halloween pusieron a los niños a*
          So then they gave gifts, then on Halloween they arranged for all of the children to

56   *pinta:::r con los padres y a los niños calaba::::zas, cosas como que nos hacía*
          paint with the parents and the children pumpkins, things that kind of made us

57   *que nos uñiera=*
          that united us

58 Ariana: *Ya*
          Yah

59 Inés: *=entonces. muy muy buena escuela.*
          so. a very very good school.

Inés's description of the support that she received in the local Head Start program began with a reference to Ignacio's deportation ("*con todo el problema que tuve*"/due to the problem that I had, line 38). She had to withdraw Fani and Junior from the program (line 40) because, when Ignacio was deported, Inés moved into a smaller apartment on the other side of town, began working two jobs, and was too far away from the Head Start to drop off and pick up the children each day. She noted how difficult it was for her to decide to withdraw the children because of the connection that she felt to the program and to the community convened by the director. Inés enumerated several attributes of the program that she found supportive: the director reserved the children's seats in the program during the family's separation and transition (line 39); the monthly parent meetings fostered Inés's connection to other families in the community (lines 43 and 47); the director created a forum for discussing pressing topics in the families' lives (line 51); and she included all the children within the families (lines 53 and 57).

In other conversations that I had with Inés in the spring of 2009, she told me that the Halloween and Christmas events described previously were the last public events that she and her family had participated in since Ignacio's deportation (in December 2008). That same spring, after receiving Pedro's report card in the mail, Inés requested a parent/teacher conference with his teacher, and I accompanied her to translate. Even though the teachers at Ridge Elementary School did not know about Ignacio's deportation, they reported that Pedro's behavior had changed and that he had begun acting withdrawn and depressed during the same period when Ignacio was in Mexico. When Ignacio returned to Millvalley, he and Inés had to find new jobs and were not able to reenroll Fani and Junior in the Head Start program; instead, they found a state-subsidized day-care center where they could take the children during the workday. Consequently, the trauma of the deportation had lasting effects on the family's feeling of safety, their connection to the larger Latino community, and the children's educational experiences.

Implications: Rethinking Parental Participation

This chapter has examined the way in which one undocumented mother and her son demonstrated their stances toward language use and learning in U.S. public schools. Inés identified at least two types of school programming that fostered her ability to support her children's learning: first, bilingual education that facilitated her interactions with school staff and supported Pedro's ability to learn English, and second, early childhood programs that provided a space for migrant Latino parents to convene to share resources and to learn about public systems such as education and immigration. The three examples underscore Inés's desire to be involved in her children's schooling and challenge persistent deficit perceptions of Latino parents who are uninterested in their children's schooling. These exchanges also provide insight into the ways that migrant children make sense of their experiences living in two languages, migrating at a young age and growing up in the United States, and being a member of an emergent student population.

These findings confirm research showing that undocumented migrants want to participate in U.S. civic life and gain a sense of "cultural citizenship" even as they face institutional practices that systematically deny them basic civil rights such as health care, living wages, and the possibility of political participation (Flores & Benmayor, 1997). At the same time, the economic structures that lead to globalization and migration continue to influence learning and development upon families' arrival to the United States (M. Suárez-Orozco, 2001). As parents adjust to new labor conditions and develop survival strategies particular to living in diasporic communities, their family's ways of interacting and learning shift as well (O'Leary, González, & Valdez-Gardea, 2008; Veléz-Ibañez & Greenberg, 1992). In addition, children attending U.S. schools develop novel identities informed by the ways others' perceive them and their own beliefs about what citizenship means across settings and national borders (Abu El-Haj, 2007; Banks, 2008).

As an undocumented parent, Inés struggled with the ongoing tension of wanting to be a visible presence in the public schools that her children attended while remaining invisible to authorities that might deport or otherwise punish her for her undocumented status. As a result, there were certain kinds of involvement that Inés sought out, and others that she avoided. On the one hand, she wanted to have the opportunity to communicate with teachers in Spanish and attend monthly parent meetings for Latino parents led by trusted educators; on the other hand, Inés often felt too anxious to attend schoolwide events at Pedro's school, was unsure about how to volunteer during the school day, and was afraid to serve as a chaperone on field trips. Baquedano-López's research on Mexican mothers' struggles to maintain bilingual *doctrina* classes within the heightened anti-Spanish and anti-immigrant climate that existed in California after the approval of Proposition 187 suggests that marginalized parents' participation in mainstream educational practices involves a series of subtle decisions about when to be a vocal advocate versus a passive observer of mainstream educative policies (Baquedano-López, 2004; Baquedano-López & Ochs, 2002). This suggests that we must be sensitive to the shifting roles and advocacy strategies taken up by undocumented parents as we identify opportunities for parental participation; a one-size-fits-all approach does not work for Mexican and migrant parents for whom immigration policies influence their ability to be active in schooling processes (see Baquedano-López, Hernandez, & Alexander, Chapter 2, this volume).

These findings suggest three major implications for school administrators and teachers. First, schools should provide opportunities for parents and children to communicate in their home language—and sediment these in programmatic policies like bilingual education or in interpersonal approaches like learning to speak the language of the parents—because this supports parental participation. Second, school leaders and staff can work to make schools available to the public constituencies that they serve. Creating forums in which parents are participants and leaders will facilitate communication among adults who can share resources that strengthen their own support systems and foster their children's development and well-being. This can work to counter the negative effects of deportations, family separations, and other forms of institutional marginalization experienced by mixed-status families (Chaudrey et. al., 2010). Third, as anti-immigrant laws are passed in states like Arizona and proposed in other states across the country, schools have to work even harder to build trusting relationships with parents. Recently, we have witnessed the exodus of Latino children from Arizona school districts, in part because their parents feared that the schools would become arms of the state's disciplinary power (Kossan, 2010). Throughout my fieldwork, I learned that these concerns reverberate through new Latino diaspora locations like Millvalley.

Teacher educators and researchers can support school leaders and teachers working in prekindergarten through twelfth-grade settings in conceptualizing ways of working in solidarity with migrant communities. In order to do so, we must begin to talk about the implication of the important Supreme Court ruling *Plyler v. Doe*, which protects students' rights to a public education regardless of their or their parents' migratory status by prohibiting educators from inquiring about their citizenship status. In order to work alongside mixed-status families, we must acknowledge that there is a tension between acknowledging that this population exists and also protecting their right to an education. Teacher educators and researchers can play a tremendous role in facilitating this type of dialogue and scaffolding conversations about recognizing the diversity of families in an era of standardization. Educators in university settings bear a particular responsibility to talk with preservice teachers about *Plyler*—being one step removed from the public school provides them with a unique opportunity to talk about this point of intersection between juridical and educational practices openly and honestly.

By conducting research that highlights the voices of these families that have often been referred to as "living in the shadows" (Ruiz, 1998), researchers can help shed light on the resources that mixed-status families bring to schools and to the communities in which they live. Continued research in this area is needed to understand the ways that migratory processes shape student learning, attendance, and motivation across the life span, in addition to the more widely documented barriers to postsecondary study based on undocumented adolescents' migratory status (Gonzales, 2008; Rogers, Saunders, Terriquez, & Velez, 2008). The goal of serving the needs of Latino children cannot be met by policies that divide them from their parents along the lines of citizenship or language, but we can begin to work against subtractive language policies (Brisk, 2006) and schooling practices (Valenzuela, 1999) furthered by deficit models that mistake undocumented parents' fear of prosecution with a lack of interest in their children's academic progress. Learning more about—and learning how to listen to—mixed-status families will help educators work alongside parents in the pursuit of more equitable schooling practices.

Stepping Back and Scaling Up: Policy Considerations on a National Level

The experiences of the Marinero-Chavez family point to three areas of educational policy in need of urgent reexamination. Policy makers, scholars, educators, and community members must find ways to collaborate in these areas if mixed-status families are to have access to the material and social capital needed to support their children's development and learning. First, we must develop educational practices that counter the invisibility of undocumented students and mixed-status families; second, we must reexamine the connections between education, immigration, and social policy instead of treating them as distinct; and third, we must shift our emphasis from securitizing the nation to promoting the social welfare of this growing population. I will briefly describe these three areas, citing examples of how activists and educators have undertaken "coordinated counteraction—the purposeful activity of making ineffective—or restraining or neutralizing—the usually ill effects of an influence by means of an opposite force, action, or influence" (Salas, P. R. Portes, D'Amico, & Rios-Aguilar, 2011, p. 128). Examples of "coordinated counteraction" give us insight into communities' concerted efforts to develop new educational practices that counter detrimental policies; it is my hope that presenting these models can broaden our vision of what is possible through sustained collaboration.

Area One: Moving from Invisibility to Visibility

The year 2012 marked the 30th anniversary of the 1982 Supreme Court case *Plyler v. Doe*, which ruled that all children have the right to a public education regardless of their migratory status. This important protective clause has been implemented through a "don't ask, don't tell" policy in which educators are mandated never to inquire about the migratory status of the families that they serve (yet, recent reports by the American Civil Liberties Union have identified numerous violations across the nation). As a result of this silence, undocumented students in U.S. public schools remain largely invisible, and we know little about their educational experiences. In addition, *Plyler* only grants educational rights through the twelfth grade; undocumented students receive few, if any, protections upon high school graduation (Gonzales, 2011).

A growing body of research shows that living in the United States as an undocumented individual or as a member of a mixed-status family is an issue that affects development and learning at critical moments across the life span (Chavez, 1998). These moments begin in early childhood (C. Suárez-Orozco, Yoshikawa, Teranishi, & M. M. Suárez-Orozco, 2011) and continue through elementary school (Mangual Figueroa, 2011) into adolescence (Abrego, 2006; Gonzales, 2011; Perez, 2009) and parenthood (Yoshikawa, 2011). Migratory status has material and psychological impacts on individuals and families whose members confront the contradiction of both belonging to and being excluded from U.S. life on a daily basis (Gonzalez, 2011; Zavella, 2011).

Undocumented youth and adults have developed a grassroots strategy of "coming out," or declaring their migratory status in public as a means of calling for support of Dream Act legislation that would provide eligible undocumented youth with a pathway to U.S. citizenship (Hing, 2011). This coordinated and strategic counteraction is evidenced by events like "Dreamers" staging sit-ins at President Obama's campaign offices around the country and risking arrest to call for more attention to the significance of the Dream Act (Ingold, 2012) and the first ever "Dream Graduation" held in San Francisco to honor the accomplishments of undocumented students and call for federal policy change (E. Murillo, personal communication). University scholars should follow this example—convening concerned stakeholders to explore the relationship between citizenship and schooling and advocating publically for the rights of children, youth, and adults living in mixed-status families. Those of us deeply committed to upholding and extending these rights are uniquely positioned to engage in this work because we are not bound by *Plyler*'s mandate of silence. We can serve as liaisons between families (who often participate in our research) and educators of good faith restrained from addressing citizenship status directly, helping parents and schools to collaborate with one another as opposed to interacting against a backdrop of fear and silence.

Area Two: Connecting the Dots

New research on mixed-status families indicates that undocumented parents endure poor working conditions, are afraid to access social services, and are socially isolated—all factors that negatively impact the cognitive and social-emotional development of their U.S.-born children during early childhood (Yoshikawa, 2011). Being undocumented shapes parents' incorporation into U.S. economic and social life (Chavez, 1998), which in turn impacts their children's experiences in public schools. Yet we continue to treat educational policy reform as distinct from immigration, economic, and social policy. Working to change policies in one area will constitute only a piecemeal approach unless we work in an integrated and systemic way to change the plight of families living in poverty who cannot access equitable social, educational, and economic opportunities (P. R. Portes, 2005).

We have increasing evidence of the ways in which immigration and education policy grow more intertwined each day. Republican congressmen have recently proposed repealing the Fourteenth Amendment that grants citizenship to children born in the United States, and that forms the basis for the *Plyler* decision, in the hopes of deterring their undocumented parents from crossing the southern border into the United States (Lacey, 2011). In the summer of 2011, the governor of Alabama signed a law requiring public schools to verify students' immigration status upon enrollment and denying undocumented students the opportunity to attend public colleges in the state (Preston, 2011). In June 2012, days after President Obama issued the Deferred Action for Childhood Arrivals (DACA) memorandum, which allows undocumented immigrants brought to the United States as children the right to request two years of deferred action on deportation and legal permission to work in the United States, the Supreme Court struck down, on points of constitutionality, several key provisions impacting education of Arizona's S.B. 1070, one of the nation's most restrictive immigration laws (Sherman, 2012). Although applauded by civil liberties groups, neither of these actions has resolved the issues for undocumented students seeking postsecondary education; although 16 states have issued laws or Board of Regents' policies allowing undocumented students to pay in-state tuition at state institutions, 3 (Georgia, Indiana, and Arizona) officially prohibit in-state tuition rates for undocumented students, and 2 states (South Carolina and Alabama) prohibit admission to undocumented students at any state institution of postsecondary education (National Conference of State Legislatures, 2013). Given the variability in state-specific legislation, the national debate about who has the jurisdiction to control immigrants' rights continues in domains ranging from law enforcement to housing and schooling (Gomez, 2012).

Around the country, activists have come out to support mixed-status families. Some of the most notable counteractions are taking place in the state of Georgia where one of the nation's most restrictive immigration laws was passed in 2012 (Shashahani, 2012). University of Georgia professors, in response to the Board of Regents' barring undocumented students from admission to the state's five most prestigious universities and colleges (Associated Press, 2011), created the "Freedom University" that offers undocumented students college-level classes. In addition, undocumented Georgia high school students have engaged in organized, peaceful acts of civil disobedience, drawing national attention to the issue (Brumback, 2011), and the American Educational Research Association (AERA) boycotted the state by relocating their 2013 annual national conference, which had been scheduled to convene in Atlanta, to another city (AERA, personal communication).

Educational leaders and politicians must support this work in vocal and public ways. This would require the national education secretary, the National Governors Association, and superintendents across the country to speak out for the civil and human rights of mixed-status families. The current educational focus on adopting Common Core State Standards and reforming high-stakes testing policies will do nothing to close the widening achievement gap if structural inequalities persist. Discussions of educational policy that ignore the reality of undocumented families—the difficulty of earning a living wage, the lack of health care and other social services, and the constant fear of deportation, among other factors—will not only fail to produce meaningful reform, they will also perpetuate a system in which individual students are blamed for what are collective failures.

Area Three: Stop Criminalizing and Start Nurturing Mixed-Status Communities

Despite the fact that migration to the United States has slowed and begun to decrease for the first time in 40 years (Passel, Cohn, & González-Barrera, 2012), and the fastest rate of growth of the Latino population is attributable to births of U.S.-born citizens (Passel et al., 2011), immigration policy and public discourse still operate as though border control is the utmost priority for addressing migration. There are currently at least 5,100 children and youth that have been placed in foster care because of the criminalization and deportation of parents (Wessler, 2011). The number of deportations has grown exponentially since President Obama took office (Slevin, 2010). Although the DACA memorandum—which calls for a halt on deportations for eligible undocumented youth who migrated to the United States before their 16th birthday (Preston & Cushman, 2012)—may quell some of the immediate fear that undocumented youth feel surrounding the threat of deportation, any policy that falls short of providing a pathway to citizenship will perpetuate a status quo in which families are separated and children live in instability and uncertainty. This discourse of criminalization and outmoded emphasis on border "security" serves only to create a permanent underclass in the United States, diverting public funds from constructive projects and fostering mistrust between public officials and mixed-status communities.

Youth activists as well as community and professional organizations are waging a concerted campaign to change the public discourse regarding migratory status by calling on individuals to pledge not to use the word "illegal" when referring to undocumented youth (see http://colorlines.com/droptheiword/). The Society of Professional Journalists has called for journalists and media outlets across the country to stop using the word "illegal," encouraging them to use the term "undocumented" instead (Scheiner, 2012). In response to public pressure, the Associated Press has updated their stylebook directing journalists to use the term "illegal" only when referring to an action, not a person except in direct quotes (Downes, 2013). Members of the Undergraduate Students Association at the University of California, Los Angeles, recently followed suit by voting to stop using the word "illegal" on campus. This decision corresponds with a change in leadership across the University of California system in which Janet Napolitano—the former head of Homeland Security—was selected to be the next president ("UCLA Student Body," 2013), further underscoring the increasing connections between education, immigration, and securitization. These counteractions point to the importance of changing the public's perception of undocumented populations as a vital first step in shifting the conversation from criminalization to humanization.

Educators and researchers who work with mixed-status families have a responsibility to push back against criminalizing discourses by helping to establish relationships between these families and other community members. At the very least, we can serve the important function of creating spaces in which undocumented individuals or their families can speak about and out of their experiences, countering the xenophobic stereotypes so often propagated by politicians and the media. Scholars of education who can find creative ways to enable mixed-status families to testify about their experiences in their own voice—whether through publication, public fora, classroom visits, or other means—will be helping, in their own small but significant way, to move beyond sound bites regarding "security" to a more nuanced sense of the human complexity of migratory status. Crucially, it will also alert scholars to grassroots strategies and counteractions developed within these communities, affording important opportunities for collaboration, and reminding us that scholars and policy makers have as much to learn as we do to teach.

TABLE 9.1 Transcription Conventions

(.)	"Micropause"	CAPS	Especially loud talk
.	Falling, or final intonation contour	o	Talk following it was quiet or soft
?	Rising intonation	↑↓	Sharper intonation rises or falls
::	Prolongation of the preceding sound	(( ))	Transcriber's description of events
_	Stress or emphasis	><	Fast or rushed talk
[	A point of overlap onset	=	Continuous utterance

Notes

1. The term *unauthorized* is used largely in the policy literature (see Passel, 2005, and reports issued by the Pew Hispanic Center), whereas the term *illegal* is prevalent in public debates about immigration reform (Mehan, 1997; Santa Ana, 1999). I use the term *undocumented* because it closely reflects the language that the focal families used. When adults talked about migrants and included themselves, they said *nosotros los indocumentados* (we the undocumented); they also referred to citizenship status by using the metaphorical adjectival phrase *tener papeles* (to have papers). The term *undocumented* reflects this emphasis on legal documentation or paperwork.
2. All of the proper names used throughout this chapter are pseudonyms.
3. To protect participants' anonymity, I cite personal communications without including the date.
4. In Pennsylvania, undocumented migrants cannot apply for a state-issued driver's license or identification card. Although Millvalley had a public system of municipal transportation, travel to and from work was difficult without a car. Due to local laws and the heightened "citizenship policing" (Villenas & Moreno, 2001, p. 671), undocumented migrants driving cars were at heightened risk of being stopped, detained, and deported.
5. I adhered to conversation analysis transcription conventions; it is important to note that "punctuation marks are *not* used grammatically, but to indicate intonation" (Schegloff, 2007, p. 267).

References

Abrego, L. J. (2006). "I can't go to college because I don't have papers": Incorporation patterns of Latino undocumented youth. *Latino Studies, 4,* 212–231.

Abu El-Haj, T. (2007). "I was born here but my home it's not here": Educating for democratic citizenship in an era of transnational migration and global conflict. *Harvard Educational Review, 77*(3), 285–316.

Alba, R. (2004, December). *Language assimilation today: Bilingualism persists more than in the past, but English still dominates.* Albany, NY: Lewis Mumford Center for Comparative Urban and Regional Research University at Albany.

Associated Press. (2011, August 25). Freedom university: Georgia profs offer course to undocumented immigrants. *Huffington Post.* Retrieved from www.huffingtonpost.com/ 2011/08/25/freedom-university-georgi_n_936296.html

Banks, J. (2008). Diversity, group identity, and citizenship education in a global age. *Educational Researcher, 37*(3), 129–139.

Baquedano-López, P. (2004). Traversing the center: The politics of language use in a Catholic religious education program for immigrant Mexican children. *Anthropology and Education Quarterly, 35*(2), 212–232.

Baquedano-López, P., & Ochs, E. (2002). The politics of language and parish storytelling: *Nuestra Señora de Guadalupe* takes on English-only. In P. Linell & K. Aronsson (Eds.), *Selves and voices: Goffman, Viveka, and dialogue* (pp. 173–191). Linkoping, Sweden: Linkoping University.

Bhimji, F. (2005). Language socialization with directives in two Mexican immigrant families in South Central Los Angeles. In A. C. Zentella (Ed.), *Building on strength: Language and literacy in Latino families and communities* (pp. 60–76). New York: Teachers College.

Brisk, M. E. (2006). *Bilingual education: From compensatory to quality schooling* (2nd ed.). Mahwah, NJ: Lawrence Erlbaum.

Brumback, K. (2011, June 28). Georgia immigration law: 6 illegal immigrants arrested during protest. *Huffington Post.* Retrieved from www.huffingtonpost.com/2011/06/28/georgia-immigration-law-illegal-immigrants-arrested_n_886622.html

Chaudry, A., Capps, R., Pedroza, J. M., Castañeda, R. M., Santos, R., & Scott, M. M. (2010, February). *Facing our future: Children in the aftermath of immigration enforcement.* Washington, DC: The Urban Institute.

Chavez, L. R. (1998). *Shadowed lives: Undocumented immigrants in American society.* Belmont, CA: Wadsworth.

Cummins, J., Editor (2000). Language interactions in the classroom. In *Language, power, and pedagogy: Bilingual children caught in the crossfire* (pp. 31–52). Clevendon, UK: Multilingual Matters.

Delgado-Gaitan, C. (1992). School matters in the Mexican-American home: Socializing children to education. *American Educational Research Journal, 29*(3), 495–513.

Downes, L. (2013, April 13). No more "illegal immigrants." *New York Times.* Retrieved from http://takingnote.blogs.nytimes.com/2013/04/04/no-more-illegal-immigrants/?_r=0

Durand, J., Telles, E., & Flashman, J. (2006). The demographic foundations of the Latino population. In M. Tienda & F. Mitchell (Eds.), *Hispanics and the future of America* (pp. 66–99). Washington, DC: National Research Council.

Fix, M., & Zimmerman, W. (2001). All under one roof: Mixed-status families in an era of reform. *International Migration Review, 35*(2), 397–419.

Flores, W. V., & Benmayor, R. (1997). *Latino cultural citizenship: Claiming identity, space, and rights.* Boston: Beacon Press.

Garrett, P., & Baquedano-López, P. (2002). Language socialization: Reproduction and continuity, transformation and change. *Annual Review of Anthropology, 31,* 339–361.

Goetze, J., & Lecompte, M. (1981). Ethnographic research and the problem of data reduction. *Anthropology and Education Quarterly, 12*(1), 51–70.

Gomez, A. (2012, April 25). Supreme Court hears arguments over Ariz. immigration law. *USA Today.* Retrieved from www.usatoday.com/news/washington/judicial/story/2012-04-24/supreme-court-arizona-immigration/54522026/1

González, N. (2001). *I am my language: Discourses of women and children in the borderlands.* Tucson, AZ: University of Arizona Press.

Gonzales, R. G. (2008). Left out but not shut down: Political activism and the undocumented student movement. *Northwestern Journal of Law and Social Policy, 3,* 219–239.

Gonzales, R. G. (2011). Learning to be illegal: Undocumented youth and shifting legal contexts in the transition to adulthood. *American Sociological Review, 76*(4), 602–619.

Gutiérrez, K., & Rogoff, B. (2003). Cultural ways of learning: Individual traits or repertoires of practice. *Educational Researcher, 32*(5), 19–25.

Hanks, W. F. (2006). Joint commitment and common ground in a ritual event. In N. Enfield & S. Levinson (Eds.), *Roots of human sociality: Culture, cognition and interaction* (pp. 299–328). Oxford, UK: Berg.

Hill, J. H. (1997). Language, race and White public space. *American Anthropologist, 100*(3), 680–689.

Hing, J. (2001, March 8). DREAMers come out: "I'm undocumented, unafraid, and unapologetic." *Colorlines.* Retrieved from http://colorlines.com/archives/2011/03/dreamers_come_out_im_undocumented_unafraid_and_unapologetic.html

Ingold, J. (2012, June 5). Immigration activists stage sit-in at Denver Obama office. *Denver Post.* Retrieved from www.denverpost.com/breakingnews/ci_20791243/immigration-activists-stage-sit-at-denver-obama-office

Kossan, P. (2010, May 28). Schools: Immigrant families leaving Arizona because of new immigration law. *Arizona Republic.* Retrieved from: www.azcentral.com/arizonarepublic/news/articles/2010/05/28/20100528arizona-immigration-law-schools.html

Lacey, M. (2011, January 4). Birthright citizenship looms as next immigration battle. *New York Times.* Retrieved from www.nytimes.com/2011/01/05/us/politics/05babies.html?pagewanted=1&emc=eta1

Lave, J., & Wenger, E. (1991). *Situated learning: Legitimate peripheral participation.* New York: Cambridge University Press.

López, D. E., & Stanton-Salazar, R. D. (2001). Mexican-Americans: A second generation at risk. In R. G. Rumbaut & A. Portes (Eds.), *Ethnicities: Children of immigrants in America* (pp. 57–90). Berkeley, CA: University of California Press.

Mangual Figueroa, A. (2011). Citizenship and education in the homework completion routine. *Anthropology & Education Quarterly, 42*(3), 263–280.

Mangual Figueroa, A. (2012). "I have papers so I can go anywhere:" Everyday talk about citizenship in a mixed-status family. *Journal of Language, Identity & Education, 11*(5), 291–311.

Mangual Figueroa, A. (in press). Giving the onion another stir: The role of citizenship status in language education policy. *Language Policy.*

Marcus, G. E. (1995). Ethnography in/of the world system: The emergence of multi-sited ethnography. *Annual Review of Anthropology, 24,* 95–117.

Mehan, H. (1997). The discourse of the illegal immigration debate: A case study in the politics of representation. *Discourse & Society, 8*(2), 249–270.

Mercado, C. (2005). Reflections on the study of households in New York City and Long Island: A different route, a common destination. In N. González, L. C. Moll, & C. Amanti (Eds.), *Funds of knowledge: Theorizing practices in households, communities, and classrooms* (pp. 233–256). Mahwah, NJ: Lawrence Erlbaum.

Moll, L. C., Amanti, C., Neff, D., & González, N. (1992). Funds of knowledge for teaching: Using a qualitative approach to connect homes and classrooms. *Theory into Practice, 31*(2), 132–141.

National Conference of State Legislatures. (2013, July). *Undocumented student tuition: Overview.* Retrieved from www.ncsl.org/issues-research/educ/undocumented-student-tuition-overview.aspx

Ochs, E. (1986). Introduction. In B. Schieffelin & E. Ochs (Eds.), *Language socialization across cultures* (pp. 1–16). New York: Cambridge University Press.

Ochs, E. (2002). Becoming a speaker of culture. In C. Kramsch (Ed.), *Language acquisition and socialization: Ecological perspectives* (pp. 99–120). London: Continuum.

Ochs, E., & Schieffelin, B. B. (2008). Language socialization: An historical overview. In P. Duff & N. H. Hornberger (Eds.), *Encyclopedia of language education: Language socialization* (2nd ed., Vol. 8, pp. 3–15). New York: Springer.

O'Leary, A. O., González, N. E., & Valdez-Gardea, G. C. (2008). Latinas' practices of emergence: Between cultural narratives and globalization on the U.S.-Mexico border. *Journal of Latinos and Education, 7*(3), 206–226.

O'Neil, D. (2008). *KINSHIP: An introduction to descent systems and family organization.* Retrieved from http://anthro.palomar.edu/kinship/default.htm

Ovando, C., Collier, V., & Combs, M. (2003). *Bilingual and ESL classrooms: Teaching multicultural contexts* (3rd ed.). Boston: McGraw-Hill.

Passel, J. S. (2005, June). *Unauthorized migrants: Numbers and characteristics.* Washington, DC: Pew Hispanic Center.

Passel, J. S. & Cohn, D. (2009, April). *A portrait of unauthorized immigrants in the United States.* Washington, DC: Pew Hispanic Center.

Passel, J. S., Cohn, D., & González-Barrera, A. (2012). *Net migration from Mexico falls to zero—and perhaps less.* Washington, DC: Pew Hispanic Center.

Passel, J. S., Cohn, D., & López, M. (2011, March). *Hispanics account for more than half of the nation's growth in the past decade. Census 2010: 50 million Latinos.* Washington, DC: Pew Hispanic Center.

Passel, J. S. & Taylor, P. (2010, August). *Unauthorized immigrants and their U.S.-Born children.* Washington, DC: Pew Hispanic Center.

Perez, W. (2009). *We ARE Americans: Undocumented students pursuing the American dream.* Sterling, VA: Stylus.

Pew Hispanic Center. (2011, July). *The Mexican-American boom: Births overtake immigration.* Washington, DC: Author.

Portes, A., & Hao, L. (1998). E Pluribus Unum: Bilingualism and loss of language in the second generation. *Sociology of Education, 71,* 269–294.

Portes, P. R. (2005). *Dismantling educational inequality: A cultural-historical approach to closing the achievement gap.* New York: Peter Lang.

Preston, J. (2009, December 22). Latino leaders use churches in census bid. *New York Times.* Retrieved from www.nytimes.com/2009/12/23/us/23latino.html

Preston, J. (2011, June 3). In Alabama, a harsh bill for residents here illegally. *New York Times.* Retrieved from www.nytimes.com/2011/06/04/us/04immig.html

Preston, J. & Cushman, J. H., Jr. (2012, June 15). Obama to permit young migrants to stay in U.S. *New York Times.* Retrieved from www.nytimes.com/2012/06/16/us/us-to-stop-deporting-some-illegal-immigrants.html?hpw

Ritchie, J., Lewis, J., & Elam, G. (2003). Designing and selecting samples. In J. Ritchie and J. Lewis (Eds.), *Qualitative research practice: A guide for social science students and researchers* (pp. 77–108). Thousand Oaks, CA: Sage.

Rogers, J., Saunders, M., Terriquez, V., & Velez, V. (2008). Civic lessons: Public schools and the civic development of undocumented students and parents. *Northwestern Journal of Law and Social Policy, 3,* 201–218.

Rogoff, B. (1990). *Apprenticeship in thinking.* New York: Oxford University Press.

Ruiz, V. L. (1998). *From out of the shadows: Mexican women in twentieth-century America.* New York: Oxford University Press.

Rumbaut, R. G., & Portes, A. (2001). Introduction—ethnogenesis: Coming of age in immigrant America. In R. G. Rumbaut & A. Portes (Eds.), *Ethnicities: Children of immigrants in America* (pp. 1–20). Berkeley, CA: University of California Press.

Salas, S., Portes, P. R., D'Amico, M. M., & Rios-Aguilar, C. (2011). Generación 1.5: A cultural historical agenda for research at the 2-year college. *Community College Review 39*(2), 121–135.

Santa Ana, O. (1999). 'Like an animal I was treated': Anti-immigrant metaphor in U.S. public discourse. *Discourse & Society, 10,* 191–224.

Schegloff, E. A. (2007). *Sequence organization in interaction: A primer in conversation analysis* (Vol. 1). New York: Cambridge University Press.

Scheiner, E. (2012, December 29). Society of professional journalist questioning 'illegal immigrant' as an 'offensive' term. *CNS News.* Retrieved from http://cnsnews.com/news/article/society-professional-journalists-questioning-illegal-immigrant-offensive-term

Shashahani, A. (2012, May 21). HB 87 negatively impacts Georgia's economy and reputation. *Huffington Post.* Retrieved from www.huffingtonpost.com/azadeh-shahshahani/georgia-immigration-policy_b_1528987.html

Sherman, M. (2012, June 25). Supreme court issues ruling on S.B. 1070. *Huffington Post.* Retrieved from www.huffingtonpost.com/2012/06/25/supreme-court-sb1070_n_1614121.html

Shohamy, E. (2003). Implications of language education policies for language study in schools and universities. *Modern Language Journal, 87,* 2–10.

Slevin, P. (2010, July 26). Deportation of illegal immigrants increases under Obama administration. *Washington Post.* Retrieved from www.washingtonpost.com/wp-dyn/content/article/2010/07/25/AR2010072501790.html

Suárez-Orozco, C., Suárez-Orozco, M. M, & Todorova, I. (2008). *Learning a new land: Immigrant students in American society.* Cambridge, MA: Belknap Harvard.

Suárez-Orozco, C., Yoshikawa, H., Teranishi, R. T., & Suárez-Orozco, M. M. (2011). Growing up in the shadows: The developmental implications of unauthorized status. *Harvard Educational Review, 81*(3), 438–472.

Suárez-Orozco, M. (2001). Globalization, immigration, and education: The research agenda. *Harvard Educational Review, 71*(3), 345–365.

UCLA student body drops term 'illegal immigrant.' (2013, September 3). *Huffington Post.* Retrieved from www.huffingtonpost.com/2013/09/03/ucla-illegal-immigrant_n_3862671.html

Vadeboncoeur, J. A., & Portes, P. R. (2002). Students "at risk": Exploring identity from a sociocultural perspective. In D. M. McInerney & S. V. Etten (Eds.), *Research on sociocultural influences on motivation and learning: An historical perspective* (Vol. 2, pp. 89–128). Charlotte, NC: Information Age.

Valdés, G. (1996). *Con respeto: Bridging the distances between culturally diverse families and schools an ethnographic portrait.* New York: Teachers College Press.

Valencia, R. R. (2002). Mexican Americans don't value education!—On the basis of the myth, mythmaking, and debunking. *Journal of Latinos and Education, 1*(2), 81–103.

Valenzuela, A. (1999). *Subtractive schooling: U.S. Mexican youth and the politics of caring.* New York: State University of New York Press.

Vásquez, O. A., Pease-Alvarez, L., & Shannon, S. M. (1994). *Pushing boundaries: Language and culture in a Mexicano community.* New York: Cambridge University Press.

Veléz-Ibañez, C. G., & Greenberg, J. B. (1992). Formation and transformation of funds of knowledge among U.S.-Mexican households. *Anthropology and Education Quarterly, 23*(4), 313–335.

Villanueva, V. (2000). Afterword: On English-only. In R. D. González & I. Melis (Eds.), *Language ideologies: Critical perspective on the official English movement. Education and the social implications of official language* (Vol. 1, pp. 333–342). Mahwah, NJ: Lawrence Erlbaum.

Villenas, S., & Moreno, M. (2001). To valerse por si misma between race, capitalism, and patriarchy: Latina mother-daughter pedagogies in North Carolina. *Qualitative Studies in Education, 14*(5), 671–687.

Wessler, S. (2011, November). *Shattered families: The perilous intersection of immigration enforcement and the child welfare system.* New York: Freed, Applied Research Center.

Whiting, B. W. (1980). Culture and social behavior: A model for the development of social behavior. *Ethos, 8*(2), 95–116.

Wiley, T. G., & de Klerk, G. (2010). Common myths and stereotypes regarding literacy ad language diversity in the multilingual United States. In M. Farr, L. Seloni & J. Song (Eds.), *Ethnolinguistic diversity and education: Language, literacy, and culture* (pp. 23–42). New York: Routledge.

Wiley, T. G., & Wright, W. E. (2004). Against the undertow: Language-minority education policy and politics in the "age of accountability." *Educational Researcher, 18*(1), 142–168.

Wong-Fillmore, L. (2000). Loss of family languages: Should educators be concerned? *Theory into Practice, 39,* 203–210.

Wortham, S., Murillo, E. G., & Hamann, E. (2002). *Education in the new Latino diaspora: Policy and the politics of identity.* Westport, CT: Ablex.

Yoshikawa, H. (2011). *Immigrants raising citizens: Undocumented parents and their children.* New York: The Russell Sage Foundation.

Zavella, P. (2011). *I'm neither here nor there: Mexicans' quotidian struggles with migration and poverty.* Durham, NC: Duke University Press.

Zentella, A. C. (2001). Language planning/policy and US colonialism: The Puerto Rican thorn in English-only's side. In T. Huebner & K. Davis (Eds.), *Sociopolitical perspectives on language policy and planning in the USA* (pp. 155–172). New York: John Benjamins.

10

TALKING THE WALK

Classroom Discourse Strategies That Foster Dynamic Interactions with Latina/o Elementary School English Learners

Ruth Harman

Latina/o students make up the largest minority group in the U.S. educational system, representing more than 20 percent of pre-K–12 students enrolled in U.S. public schools, most of whom report Spanish as being the language spoken at home (U.S. Department of Education & White House Initiative on Educational Excellence for Hispanics, 2011). In spite of these demographic trends, high-stakes government policies, such as the No Child Left Behind Act of 2001 (NCLB) and state-level English-only mandates (e.g., in California, Colorado, and Massachusetts), have put increasing pressure on urban school districts to adopt reductive monolingual literacy practices and curricula materials that fail to validate the rich cultural and linguistic resources of this fast-growing school population (August & Shanahan, 2006). For example, after the passage of English-only legislation in Massachusetts in 2002, several English-as-a-second-language (ESL) and bilingual schoolteachers that I worked with during the course of this research study said they had been ordered by administrators to stop using Spanish in classrooms and hallways. In one instance, the school librarian was told to "get rid of all the Spanish language materials" in the library (field notes, ACCELA, 2006). Without institutional or classroom validation of their multilingual and cultural backgrounds, Latino/a English learners (ELs), newly arrived immigrants in particular, often struggle to acquire content-area knowledge as well as the cultural and linguistic norms of school English (Menken, 2008; Wells & Chang-Wells, 1992).

Although reform efforts such as NCLB have sought to hold schools and educators accountable for students' progress, their methods have disadvantaged ELs (Gebhard & Harman, 2011). In Massachusetts, for example, students are required to take regular assessment exams (Massachusetts Comprehensive Assessment System, MCAS), the results of which determine if schools have met NCLB's annual yearly progress (AYP) standard. The MCAS, like assessment systems in other states, cover academic subject matter and include sections in English Language Arts, Mathematics, and Science and Technology/Engineering (Massachusetts Department of Elementary and Secondary Education, 2011). Urban schools with higher EL populations have been more likely to receive "underperforming" assessments. As such, as analysis of NCLB policies suggests, pressure on school districts to achieve AYP can also create a counterincentive to keeping and supporting ELs in the school system (Darling-Hammond, 2006). To avoid sanctions and potential corporate takeovers of their schools if their AYP did not meet government standards[1] (e.g., see regulations of NCLB, 2001), for example, the teachers in River Town, the research site of this study, often felt pressured by administrators to focus exclusively on test materials and preparation, even in early elementary grades (Wright, 2005). Thus, classroom interactions were sometimes limited to "teaching to the test," which resulted in reductive question/answer discourse and time-consuming test-taking practice.

A major challenge for urban multicultural educators, therefore, is to develop discourse strategies that acknowledge immigrant students as vital partners in building classroom knowledge of new concepts despite English-only mandates and high-stakes school reform (see Gebhard & Harman, 2011; K. D. Gutiérrez, 1993). Informed by this perspective, the purpose of the current study is to analyze the discourse strategies used by two early elementary urban schoolteachers, Angela Holman and Helen Chatel,[2] while teaching English literacy in two "underperforming" elementary school classrooms. How did their classroom discourse practices foster or constrain Latino/a students from engaging in dynamic interactions with their peers and teacher? What contextual factors may have informed the differences in their approach?

Such inquiry into classroom practices and the contextual factors that shape them is important for education policy makers, researchers, and educators who need to consider how classroom practices impact the academic trajectory of Latino students. In other words, classroom discourse, shaped not only by idiosyncratic styles of individual teachers but also by top-down language policies, is integrally connected to education equity and access.

Sociocultural Perspectives on Learning

Recent research on second-language literacy has focused on the importance of using sociocultural perspectives of language and literacy learning to support the academic needs of immigrant students, a vast majority of whom are Spanish speakers (e.g., K. D. Gutiérrez, Baquedano-López, & Alvarez, 2001; Martínez-Roldán & Fránquiz, 2009; Moll, 2001; Nieto & Bode, 2008; Valdés, 2001). Informed by Vygotskyian theories of learning, sociocultural theory (SCT) emphasizes the role of social interaction and cultural artifacts such as a student's primary language as key tools in supporting changes in an individual's cognitive understanding of how and what to communicate in particular sociocultural contexts (Moll, 2001). As Wells and Chang-Wells (1992, p. 33) point out, "Talk, far from being an unimportant accompaniment to the real business of learning and teaching, is seen to be a central and constitutive part of every activity."

As opposed to reductive approaches to teaching that encourage use of display questions and rote learning, the SCT approach promotes dynamic apprenticeship and jointly constructed social interaction, where the more knowledgeable partner (e.g., the teacher) supports the novice (the student) in learning the cultural and linguistic norms of a particular activity or concept (Rogoff, 1990). Within this framework, learning, as opposed to being merely the transfer of knowledge, is accomplished through the appropriation of cultural resources and practices during co-constructed activities that are carefully orchestrated by the teacher.

Classroom Context and Student Identity

Many factors contribute to how students participate in classroom interactions. At the forefront are the identities they are afforded at school. As Cazden (2001) states, "One of the most important influences on all talk . . . is the participants themselves—their expectations about interactions and their perceptions about each other" (p. 67). Research such as that by Diaz and Flores (2001) highlights how Latina/o students from lower socioeconomic districts experience difficulty in their academic trajectories because of their teachers' deficit discourses, manifest in classroom interactional and instructional practices. Willett's (1995) ethnographic study of first-grade ELs also found that students' level of language depended largely on the type of social identities they were afforded in their interactions with peers and teachers. In other words, the potential to learn is determined by how students are positioned within the "social structure of the community of practice, its power relations and its conditions for legitimacy" (Lave & Wenger, 1991, p. 98). Indeed, for newly arrived Latina/o immigrant students, the consequences of negative classroom interactions can be dramatic because their lived experiences, languages, and histories often have been effectively erased from the common literacy curriculum (K. Gutiérrez & Larson, 1994; Harklau, 1994).

Walking the Talk

Despite recent research on the potentially inhibiting nature of rigid turn taking and participation structures for second-language acquisition, a lot of research on classroom discourse has found that elementary teachers tend to privilege display questions with a normative use of initiation-response-evaluation (IRE) exchanges—discussions initiated by a teacher with a question that calls for student response(s) that the teacher then deems right or wrong—that promote chorus recitation over authentic elaboration of ideas (Boyd & Rubin, 2002; Wells, 1999). As Rymes (2009) notes, ELs may be silenced by the IRE sequence based on having a lack of experience with the format and also because ELs often have more difficulty determining the "right answer" sought by the teacher.

To provide students with optimal learning environments, Diaz and Flores (2001) recommend that teachers, informed by SCT theories of learning, develop ways of examining, reflecting, and transforming classroom discursive practices. This includes examining discourse elements such as wait times, contextualization cues, and lexical choices, which have been shown to foster and constrain ELs' willingness to participate. Gibbons (2002, 2009) illustrates how culturally responsive teachers use particular patterns of contextualization cues (e.g., intonation and body gestures) and lexical choices to support ELs in gaining access to mainstream content literacies. Recent research also recommends critical discourse analysis as a tool for teachers and researchers to reflect on how language is embedded in particular sociohistorical and sociocultural contexts that shape classroom literacy practices (e.g., Harman & McClure, 2011; Rymes, 2009).

In sum, recent research highlights how classroom discourse not only serves not only a regulatory or instructional function in the classroom but is also an important component in validating or negating multilingual and multidialectal voices and cultures (identities), building academic discourse communities, and generating critical language awareness—all critical components of literacy learning and all connected to Latina/o ELs' ability to co-construct knowledge through participation.

Context and Methods

Teacher Development Initiative—ACCELA

To support the teachers and students in the River Town school district, a federally funded university-school alliance called Access to Critical Content and English Language Acquisition (ACCELA) was set up among university faculty, school administrators, teachers, and community members in 2002 (Gebhard, Willett, Jimenez, & Piedra, 2010). The ACCELA Master's in Education and Licensure Program encouraged teachers to teach "against the grain" in their urban schools (Cochran-Smith, 2001). In their on-site ACCELA master's course work, teachers read about research and praxis of critical literacy, systemic functional linguistics, and multicultural education, and they developed critical language curricula with the help of on-site university researchers.

This study investigates how, in the implementation of their curricular initiatives, two ACCELA teachers used discourse strategies that included, or excluded, their Latino EL students from engaging in authentic interactions. Did teachers "walk the talk" by using discourse strategies that encouraged student participation? Informed by a broader ethnographic approach, the study also explores what contextual factors may have contributed to differences in their discourse patterns.

Setting and Participants

River Town is a midsized, economically struggling city in Massachusetts that experienced rapid demographic shifts from predominantly White to predominantly Latino between 1990 and 2000. An Irish-born language teacher in public schools and university contexts, I taught ACCELA courses to teachers participating in the master's program and supported their inquiry-based classroom research from 2003 to 2007. In this capacity, I worked with eight elementary and middle school teachers in developing and analyzing curricula that would support Latina/o EL students in developing academic literacy and critical language awareness.

The two teachers, Angela Holman and Helen Chatel, were selected for this current study because they both were working with early elementary school classes in which immigrant children were already being labeled as deficient by the institutions. From 2004 to 2006, I worked with both teachers in their elementary schools. Angela Holman is a Native American/Italian American woman with eight years' experience teaching in urban public schools. In 2004–2005, I worked with Angela and her small group of Latino and African American second-grade students, who were constructed by the school community as "behaviorally difficult" (Angela Holman, interview, April 2005). Helen Chatel is a Euro-American teacher who at the time of this study had four years of teaching experience in the public school system. I worked with Helen in the 2005–2006 school year when she provided reading/writing instruction to a small group of Latino and African American children who were being constructed by assessments and the school as "at risk" for reading failure.

The following types of data were collected for each research site: audio and video recordings of classroom interactions and interviews, students' texts, scanned instructional materials, interviews with the teachers, and field notes. Also used as secondary data, in my capacity as an ACCELA instructor, 2003–2007, I collected a large archive of ethnographic data and narratives about the two schools and the school district, such as observation notes, videotapes of other classroom curricular units, school district and state policy documents, and recordings of meetings and interviews with teachers and school administrators.

Data Analysis

Informed by an ethnographic approach to data collection and analysis (e.g., long-term participant observation and qualitative inquiry into cultural patterns in the institutional settings), critical discourse analysis was used to explore the interconnections between social practice, institutional context, and interactional norms of the two classrooms (see Fairclough, 1992). The first stage of inquiry involved a review of contextual factors at play in the River Town school district. For example, a broad contrastive analysis of field notes, policy documents, and ethnographic data collection from both schools showed a marked difference in morale and discursive practices in the two institutions.

The second level of inquiry involved a close discourse analysis of classroom interactions representative of the contrasting approaches employed by the teachers. Informed by an interactional, sociolinguistic analytic framework, this involved an investigation of the teachers' contextualization cues (e.g., intonation and gestures) and lexical choices in their questioning exchanges with students when engaged in reading/writing events (e.g., Bloome, Carter, Christian, & Otto, 2004; Rymes, 2009). Specifically, this lens helped explore how the teachers were orchestrating participation structures and patterns of turn taking through their questioning strategies. The type of questions posed by the teacher in these sequences, how the teacher evaluated a student response, and the amount of wait time allowed for a response were analyzed, as well as how students responded. In sum, analysis of question/answer sequences and turn taking supported investigation of how discourse patterns in both classrooms enabled or stifled participation.

Findings

Even though both schools were in the same district, contextual analysis showed how sociopolitical factors created a much more positive teaching environment in Angela's school (see Harman, 2008, for an extended description of Angela's school). For example, when Angela felt uneasy because the school was labeling her students as "behaviorally difficult," a colleague volunteered to work with her in a cross-grade literacy project that expanded the level of community support for Angela and her students (see Willett, Harman, Lozano, Hogan, & Rubeck, 2007). Helen, on the other hand, reported feeling increasingly anxious and isolated over the course of the two years we worked together. Indeed, because of the low morale in the school, of all of the teachers from her school who participated in ACCELA, she was the only teacher to complete the master's program.

In addition, although both teachers were part of ACCELA's master's program and had developed dynamic curricular units informed by a critical genre-based approach to literacy (e.g., Gebhard, Harman, & Seger, 2007), analysis of classroom interactions reflected that their discourse practices in leading discussions positioned language learners in very different ways. In Helen's case, her questioning strategies, evaluative responses, and contextualization cues, such as a rapid pacing of lesson sequences, tended to close off meaningful discussion and elaboration of students' lived experiences. In contrast, Angela's use of strategies such as recasting of students' responses and longer wait times for ELs encouraged the students to share and reflect on their own experiences and connect them to the literacy events. In sum, analysis of the two classrooms highlighted a very different set of institutional and classroom discourse practices at play.

Case Study 1: Helen Chatel and Her Students

The first set of classroom interactions comes from Helen's curricular unit on writing for her first graders during the 2005–2006 school year. She provided reading/writing instruction to a small group of eight Latino and African American students who were constructed as "at risk" for reading failure. According to Helen, her work environment was particularly stressful that year because of increased scrutiny and accountability in the school, as well as requirements that her students be on grade level by the end of the year (R. Harman, field notes, April 2006). She was charged with providing her small group with a solid foundation in writing so that they could be prepared to take the English Language Arts portion of the state's mandated high-stakes testing, in third grade. In the context of the ACCELA second-language literacy courses, Helen developed a critical genre-based approach that involved explicit scaffolding of genre features, use of an authentic audience, and incorporation of student interests (see Gebhard & Harman, 2011). For example, when she realized that the students were fascinated with anything to do with fire (e.g., fire hoses and firemen) she organized a five-day sequence in her curricular unit around this. She organized a field trip to a local fire station, invited guest speakers, and selected nonfiction and fiction children's literature that focused on issues related to fire safety and fire stories. In the transcript excerpts presented subsequently, the students were learning to write recounts, a genre in which the writer tells the reader in sequential order about an event that has happened in the past (Knapp & Watkins, 2005). Their final project in the curricular unit was to create multimodal recounts of their fire stories and read them to an invited audience.

Rigidity in IRE Sequences

In the reading/writing block the day before the literacy event described subsequently, the students created a list of temporal connectors (e.g., time order words) that they were encouraged to use in writing their recounts about their fire station visit. The speech event began with a teacher-guided recall of these temporal connectors and when they would be used, using word cards as a learning aid. (A key of the transcript conventions used in the following transcript excerpts is located in Appendix A, at the end of this chapter.)

TRANSCRIPT 1

Students	Helen
01	What's a word that we put on
02	our list ye:sterday that told <u>when</u>
03	something ↓happened.
04 ((*coughing and muffled sounds in the background*))	
05	<Raise your hands please.>=
06 ((*Jesus quickly raises his hand.*))	
07	=<u>Je</u>:sus.
08 Jesus: Umm ⋆(hmmm)⋆ =	
09	((*shuffling through deck of word cards*)) =We came up with some
10	words for example, to:da:y.
11	((*holds up word card as she says today*))
12	
13	
14 Ss: >To:da:y< ((*chorus reading*))	
15	We are talking about time order
16	words (.) to:da:y.
17	So <for example, like I said>
18	something could happen <u>toda:y</u>.
19	When did it ↑happen? =
20 Ss: =<u>Toda:y</u>. . . ((*chorus*))	

The interaction described previously illustrates Helen's frequent use of display questions in her interactions with students to get them responding in chorus fashion to her prompts. Certain contextualization cues in this excerpt (and common to several other interactions) highlight how Helen quickly became frustrated with the students. For example, in line 5 (see Transcript 1) she sped up her delivery of an imperative to the students. In line 9, after asking Jesus, a Latino EL, to respond to the question, she overlapped his hesitant response, a signal that he was not responding promptly enough to her question. In other words, her contextualization cues signaled to the students that they needed to respond within a particular time frame and that the answers needed to match her expectations. The fast pace, lack of wait time, and the requirement that the answer be the "right" one, as illustrated in the exchange described previously above, led Jesus often to be hesitant about participating in classroom interactions. Indeed, although display questions and fast-paced IRE structures where the teacher expects a certain answer are efficient when used as quick way of getting students to recall information, research has shown that the approach often does not support ELs in learning how and when to interact in literacy events (e.g., Gibbons, 2009; Mehan, 1979).

As the speech event continued, Helen moved from a formulaic questioning to a seemingly more exploratory line of questioning in the sense that students were now expected to share their own experiences. However, they still needed to use the time order word sequence that Helen modeled for them (see Transcript 2).

TRANSCRIPT 2

Students		Helen
37		Today. Today, what did we do today?
38		Ss: Um. . .
39		<Somebody tell me>. . .
40		
41		>Today I. . .<
42		
43		what? (.)
44		
45		Toda:y, I came to school.
46 Siena:	Toda:y I	
47	<brushed my teeth>=	
48		=Toda:y I < brushed my teeth↓>
49 Maria:	Today <I woke up>	
50		[Nyata. . .today?]

Helen's quickened delivery of line 39, "Somebody tell me," and the subsequent statement starting with the elongated vowel sound in "Today," signaled to the students that they needed to essentially fill in the blanks. Siena's response introduced what could have led to a short recount about her early morning routines. Instead of getting Siena to elaborate, however, Helen cut her off by repeating the response in an accelerated pace and with falling intonation. Maria imitated this quickened response in telling the class, "Today I woke up." Because of these types of discourse patterns in Helen's orchestration of whole class literacy events, students interpreted the routine as formulaic turns of talk that needed to occur in rapid response sequences in a particular length of time—the focus was on the form of the responses and not on the meaning.

However, despite the focus on students offering prompt and formulaic responses to the questions, Helen also indicated that these answers needed to be "true." This left some students confused, especially Felipe, a Latino language learner who already had been moved from school to school and into foster care several times at an early age.

TRANSCRIPT 3

Students	Helen
55	Felipe, to:da:y, ((*tap, tap, tap*))
56	what'd you do today?
57 Felipe: Um, <Play outside>	
58	You ↑played **out**↑**side** to↑day? (.)
58	Before ↑school (.) ↑Real↓ly?
59 Siena: At home.	
60	Interesting.
61 Janita: Um, **I know**. . . ((*raising hand*))=	
62	=Janita
63 Janita: Today my mom <did my nails before work.>	
64	Today my mom did my nails.
65	What else?

Through Helen's continued modeling of evaluative repetition of their responses, most of the students, including Janita in line 63 (see Transcript 3), provided Helen with the expected type of responses about activities that had *already happened*. However, because the teacher recognized that the freezing cold February weather in Massachusetts made it unlikely Felipe "play[ed] outside," his response did not meet expectations for realistic details. As a language learner, Felipe might have been suggesting an activity that he *could* do or that he *would* do later "today," either of which could be constructed as a valid contribution. However, Helen did not ask for any elaboration of his response. Instead, she used rising intonation and several questions to indicate her incredulity that he could have played outside. In this way, she sequentially deleted his response from the sequence of exchanges (Rymes, 2009). The other students quickly picked up on how Felipe was being positioned. For example, Janita put stress on the second word, "I *know*," in her response, indicating that she had the right response compared to Felipe's erroneous one.

Overall, although Helen spent considerable time developing a genre-based approach to writing in her ACCELA courses, inspired by readings on critical and permeable literacy approaches (e.g., Dyson, 2003), her contextualization cues and lexical choices silenced her students and inhibited them from co-constructing learning. Her teacher *talk* did not conform to how she wanted to *walk* with her students. As Vygotskian scholars have underlined, Helen's constricted classroom discourse mediated a narrow and scripted understanding of what literacy is among her students by foreclosing them from contributing to discussion with their unique perceptions and experiences. Importantly, it afforded ELs like Felipe a very limited range of social identities that most likely would be reinforced by other deficit discourse practices in the same school and elsewhere. As Diaz and Flores (2001) point out, young children like those in Helen's classroom

> enter the classroom at an actual level of development that has been a function of their everyday familial, cultural, and communal experiences. If the teacher does not respect and properly take into account these previous experiences as indicative of the students' actual level of development, then the child is put "at risk" within the socio-educational contexts. (p. 33)

Case Study 2: Angela Holman and Her Students

In classrooms such as Helen Chatel's and Angela Holman's, curriculum design and careful orchestration of discourse are especially important, given the fact that bilingual and bidialectal students in low socioeconomic districts are frequently marginalized within the school (Moll, 2001). In Angela's classroom, this type of top-down deficit discourse was evident in the school's designation of her multidialectal and multilingual group of students as "behaviorally difficult." Frequently afforded stigmatizing social identities at school, Angela's students had difficulty focusing on academic literacy activities. To counteract their negative experiences, Angela selected trade books and teaching materials that would support the children in telling their own stories, in reenacting scenes from children's literature that resonated for them, and in creating multimodal narratives that linked their lived experiences to characters they encountered in children's books (see Willett et al., 2007). Angela was supported in creating this curricular approach through a literacy partnership with an ACCELA colleague and fifth-grade Fuentes teacher. As described in an earlier ethnographic study, the collegial atmosphere and level of administrative support at Fuentes was much stronger than in other elementary schools in the same district (see Harman, 2008).

Compared with the predominance of IREs in Helen's classroom that students learned to interpret as cues to close off meaningful interaction, Angela often supported students learning and collaborative interaction by being contingently responsive to the ways they were engaging in discussion (Wells & Chang-Wells, 1992). In other words, she listened to her students and elaborated on their responses in ways that validated and built on their contributions. For example, in activating personal and family connections to class readings, Angela supported students in taking longer turns of talk to explain parallel stories that connected to the class reading or to other student stories. The following transcript provides an example of Angela's orchestration of classroom discourse. In this representative literacy event, the students moved into a whole-class group reading discussion about *Matthew and Tilly* (Jones, 1991).

As distinct from Helen's controlled use of display questions, Angela opened storytelling and reading discussions with open-ended questions to get students thinking of connections between their own lives and the protagonists' in children's literature. Often, during these events, she also prolonged student turns of talk by using additional open-ended questions, as evidenced in line 17 of a typical discussion excerpted subsequently (see Transcript 4). This speech event began with Angela reading a passage from the book about how the main characters sold lemonade together and also played sidewalk games when business was slow. She then asked the children if they had ever had a lemonade or Kool-Aid stand. Alyssa, an African American student, explained how she sold "chicken dogs" with her friends, but Daniel, a Latino EL, did not understand what she meant. The students were seated on the carpet in a circle, facing Angela, who sat in a chair at the front.

TRANSCRIPT 4

Students		**Angela**
13		↑Oh like a chicken ↑dog
14 Students:	((*laughter*))	
15 Daniel:	What's **chicken** dog↑	
16		You put the chicken on a on
	((*Alyssa nods*))	a stick↓ ((*gestures stick*)) and then ((*turns to Alyssa*)) you sold that (1.0)
17		Did you make a lot of money?
18 Alyssa:	Yeah =	
19 Janika:	= (All those chick) you put on the sticks and then you ate it on the stick	

As evidenced in the interaction described previously, Angela limited her role as teacher and served more as a facilitator in this event. For example, when Daniel asked for a definition of a "chicken dog" in line 15, Angela embedded her answer to his question in a direct statement to Alyssa:

> You put the chicken on a stick↓ ((*gestures stick*)) and then ((*turns to Alyssa*)) you sold that (1.0).

In line 19, Janika, another African American student, responded to Daniel's question with an additional description of a chicken dog. Daniel, in this way, was ratified as a legitimate contributor to the conversation and not singled out as different from the other contributors.

For language learners like Daniel, these types of authentic interactions support development not only of lexico-grammatical knowledge of English but also discourse competence. For example, they become engaged in using and noticing cultural use of turn taking, wait time, and intonation patterns in a particular discourse community (Cazden, John, & Hymes, 1972). In addition, the incorporation of personal and cultural stories into classroom instruction validates student voices in ways that formulaic use of sharing time often does not (Boyd & Rubin, 2002; Michaels, 1984).

In a later sequence of exchanges in the same discussion, the students began to provide more detailed descriptions of their activities, which were prompted by another open-ended question by Angela. Similar to the first sequence of interactions, Angela safeguarded the turns of talk of Janika and Felicia through strategic use of contextualization cues and lexical choices. For example, in line 34 (see Transcript 5) she signaled to the boys that they needed to be quiet and listen to Janika's story, and in the following line, she repeated Janika's final statement to signal that she still had the floor. She also ensured that Felicia, a Puerto Rican EL, was validated in sharing her experiences. When Felicia explained how she owned a new type of jump rope, Angela and two other students acknowledged and elaborated on her story by asking questions and making additional comments to show their interest. Most importantly, with contextualization cues such as long wait times (e.g., long pauses between lines 36 and 37) and nonverbal gestures, Angela signaled to the speakers that their stories were important and they could spend as much time as needed reconstructing the events.

TRANSCRIPT 5

Students		Angela
25		What kind of sidewalk games did you play with a friend↓
26 Janika:	Hopscotch	
27		Hopscotch.
28		((*Turns to Jairus*)) Have you done that ↑before?
28 Jairus:	No, I don't have no chalk	
29		Okay
30 Janika:	Jump rope	
31 Sasha:	Where's it↑	
32 Hogan:	Jump rope is on the sidewalk ((*points at Janika*))	

33 Janika:	Because I remember it from the summer (1.0) in my backyard (.) and my mom ((*gestures with hands as if jumping rope*)) take turns jump roping	
34		[Are you listening?] ((*points at boys who are talking*))
35		Take turns jump roping
36 Felicia:	Ms. Holman I got (1.0) summertime it's the jump rope (2.0) that umm it got to one side spinning and it's go the other side	
37		That's the new one that came out Right↑
38 Sasha:	Oh, that's the new one	
39 Janika:	I know that because you turn it and ( ) my sister (inaudible)	

In discussing academic literacy development in elementary school, Schleppe-grell (2004) writes about the importance for language learners to be given the opportunity to explain and share information and experiences in ways that position them as authorities on different topics. In Daniel and Felicia's case, for example, their interactions with Angela and their classmates can help to deepen metalinguistic awareness by providing opportunities to articulate and evaluate their understanding of English language and culture.

In Angela's classroom, the fact that institutional discourses already had positioned her second-grade children as behaviorally difficult made validation of student voices and use of contingently responsive discourse of upmost importance (Moll, 2001). Through inclusive discussion and incorporation of multiple voices, Angela connected school literacy to real-life events, thereby supporting academic development and personal agency (Rymes, 2009).

Discussion

Rymes and Pash (2001) offer the simple, yet profound statement that "the practice of questioning a student is always simultaneously a practice of questioning a student's *identity*" (p. 278). This statement sheds light on the dynamics in linguistically diverse classroom, an environment where the issue of self-identity is even more complex than in monolingual classrooms, because many students have not yet created their identity in the target language and yet where their primary cultural identities are often silenced or negatively portrayed. Indeed, in states like Massachusetts where English-only mandates have been passed, school curricula and discourse actively erase children's dynamic multicultural and multiliterate identities (Nieto & Bode, 2008). Analysis of the two main discourse approaches in this study, one offering more rigid questioning and pacing, the other more open-ended and exploratory questioning, highlights the pivotal role of the teacher as a key mediator in supporting academic learning in the classroom, particularly for immigrant language learners (Cazden, 2001; Diaz & Flores, 2001).

The different findings from Helen and Angela's classrooms highlight the importance of supporting teachers in developing democratic discourse strategies that *talk the walk* with multilingual students. In Helen's case, her rigidity in use of display questions and contextualization cues inhibited students from using co-constructed linguistic scaffolds to expand and elaborate on their understanding of new concepts. Angela's contingent scaffolding, on the other hand, promoted intertextual connections to home practices and co-constructed learning.

However, a glaring absence from both classroom practices was the use of Spanish or other primary languages in both the official classroom discourse and in student–student interactions. Inherent in this English-only classroom discourse is the violent erasure of the complex linguistic resources that the immigrant students bring to the classroom. Helen and Angela developed their teaching practices in the context of ACCELA Alliance to counteract this cultural hegemony, but it remained the "elephant in the room." To counteract this symbolic violence (Bourdieu, 1991), fostering unofficial use of the primary languages of children needs to be an integral element of classroom discourse strategies in English-only states, whenever possible.

In sum, findings from this study highlight the importance for teacher education programs to support preservice and in-service teachers in developing awareness of how English-only mandates and classroom interaction inhibit and facilitate academic learning and dynamic discourse communities.

Policy Considerations

For policy makers and researchers, the findings from this study suggest, first, that second-language research studies need to connect microlevel analyses of classroom interactions with an exploration of policies and practices within local, state, and national institutions if we are to even begin challenging the top-down set of deficit policies about language learning in place in the United States (e.g., Gebhard & Harman, 2011). For example, it would be easy to use differences in Helen's and Angela's classrooms to just showcase more and less effective instructional practices. However, interwoven with any microlevel discussion of classroom practices, there needs to be discussion of longitudinal ethnographic findings that explore connections to macrolevel contextual factors. For example, my qualitative inquiry into the institutional practices at Helen's school highlights how distrust and fear were prevailing emotions among the teachers. In other words, the school administrators reacted to the top-down policies by putting more and more pressure on the teachers to teach to the test and enforce mandated curricula that did not address students' needs or interests. In Angela's case, although there was pressure to teach to the high-stakes test, the collaboration among teachers that had developed through a series of professional development alliances with a local university promoted a very different set of literacy practices in the school (see examples of this collaboration in Gebhard et al., 2007; Gebhard, Shin, & Seger, 2011). Such findings are important for education policy makers and educators because they show the deleterious impact that policies such as NCLB have on school morale and leadership. For educators, the findings also show the importance of collective local action as a means to challenge prevailing policies. Angela's approach was not unique in her school but emerged from a collective local response to the sociopolitical context.

Findings also highlight how current U.S. government policies, such as NCLB and Race to the Top, actively promote reductive literacy practices and teachingto-the-test mentality (K. D. Gutiérrez, Asato, Santos, & Gotanda, 2002), practices that often perpetuate a deficit education model in relation to Latina/o language learners. In Helen's case, her fear of the administration and the low morale in her school impacted how she related to her students, despite her participation in a professional development initiative. Classroom discourse is a crucial gatekeeper to more or less education equity, yet it is often disregarded as an important factor in school learning as evidenced by the increasing national pressure to teach to the test and to adhere to national and state curriculum mandates without any reflection by policy makers on how these policies impact dynamic learning in multicultural classrooms. As Cazden (2001, pp. 2–3) states: "Creating the conditions for the interdependent goals of academic and language development for all students requires changes in classroom language use . . . but those who help shape the contexts that surround the classroom have to realize their responsibility as well."

To conclude, the ability of U.S. K–12 schools to support their Latina/o ELs in achieving high school diplomas and gaining access to higher education is critical toward their future success in the workforce. As the world economy becomes further globalized, the majority of jobs will require higher levels of training or postsecondary education. Latina/o's currently make up more than 16 percent of the U.S. population, a significant portion of the workforce already, and over the next 45 years, they are estimated to account for 60 percent of all population growth. President Obama has highlighted the significance of these numbers in a recent report, *Winning the Future: Improving Latino Education*: "Latino success in education and in the labor market is of both immediate and long-term important to America's economy" (U.S. Department of Education & White House Initiative on Educational Excellence for Hispanics, 2011). As this study about classroom practice suggests, any national commitment to addressing inequities in U.S. education for Latina/o's must involve continued research and evidence-based policies that support all Latina/o students now.

Appendix A: Key of Transcript Conventions

=	Latching (response immediately after)
[ ]	Simultaneous (overlapping speech)
(.)	Short pause
<>	Speeding up
><	Slowing down
<u>Text</u>	Emphasis
CAPS	Screaming (volume)
Bold	Loud voice
★pst★	Quiet voice
(. . .)	Inaudible
(( ))	Gestures/other noises
↓	Lowered pitch
↑	Raised pitch
No:	Elongated vowel

Notes

1. If a school district fails to meet AYP for four consecutive years, the state can (1) ask the school to modify its curriculum program, (2) withhold Title III funds, or (3) replace the teaching staff at the school (Wright, 2005, p. 26).
2. All names of teachers and students are pseudonyms.

References

August, D. & Shanahan, T. (2006). Developing Literacy in Second Language Learners: Executive Summary of The National Literacy Panel on Language-Minority Children and Youth. Mahwah, NJ: Lawrence Erlbaum Associates, Publishers.

Bloome, D., Carter, S. P., Christian, B. M., & Otto, S. (2004). *Discourse analysis & the study of classroom language & literacy events: A microethnographic perspective.* Mahwah, NJ: Lawrence Erlbaum.

Bourdieu, P. (1991). *Language and symbolic power* (John B. Thompson, Ed.; G. Raymond & M. Adamson, Trans.). Cambridge, UK: Polity Press.

Boyd, M. P., & Rubin, D. L. (2002). Elaborated student talk in an elementary ESoL classroom. *Research in the Teaching of English, 36*(4), 495–530.

Cazden, C. B. (2001). *Classroom discourse: The language of teaching and learning* (2nd ed.). Portsmouth, NH: Heinemann.

Cazden, C. B., John, V. P., & Hymes, D. H. (1972). *Functions of language in the classroom.* New York: Teachers College Press.

Cochran-Smith, M. (2001). Learning to teach against the (new) grain. *Journal of Teacher Education, 52*(1), 3–4.

Darling-Hammond, L., (2006). Assessing teacher education: The usefulness of multiple measures for assessing program outcomes. *Journal of Teacher Education, 57*(2), 120–138.

Diaz, E., & Flores, B. (2001). Teaching as a sociocultural, sociohistorical mediator. In J. J. Halcon & M. de la Reyes (Eds.), The Best for Our Children: Critical Perspectives on Literacy for Latino Students (pp. 29–47). New York: Teachers College Press.

Dyson, A. H. (2003). *The brothers and sisters learn to write: Popular literacies in childhood and school cultures.* New York: Teachers College Press.

Fairclough, N. (1992). *Discourse and social change.* Cambridge, UK: Polity Press.

Gebhard, M., & Harman, R. (2011). Reconsidering genre theory in K-12 schools: A response to school reforms in the United States. *Journal of Second Language Writing, 20*(1), 45–55.

Gebhard, M., Harman, R., & Seger, W. (2007). Reclaiming recess: Learning the language of persuasion. *Language Arts, 84*(5), 419–430.

Gebhard, M., Shin, D., & Seger, W. (2011). Blogging and emergent L2 literacy development in an urban elementary school: A functional perspective. *CALICO Journal, 28*(2), 278–307.

Gebhard, M., Willett, J., Jimenez, J., & Piedra, A. (2010). Systemic functional linguistics, teachers' professional development, and ELLs' academic literacy practices. In T. Lucas (Ed.), *Preparing all teachers to teach English language learners* (pp. 91–110). Mahwah, NJ: Lawrence Erlbaum.

Gibbons, P. (2002). *Scaffolding language, scaffolding learning: Teaching second language learners in the mainstream classroom.* Portsmouth, NH: Heinemann.

Gibbons, P. (2009). *English learners, academic literacy, and thinking: Learning in the challenge zone.* Portsmouth, NH: Heinemann.

Gutiérrez, K., & Larson, J. (1994). Language Borders: Recitation as hegemonic discourse. *International Journal of Educational Reform, 3*(1), 22–36.

Gutiérrez, K., Moll, L., Asato, J., Pacheco, M., Olson, K., & Horng, E. L. (2002). "Sounding American": The consequences of new reforms on English language learners. *Reading Research Quarterly, 37*(3), 328–343.

Gutiérrez, K. D. (1993). How to talk, context, and script shape contexts for learning: A cross-case comparison of journal sharing. *Linguistics and Education, 5*(3–4), 335–365.

Gutiérrez, K. D., Asato, J., Santos, M., & Gotanda, N. (2002). Backlash pedagogy: Language and culture and the politics of reform. *Review of Education, Pedagogy, & Cultural Studies, 24*(4), 335–51.

Gutiérrez, K. D., Baquedano-López, P., & Alvarez, H. H. (2001). Literacy as hybridity: Moving beyond bilingualism in urban classrooms. In M. Reyes & J. Halcón (Eds.), *The best for our children: Critical perspectives on literacy for Latino students.* New York: Teachers College Press.

Harklau, L. (1994). Jumping tracks: How language minority students negotiate evaluations of ability. *Anthropology and Education Quarterly, 25*(3), 347–363.

Harman, R., & McClure, G. (2011). All the school's a stage: Critical performative pedagogy in urban teacher education. *Equity & Excellence in Education, 44*(3), 379–402.

Harman, R. M. (2008). *Systemic functional linguistics and the teaching of literature* (M. O'Donnell, Ed.). Retrieved from the International Systemic Functional Linguistics Association website: www.isfla.org/Systemics/Print/index.html

Jones, R. (1991). *Matthew and Tilly.* New York: Puffin.

Knapp, P., & Watkins, M. (2005). *Genre, text, grammar: Technologies for teaching and assessing writing.* Sydney: UNSW Press.

Lave, J., & Wenger, E. (1991). *Situated learning: Legitimate peripheral participation.* Cambridge, UK: Cambridge University Press.

Martínez-Roldán, C., & Fránquiz, M. E. (2009). Latina/o youth literacies: Hidden funds of knowledge. In L. Christenbury, R. Bomer, & P. Smagorinsky (Eds.), *Handbook of adolescent literacy research* (pp. 323–342). New York: Guilford Press.

Massachusetts Department of Elementary and Secondary Education. (2011). *Requirements for the participation of English language learners in MEPA and MCAS.* Retrieved from www.doe.mass.edu/mcas/participation/lep.pdf

Mehan, H. (1979). "What time is it, Denise?": Asking known information questions in classroom discourse. *Theory into Practice, 28*(4), 285–294.

Menken, K. (2008). *English learners left behind: Standardized testing as language policy.* Clevedon, UK: Multilingual Matters.

Michaels, S. (1984). Listening and responding: Hearing the logic in children's classroom narratives. *Theory into Practice, 23*(3), 218–224.

Moll, L. C. (2001). The diversity of schooling: A cultural-historical approach. In M. Reyes & Halcon (Eds.), *The best for our children: Critical perspectives on literacy for Latino students. Language and literacy series.* New York: Teachers College Press.

Nieto, S., & Bode, P. (2008). *Affirming diversity: The sociopolitical context of multicultural education* (5th ed.). Boston: Pearson/Allyn and Bacon.

Rogoff, B. (1990). *Apprenticeship in thinking: Cognitive development in social context.* New York: Oxford University Press.

Rymes, B. (2009). *Classroom discourse analysis: A tool for critical reflection.* Cresskill, NJ: Hampton Press.

Rymes, B. R., & Pash, D. (2001). Questioning identity: The case of one second language learner. *Anthropology & Education Quarterly, 32*(3), 276–300.

Schleppegrell, M. J. (2004). *The language of schooling: A functional linguistics perspective.* Mahwah, NJ: Lawrence Erlbaum.

U.S. Department of Education. (2011). *Budget 2012: Supporting English learners.* Retrieved from www2.ed.gov/about/overview/budget/budget12/crosscuttingissues/englishlearners.pdf

U.S. Department of Education & White House Initiative on Educational Excellence for Hispanics. (2011). *Winning the future: Improving education for the Latino community.* Retrieved from www.whitehouse.gov/sites/default/files/rss_viewer/WinningTheFutureImprovingLatinoEducation.pdf

Valdés, G. (2001). *Learning and not learning English: Latino students in American schools.* New York: Teachers College Press.

Wells, C. G. (1999). *Dialogic inquiry: Towards a sociocultural practice and theory of education.* New York: Cambridge University Press.

Wells, C. G., & Chang-Wells, G. L. (1992). *Constructing knowledge together: Classrooms as centers of inquiry and literacy.* Portsmouth, NH: Heinemann.

Willett, J. (1995). Becoming first graders in an L2: An ethnographic study of L2 socialization. *TESOL Quarterly, 29*(3), 473–503.

Willett, J., Harman, R., Lozano, M. E., Hogan, A., & Rubeck, J. (2007). Generative routines: Using the everyday to create dynamic learning communities for English language learners. In L. Verplaetse & N. Migliacci (Eds.), *Inclusive pedagogy for English language learners: Research informed practices* (pp. 33–54). Mahwah, NJ: Routledge.

Wright, W. E. (2005). English language learners left behind in Arizona: The nullification of accommodations in the intersection of federal and state policies. *Bilingual Research Journal 29*(1), 1–29.

11

CHANGING THE PEDAGOGICAL CULTURE OF SCHOOLS WITH LATINO ENGLISH LEARNERS

Reculturing Instructional Leadership

Noni Mendoza Reis and Barbara Flores

In this chapter, we draw attention to the importance of school leadership on the academic achievement of Latino English learners (ELs) to argue for the critical role of administrators in advocating for access, equity, and achievement policies that will improve K–12 outcomes of that growing segment of the U.S. school population. We know that in terms of within-school factors related to student achievement, school leadership quality is second only to the effects of the quality of curriculum and teacher instruction (Heck, 2000; K. A. Leithwood & Riehl, 2003, 2005). The literature is also clear on the fact that the influence school leadership has on student learning is not so evident in low-performing schools (Riordan, 2003). Studies on the principal labor market, while scarce, document the unequal distribution of school leader quality. Loeb, Kalogrides, and Hornig (2010) report that low-income students, students of color, and low-performing students are more likely to attend schools led by novice or temporary principals, leaders who do not hold an advanced (master's) degree, and leaders who attended less selective colleges. This uneven distribution in quality of school leadership places ELs in jeopardy before they even begin the schooling process—and perhaps even more, those ELs of Latino heritage. How to improve the quality of leaders who can successfully transform schools with English-language learners is a pressing issue for everyone, particularly for leadership preparation programs and district, state, and national agencies.

We posit that principal quality in schools with ELs can be improved through a renewed focus on instructional leadership that addresses their specific needs. We know today that transformative change begins with effective leadership. Without vision, pedagogical knowledge, understanding, and wisdom, educational transformation cannot succeed. Without personal and ideological clarity, a shift from a deficit school culture to a respectful and culturally inclusive one, a school (leader, teachers, staff, students, parents, and community) cannot effectively transform. Specifically, we propose that a reculturing in schools will occur when school leaders do the following: practice an advocacy stance toward ELs, improve their own knowledge base about the teaching and learning of ELs, and develop an ideological clarity that will transform schools for ELs. We propose a trilevel framework that addresses the combination of institutional, pedagogical, and personal levels (see Figure 11.1).

At the institutional level, we suggest that leadership in schools with ELs engage in an advocacy leadership that challenges the existing status quo and the role that schools play in maintaining a system of disproportionate school failure among nondominant students, in particular, those students still developing proficiency in English. School leaders must be ready to examine and interrupt all school and district policies that lead to institutional inequities. They must analyze, disrupt, and transform the structural barriers that contribute to such policies. At the pedagogical level, we focus on a reculturing of instructional leadership that goes beyond mainstream approaches. We propose that school leaders overseeing the education of ELs have a sound pedagogical knowledge base that addresses a strong foundation in professional development, language and (bi)literacy development, knowledge about culturally relevant instructional practices and language acquisition/development (oral/written and first [L1] and second [L2] languages) theories, and best practices. At the personal level, we stress the importance of school leaders' ideological clarity (Bartolome, 2000), as well as the ongoing personal critical reflection and transformation of deficit assumptions, beliefs, and attitudes about ELs. We believe that when school leaders have ideological clarity, they are able to lead their school personnel through similar transformational processes.

Institutional Level	Pedagogical Level	Personal Level
Identifying and addressing institutional inequities by identifying structural barriers to student achievement and taking an "advocacy stance" as leaders	Instructional leadership that defines content knowledge necessary for leading schools with ELs: Pedagogical Knowledge Sociocultural Knowledge Culturally Relevant Pedagogy L1/L2 Language and Literacy Acquisition and Development	Exhibiting ideological clarity by self-examination and transformation of deficit assumptions, beliefs, and attitudes about ELs; and naming, interrogating, and transforming deficit assumptions, beliefs, and attitudes about ELs with teachers

FIGURE 11.1 Reculturing Instructional Leadership

A conceptual model adapted from Mendoza-Reis, Flores, and Quintanar (2009).

We set the context of this chapter with an overview of the academic achievement gap for ELs. We review literature that includes advocacy leadership, instructional leadership, teacher and principal development, and professional development. We suggest that to improve the quality of principals in schools with ELs, instructional leadership must be mediated through different approaches and a certain knowledge base. We highlight an exemplary model of culturally responsive professional development for teachers of ELs, the Instructional Conversation Model—a research project from the Center for Latino Achievement and Success (CLASE) in Athens, Georgia—as the type of professional development that instructional leaders ought to engage in to transform schools for ELs. We conclude this chapter with recommendations to policy makers in the form of essential steps in reculturing instructional leadership.

ELs and the Achievement Gap

ELs are the fastest growing sector of the public school population—and the majority of those learners are of Latino heritage. Over the past 15 years, the number of ELs has nearly doubled to about approximately 5 million. By 2015, it is projected that ELs' enrollment in U.S. schools will reach about 10 million. And, by 2025, it is predicted that nearly one out of every four public school students will be an EL (Chapa & De La Rosa, 2004; National Council of La Raza, 2007). However, as the authors of many of the chapters assembled in this volume have noted, the academic performance levels of Latino ELs remain stubbornly and significantly below those of their peers in nearly every measure of achievement (cf. Gándara & Contreras, 2010; Gándara & Orfield, 2010).

In their examination of ELs in California schools, Gándara, Rumberger, Maxwell-Jolly, and Callahan (2003) reported that the academic achievement of ELs lagged considerably behind the achievement of students from English-speaking backgrounds. They concluded that the achievement gap for ELs could only be attributed to seven conditions of inequity severely influencing their opportunities to learn: (1) inequitable access to appropriately trained teachers; (2) inadequate professional development opportunities to help teachers address the instructional needs of ELs; (3) inequitable access to appropriate assessment to measure EL achievement, gauge their learning needs, and hold the system accountable for their progress; (4) inadequate instructional time to accomplish learning goals; (5) inequitable access to instructional materials and curriculum; (6) inequitable access to adequate facilities; and (7) intense segregation into schools and classrooms that place them at particularly high risk for educational failure.

As one can see, these inequities are significant. A position that "blames the victim" can no longer be accepted as a rationale for the "lack of achievement" of ELs, in particular, ELs of Latino backgrounds. Given this context, we argue that school leaders need to be supported to develop the knowledge, skills, and dispositions necessary to address these inequities so that they can fully participate in developing equitable policies that in turn can lead to the implementation of educational practices that will contribute to closing the achievement gap for this specific, critical school population.

Level One: Institutional Level—Advocacy Leadership

For many years, while our student population in our public schools was becoming increasingly diverse, our leadership preparation programs remained focused on a universal, one-size-fits-all model of leadership (Mendoza Reis & Smith, 2013). More recently, studies of educational leadership generally acknowledge that contemporary administrators must be equipped with different skill sets in order to be successful and that these are centered around an advocacy stance and cultural proficiency (Cambron-McCabe & McCarthy, 2005; Scheurich & Skrla, 2003). In this chapter, we also support the idea that schools with diverse students require a new kind of thinking, different lenses, and new kinds of dynamic leaders who can effectively close the academic achievement gap between mainstream students and ELs.

Arguing for a postreform agenda in education, Anderson (2010) notes that "an advocacy leader believes in the basic principles of a high quality and equitable public education for all students and is willing to take risks to make it happen" (p. 13). To that that end, Anderson argues for a rethinking of leadership that includes both authenticity and advocacy that will challenge the status quo. Advocacy leaders such as those he posits are necessary for sustainable achievement and are prepared to identify and change policies on behalf of ELs. Additionally, in their description of what "cultural proficiency" in educational leadership means, Lindsey, Roberts, and Campbell-Jones (2005) pinpoint "the state of honoring the differences among cultures, seeing diversity as a benefit, and interacting knowledgeably and respectfully among a variety of cultural groups" (p. 4). Lindsey et al. describe six essential elements that school leaders use to develop cultural competence: valuing diversity, assessing school culture, managing the dynamics of difference, adapting diversity, institutionalizing cultural knowledge and resources, and inclusiveness. They also describe a culturally proficient school culture as a nexus of "policies and practices of a school or the values and behaviors of an individual that enable the school or person to interact effectively in a culturally diverse environment" (p. 146).

Both advocacy leaders and culturally proficient leaders do not hesitate to confront a pedagogical school culture that creates obstacles and barriers toward closing the achievement gap. Instead, they reject "subtractive schooling" (Valenzuela, 1999) and challenge inequitable policies at local, regional, and national levels that may affect academic achievement. They also engage in interrogating such policies with teachers, district offices, communities, and families, and they challenge the "sacred cows" in education, such as teacher and student placements, discipline policies, assessment, and transportation decisions that may have contributed to the inequity they witness. In sum, these new leaders change the pedagogical culture of their schools by ensuring that teachers develop advocacy and cultural proficiency skills in order to transform schools with ELs.

Level Two: Pedagogical Level—Instructional Leadership

There is substantial research that supports the critical role the principal plays in supporting teachers and leading schools in their efforts to implement effective practices that boost student achievement (K. A. Leithwood & Riehl, 2005; Levine, 1991; Robinson, Lloyd, & Rowe, 2008). In this regard, instructional leadership must include, among other things, but perhaps above all, a commitment to effective and meaningful teaching and student learning. Some 30 years ago, Purkey and Smith (1983) reviewed the literature on effective schools and found strong leadership to be a major component of successful schools. A little more than 10 years after the Purkey and Smith review, Hallinger and Heck (1998) conducted a meta-analysis of the relationship between leadership and student achievement and found similar results. Finally, K. Leithwood, Seashore Louis, Anderson, and Wahlstrom (2004) concluded that school leadership "is second only to teaching among school-related factors in its impact on student learning" (p. 5). These and other studies have contributed to the current stance that instructional leadership is an important component of school improvement. However, as noted earlier, it is the low-performing schools attended by nondominant students, in particular, ELs, that are most likely not to have leaders with the necessary instructional background to lead school improvement efforts.

How then do these leaders supplement their preparation so that they can be effective in schools with ELs? How do they become instructional leaders? The answer lies in the types of professional development planned and enacted at schools. It is thus important for all school leaders, particularly those who lead schools with ELs, to understand what constitutes quality professional development. We suggest that, in order to recognize quality professional development and to effectively lead schools, principals must first possess a deep knowledge base about teacher development, in particular, a deep knowledge about how teachers change practice in terms of their own developmental scale. Useful here is a pedagogy guided by sociocultural theory, culturally relevant pedagogy, and language acquisition/development across curricular contexts. Vygotsky's sociocultural theoretical framework related to teaching, learning, and development is pivotal in understanding how to organize the teaching/learning of ELs to their potential. From a sociocultural perspective, educators frame knowledge as socially constructed. It is through social interaction ("instructional conversations" [ICs]) that knowledge is first shared and then internalized at the psychological level. The zone of proximal development is the distance between where the learner is developmentally and his/her potential. Educators must teach to learners' potential and not merely to their developmental level. Additionally, from a Vygtoskian perspective, in order for the teacher to teach to learners potential, teachers must use meditational tools to bridge and make visible the goals, processes, and the learners' "coming to know." As such, once learners internalize or "own" knowledge, they can then appropriate it (i.e., make it their own to then use and apply across multiple social contexts). Within such a framework, the teacher is reframed as a sociocultural mediator, a human tool that scaffolds/mediates deliberately with intent to organize teaching/learning to the potential and across social context. Once internalized, knowledge then can be used by the learners to innovate and create new knowledge. These are important sociocultural principles that locate learning and the school as a microcosm of the necessary integration of social and cultural histories and trajectories (Portes & Salas, 2011).

Level Three: Personal Level—Ideological Clarity

By examining, naming, and interrogating the deficit assumptions, beliefs, and attitudes about ELs, educational leaders are able to not only address these insidious perceptual roadblocks to academic success, but also be able to transform and reculture the school's teaching/learning social, political, and personal environment (Flores, Cousin, & Diaz, 1991; Portes, Gallego, & Salas, 2009; Portes & Salas, 2010; Valdés, 1996, 2001). Freire (1990) posits that we as educators need to name and interrogate our generative themes and pose them as problems before we can transform our world. In our schooling practices related to ELs, one of our generative themes is that of the deficit ideology about language, culture, and class. Thus, in order to dismantle and transform this perspective in ways that shift from a debilitating paradigm to a productive and humane one (Portes, 2005), we first have to name these myths. The following are but a few of the deficit "myths" concerning ELs: ELs are "at risk" of failing school because they do not know English and lack prior knowledge, experiences, and vocabulary; ELs fail because their parents do not care, cannot speak English, and do not read to them; and, ELs do not do well on achievement/standardized tests because they are poor, do not care, and do not speak English. In the sections that follow, we offer a counterresponse to these myths in the hopes of advancing ideological clarity.

Myth One—ELs Are "At Risk" of Failing School because They Do Not Know English and Lack Prior Knowledge, Experiences, and Vocabulary. This myth is only true because we believe that it is true. Every child or student brings a wealth of "funds of knowledge" (González, Moll, & Amanti, 2005) to school that includes social, cultural, and linguistic assets and social networks (see also, e.g., de la Piedra, 2013; Delpit, 1995; Heath, 1983; Moll & Ruiz, 2002; Pacheco, 2012; Souto-Manning, 2010). A child's or student's mother tongue is an asset, not a detriment. A student's culture and family experiences are assets, not disadvantages. Moreover, a child's or student's "vocabulary" repertoire is always growing across

the life span. By focusing on the "lack of" assets, we undermine the students' academic success from the start. Vygotsky (1978) might posit that we are organizing failure through the creation of a "negative zone" that underestimates what ELs can do when supported in rich and additive environments for teaching and learning.

Myth Two—ELs Fail because Their Parents Do Not Care, Cannot Speak English, and Do Not Read to Them. Many educators believe this myth because ELs' parents do not come to the school or do not participate in open house or other school functions. Many Latino parents abide by the cultural beliefs that teachers hold a position of high regard around the notion of *encargamos a nuestros niños a los maestros* (We entrust our children to you, the teachers) (see Flores et al., 1991). In addition, administrators and teachers fail to realize that parents and grandparents and other community educators, such as Sunday school teachers, for example, engage children in sustained literacy practices daily or in a weekly basis (see, e.g., Baquedano-López, 2008). As has been amply documented in the literature of Latino parents, parents do care, but they may not know how to help their children navigate institutional requirements. This is very different than assuming that parents do not help their children at home.

Myth Three—ELs Do Not Do Well on Achievement/Standardized Tests because They Are Poor, Do Not Care, and Do Not Speak English. Although these ideas may find correlates in some achievement measures, educators need to take into consideration that standardized tests are culturally biased and are not usually normed on working-class students. Indeed, why would we require a non-proficient EL to take a standardized test in English when s/he is not a proficient speaker, reader, or writer of English? The obvious result is that the student does poorly on the test.

The process of engaging oneself and the cadre of teachers at a school site has to be very strategic and focused. For example, we recommend that these myths be typed on a sheet of paper, and that under each one, pairs or triads have to discuss and write down rationales regarding why one would believe or not believe that the myth is true. Afterward, each group would share and critically discuss these points of view with the rest of their colleagues. Shared readings and presentations of accessible educational research literature would likewise be helpful in stimulating teachers' reflection on and discussion about how negative "labels" have been used to describe ELs. Such derogatory labels and deficit ideology impede students' growth as the "Pygmalion effect" has documented (i.e., beliefs and perceptions taint/guide a person's behavior).

Bartolome (2000) states that ideological clarity requires that teachers' personal practice theories, visions, and beliefs about their students be compared and contrasted with those propagated by the dominant society. By critically juxtaposing ideologies, teachers examine to what extent the way they conceptualize ELs is shaped by dominant discourse and Anglo, middle-class culture. Leaders and teachers need to not only denounce harmful ideological practices, but also transform them to more caring and supportive ways of teaching within our schooling contexts. Similarly, Bartolome (2008) writes about the ideological and political aspects of teachers' caring and love but warns of condescending and deficit views on students of color. She then raises the issue of "authentic caring" or *cariño* as not enough to provide high-quality instruction. Instead, she argues for genuine communication (verbal and nonverbal) done in respectful and caring ways. Through the engagement of "authentic caring" and *cariño*, leaders and educators can embrace change and transform the deficit ideology that paralyzes teachers to move beyond the status quo and the perception of low-status groups as deficient across the dimensions of language, culture, and cognition.

An Illustrative Case: CLASE and the IC

Most recently, the CLASE at the University of Georgia, Athens, has been active in building on the IC concept first developed by the Center for Research on Education, Diversity and Excellence Center and working from the premise that culturally and linguistically diverse students' comprehension is increased through informal discourse (talk) with teacher and peers. In this model, the teacher assists students' learning throughout the conversation by modeling, questioning, restating, praising, and encouraging. In ongoing research conducted by the CLASE, the focus is on deconstructing the IC in ways that teachers can readily adopt for use in their classrooms. The program includes the following components.

Workshop-Model Training

A five-day, all-day workshop providing orientation to IC pedagogy. The workshop includes theory, research, practice, and planning guidance integrated to model the activity and interaction in an IC classroom. The workshop involves teachers in role-playing as students in IC with the leader and as the teacher in simulated IC with peers.

Online National Education Association (NEA) Course: Effective Teaching in Diverse Classrooms

This 20-hour course contains explicit instructions; supporting articles and other text; suggested trial activities; self-assessment tools; and, most important, high-end performance of IC, shown in professional-quality video, in English-language learner classrooms much like their own. Teachers are expected to complete this course in the fall of implementation.

Individual Coaching

A coach is assigned to visit each teacher or classroom in the treatment group on a biweekly basis from September through April. Each visit includes a discussion of the teachers' goals, a classroom observation and data collection, and a coach—teacher debriefing, providing data and dialogue about the performance of the teacher and students, as compared with the indicators of the teacher's phase-in plan for implementing the pedagogy standards.

Follow-through Coaching

Coaches and the teachers in the treatment group in each building meet regularly to discuss their IC classrooms' development, share activities and experiences, problem solve, and offer ideas and suggestions.

Teachers participate in the study for two years, the first of which provides time to practice and perfect the intervention, whereas the second comprises the experimental year. During the two-year cycle, teachers are observed (1–2 hours) by researchers and videotaped twice yearly for both research purposes and improvement of practice. Their coaches visit them on a biweekly basis during their practice year and as needed during the experimental year. Students report liking this participatory pedagogy where teachers talk less, challenge students at higher levels to learn by sharing their thinking aloud, and thus expose their zones of proximal development regularly. Our assessment of the CLASE's Instructional Conversation Model is that it meets all the criteria for productive professional development, and we consider it has the potential to effect needed changes in teacher practice not only for ELs but for all students. Unfortunately, most school leaders are not familiar with such advances nor understand the connection it has to meeting common core state standards.

Concluding Remarks and Policy Recommendations

In this chapter, we have addressed the issue of principal quality in schools with English-language learners. We have suggested that for leaders of these schools, the traditional leadership preparation models are not sufficient. We have proposed a model for improving the instructional leadership skills of school principals using a trilevel framework that focuses on the institutional, pedagogical, and personal. In closing, we offer the following policy recommendations.

Effective Curricular Leadership. Leadership is perhaps the cornerstone of the transformation of a low-performing school to a high-performing school despite poverty, underfunding, and everyday instructional challenges. The essential elements of curricular leaders are threefold: they possess and use leadership advocacy, they implement effective pedagogical knowledge, and they engage staff in systemic ideological clarity. Therefore, it is highly recommended that principals with children who are English-language learners embrace and develop these *reculturing* curricular elements.

Effective Professional Development. Professional development is most effective when it is intensive, sustained, job related, and focused on the content of the subject that teachers teach. This may also include coaching. Thus, we highly recommend implementation of an integrated model such as the one we outline in this chapter.

Rejection of Deficit Ideology about Class, Culture, Language, and Race/ Ethnicity. This is perhaps one of the most pivotal goals in order to move beyond the pervasive "blaming the victim" syndrome that we find rampant in our schools. We highly recommend that school staff name, interrogate, and transform these deficit views of children of color, children of poverty, and children who speak a language other than English.

Engaging in Ideological Clarity. Ideological clarity is healthy and necessary in order to acknowledge how one's beliefs, assumptions, and attitudes govern leaders' actions, especially regarding the teaching/learning and assessment of the children/ students with whom schools are entrusted. We highly recommend that principals lead their staff in the ideological clarity process in order to transform the culture of the school to a "can do" one.

Reframing the Teaching of English-Language Learners. In a sense, this approach rejects deficit ideology and engages ideological clarity. This reframing develops pedagogical knowledge about the teaching/learning of language, literacy, and culture in L1 and L2; employs culturally relevant pedagogy; and uses foundational and current language acquisition theories and practices.

References

Anderson, G. L. (2010). *Advocacy leadership: Towards a post-reform agenda in education.* New York: Routledge Press.

Baquedano-López, P. (2008). The pragmatics of reading prayers: Learning the Act of Contrition in Spanish-based religious education classes (doctrina). *Text & Talk, 28*(5), 582–602.

Bartolome, L. I. (2000). Democratizing bilingualism: The role of critical teacher education. In Z. F. Beykont (Ed.), *Lifting every voice: Pedagogy and politics of bilingualism* (pp. 167–186). Cambridge, MA: Harvard Education.

Bartolome, L. I. (2008). Authentic cariño and respect in minority education: The political and ideological dimensions of love. *Critical Pedagogy, 1*(1), 1–17.

Cambron-McCabe, N., & McCarthy, M. (2005). Educating school leaders for social justice. *Educational Policy, 19*(1), 201–222.

Chapa, J., & De La Rosa, B. (2004). Latino population growth, socioeconomic and demographic characteristics, and implications for educational attainment. *Education and Urban Society, 36*(2), 130–149.

de la Piedra, M. T. (2013). Consejo as a literacy event: A case study of a Border Mexican woman. *Language Arts, 90*(5), 339–350.

Delpit, L. (1995). *Other people's children: Cultural conflict in the classroom.* New York: The New Press.

Flores, B., Cousin, P., & Diaz, E. (1991). Transforming deficit myths about language literacy, and culture. *Language Arts, 68*(5), 369–379.

Freire, P. (1990). *Pedagogy of the oppressed.* New York: Continuum.

Gándara, P., & Contreras, F. (2010). *The Latino education crisis: The consequences of failed social policies.* Boston: Harvard University Press.

Gándara, P., & Orfield, G. (2010). *A return to the "Mexican Room": The segregation of Arizona's English learners.* Retrieved from http://civilrightsproject.ucla.edu/research/k-12-education/language-minority-students/a-return-to-the-mexican-room-the-segregation-of-arizonas-english-learners-1/

Gándara, P., Rumberger, R., Maxwell-Jolly, J., & Callahan, R. (2003). English learners in California schools: Unequal resources, unequal outcomes. *Educational Policy Analysis Archives, 11*(36), 1–52.

González, N., Moll, L. C., & Amanti, C. (2005). *Funds of knowledge: Theorizing practices in households, communities, and classrooms.* Mahwah, NJ: Lawrence Erlbaum.

Hallinger, P., & Heck, R. H. (1998). Exploring the principal's contribution to school effectiveness: 1980–1995. *School Effectiveness and School Improvement, 9*(2), 157–191.

Heath, S. B. (1983). *Ways with words: Language, life, and work in communities and classrooms.* New York: Cambridge University Press.

Heck, R. H. (2000). Examining the impact of school quality on school outcomes and improvement: A value-added approach. *Educational Administration Quarterly, 36*(4), 513–552.

Leithwood, K., Seashore Louis, K., Anderson, S., & Wahlstrom, K. (2004). *How leadership influences student learning: Review of research.* New York: The Wallace Foundation.

Leithwood, K. A., & Riehl, C. (2003). *What we know about successful school leadership.* Philadelphia, PA: Laboratory for Student Success, Temple University.

Leithwood, K. A., & Riehl, C. (2005). What we know about successful school leadership. In W. Firestone & C. Riehl (Eds.), *A new agenda: Directions for research on educational leadership* (pp. 22–47). New York: Teachers College Press.

Levine, D. U. (1991). Creating effective schools: Findings and implications from research and practice. *Phi Delta Kappan, 72*(5), 389–393.

Lindsey, R., Roberts, L., & Campbell-Jones, F. (2005). *The culturally proficient school.* Thousand Oaks, CA: Corwin Press.

Loeb, S., Kalogrides, D., & Hornig, E. L. (2010). Principal preferences and the uneven distribution of principals across schools. *Educational Evaluation and Policy Analysis, 32*(2), 205–229.

Mendoza-Reis, N., Flores, B., & Quintanar, R. (2009). *Webinar: Re-culturing instructional leadership using a sociocultural lens.* Washington, DC: National Education Association.

Mendoza Reis, N., & Smith, A. (2013). Rethinking the universal approach to the preparation of school leaders: Cultural proficiency and beyond. In L. C. Tillman & J. J. Scheurich (Eds.), *Handbook of research on educational leadership for equity and diversity* (pp. 651–669). New York: Routledge.

Moll, L. C., & Ruiz, R. (2002). The schooling of Latino children. In M. M. Suárez-Orozco & M. Páez (Eds.), *Latinos: Remaking America* (pp. 362–374). Berkley, CA: University of California Press.

National Council of La Raza. (2007). *Hispanic education in the United States.* Washington, DC: Author.

Pacheco, M. (2012). Learning in/through everyday resistance: A cultural-historical perspective on community resources and curriculum. *Educational Researcher, 41*(4), 121–132.

Portes, P. R. (2005). *Dismantling educational inequality: A cultural-historical approach to closing the achievement gap.* New York: Peter Lang.

Portes, P. R., Gallego, M. A., & Salas, S. (2009). Dismantling group based inequality in a NCLB era, effective practices, and Latino students placed at risk. In E.G.J. Murillo, S. A. Villenas, R. T. Galvan, J. S. Munoz, C. Martinez, & M. Machado-Casas (Eds.), *Handbook of Latinos and education: Research, theory and practice* (pp. 438–449). Mahwah, NJ: Lawrence Erlbaum.

Portes, P. R., & Salas, S. (2010). In the shadow of Stone Mountain: Identity development, structured inequality, and the education of Spanish-speaking children. *Bilingual Research Journal, 33*(2), 241–248.

Portes, P. R., & Salas, S. (Eds.). (2011). *Vygotsky in 21st century society: Advances in cultural historical theory and praxis with non-dominant communities.* New York: Peter Lang.

Purkey, S. C., & Smith, M. S. (1983). Effective schools: A review. *Elementary School Journal, 83*(4), 426–452.

Riordan, K. (2003). Teacher leadership as a strategy for instructional improvement: The case of the Merck Institute for Science Education. Philadelphia, PA: Consortium for Policy Research in Education.

Robinson, V.M.J., Lloyd, C. A., & Rowe, K. J. (2008). The impact of leadership on student outcomes: An analysis of the differential effects of leadership types. *Education Administration Quarterly, 44*(5), 635–674.

Scheurich, J. J., & Skrla, L. (2003). *Leadership for equity and excellence: Creating high achievement classrooms, schools and districts.* Thousand Oaks, CA: Corwin Press.

Souto-Manning, M. (2010). Teaching English learners: Building on cultural and linguistic strengths. *English Education, 42*(3), 248–262.

Valdés, G. (1996). *Con respeto: Bridging the distances between culturally diverse families and schools: An ethnographic portrait.* New York: Teachers College Press.

Valdés, G. (2001). *Learning and not learning English: Latino students in American schools.* New York: Teachers College Press.

Valenzuela, A. (1999). *Subtractive schooling: U.S.-Mexican youth and the politics of caring.* Albany, NY: State University of New York Press.

Vygotsky, L. S. (1978). *Mind in society: The development of higher psychological processes* (M. Cole, V. John-Steiner, S. Scribner, & E. Souberman, Trans.). Cambridge, MA: Harvard University Press.

12

BEYOND EDUCATIONAL STANDARDS?

Latino Student Learning Agency and Identity in Context

Richard P. Durán

Introduction

Over the past three decades, several successive waves of education reform have built on the idea that strong and clear educational standards are central to efforts to improve the schooling achievement of students in order to turn around a crisis in U.S. education (Hamilton, Stecher, & Yuan, 2008; McDermott, 2011). This belief is also held key to reducing evidence of persistent gaps in achievement test scores between low-scoring ethnic/racial minority groups, such as many Latinos, and White students, largely of northern European heritage, who score much higher on tests. The sentiment is that educational standards can make clear what students are expected to learn and be able to do at various grade levels and cumulatively across grades, supported by instruction. Subsequently, performance on annual tests based on standards would show concomitant improvement in students' achievement. These aspirations have proved elusive and grossly unmet, yet they remain central to reform arguments used by policy makers and educators (Hought & Elliot, 2011).

Adoption and implementation of achievement standards are complex endeavors; standards allegedly set clear goals for student learning. Their effective implementation requires an appropriate, aligned curriculum and learning materials, a trained teaching force that can provide students with necessary and effective instruction targeting achievement standards, and carefully designed assessment systems capable of detecting students' cumulative and progressive gains in achievement (Shephard, Hannaway, & Baker, 2011). Further, it is important to note that successful implementation of educational reform based on standards requires state education agency and local education agency system planning, adequate staffing and financial resources, and public will to prioritize education as a policy goal.

Let us suppose that all of the previously mentioned issues are considered. What else may be missing? It is proposed here that we need explicit attention to curriculum design to make enactment of standards-informed instruction possible and that students themselves need to understand how classroom learning activities and their engagement in these activities promote their learning and the creation of their identities as learners in the classroom. It also needs to be said that teachers and students, and educators at large, need to perceive learning communities in classrooms as connected to other forms of community extending beyond classrooms. Schools and their staff and other educational stakeholders need to see the empowerment of students as learners as a restructuring and transformation of the role of schools—they need to be seen as resources for the development of human potential and civic engagement.

It is contended here that based on previous research findings and contemporary theories of learning and development, there is something fundamentally misguided regarding how educators and the public at large have come to view learning, instruction, and academic achievement. The error is that many view students' opportunity to learn effectively in classrooms as being about students' isolated learning of skills and knowledge encapsulated in discrete learning assignments and in activities that can be mapped against statements of standard frameworks. Despite the damaging consequences of this perspective, it is subject to transformation leading to positive change. Let us consider some of these discrepant views regarding teaching and learning performance as they are treated by most educational reformers and the ways that such views contrast with what we know from the research literature that would ameliorate these beliefs and lead to a transformed view of educational reform serving Latino students.

To begin, there is the fundamental misconception that performance on tests adequately captures students' learning. Related to this misconception, there is the misguided notion that students' learning can be adequately represented by mastery of discrete skills and pieces of knowledge divorced from the embodied social and cultural contexts in which skills and knowledge are learned, exercised, and made meaningful and generalizable.

Researchers in the learning sciences (see, e.g., Bransford, National Research Council Committee on Developments in the Science of Learning, & National Research Council Committee on Learning Research and Educational Practice, 2000; Jonassen & Land, 2000; Kafai, Sandoval, Enyedy, Nixon, & Herrera, 2004; Sawyer, 2006) and cultural historical activity theory (CHAT) (see, e.g., Cole, 1996; Daniels, 2001; Portes & Salas, 2011; Rogoff, 2003) synthesize a considerable body of theoretical and empirical evidence supporting the notion that human functioning and development of problem solving competence is fundamentally tied to acquisition and exercise of agency, and to the development of identity in specific sociocultural contexts. This agency is more than the capability of answering questions on tests, and more than performing isolated classroom tasks and assignments well. One's exercise of competence—here competence in functioning academically in ways addressed by reform initiative standards—cannot be divorced from authentic embodied environments where individuals make personal meanings associated with the skills and knowledge indexed by standards.

The foregoing points, for example, are reinforced forcefully and in detail in research findings by Herrenkohl and Mertl (2010) who reported case studies of two classrooms of fourth-grade students' language interaction in science learning activities—following Cohen's complex instruction paradigm, featuring, but not exclusively utilizing, cooperative learning (see, e.g., Cohen & Lotan, 1997). The classes in question included Latino students, some of whom were transitional to English-language instruction. Interestingly, Herrenkohl and Mertl used discourse analysis methods to trace how students' enactment of different roles as learning community members, such as small-group contributor and coanalyst of information, whole class reporter of information, and whole class recipient/reactor to information, were socialized into classroom life and student identity. It is noteworthy that students' enactment of the various roles was centrally about communicating and elaborating science content knowledge and using this knowledge to conduct science problem solving. This involved "learning to be a student" and, further, "learning how to think like an apprentice scientist," within a learning community concerned with mastery of science subject matter.

The foregoing research and other similar findings (see, e.g., Gutiérrez & Larson, 2007; Moll & Díaz, 1987; Pacheco, 2012; Solís, Kattan, & Baquedano-López, 2009) suggest that a deeper understanding of how Latino students develop complete identities as learners in classroom communities can inform attaining the goals of current educational reformers in an impactful way. However, it is claimed here that a transformation is needed in how educators and policy makers understand the power of social relations in classrooms, and that connections to students' linguistic, social, and cultural identities will make such positive change possible. This transformation will require that educators and policy makers recognize more fully the necessity of having classroom learning activities build on the cultural and linguistic background of Latino students and the incorporation of community values as the foundation for classroom values and learning. Further, even with these concerns addressed, there is no simple automatic path that will support students' acquisition and mastery of the deep linguistic conventions that underlie students' being able to process complex texts efficiently. Simply put, the design of effective subject matter instruction aligned with standards will require that students be asked to work consciously, and with effort, to master advanced linguistic conventions tied to academic genre with appropriate feedback and motivational support in culturally responsive classrooms. Again, students will also have to learn in increasing detail the ways of thinking, problem solving, and information manipulation required to develop into an expert in a discipline.

It is interesting to note that this insight into the value of fusing concern for sociocultural identity, linguistic repertoire, and analytic skills as fundamental to understanding culture and learning was foreseen early on in the development of

CHAT—see, for example, the classic paper by Scribner (1979) entitled "Modes of Thinking and Ways of Speaking, Culture and Logic Reconsidered." In this paper, in the context of a Soviet Union study of reasoning by persons with limited access to formal schooling, Scribner argues that thinking, reasoning, and learning practices are fundamentally connected to the ways that people perceive themselves as sense makers and how they learn to use language in their daily ecological settings. These findings have relevance to students now faced with the expectation of performing in schools in ways that show evidence of their mastery of academic standards, yet with limited academic background knowledge. In more recent times, Lee (2000) has advanced the notion of *cultural modeling* to capture Scribner's understanding. Individuals as social and cultural beings learn cultural models for how to act and interact competently as meaning makers by enacting roles, and thinking and language practices appropriate to the *activity systems* (Engeström, Miettinen, & Punamäki, 1999) they engage in jointly with other participants in learning settings.

The suggested path toward making learning more meaningful for Latino students while helping them show evidence of mastering academic standards is not an easy one. It will require that educators and policy makers attend carefully to the moral will and human understanding of Latinos, their cultural and linguistic resources, and their communities as they are experienced in everyday settings—matters so often cast aside by the current education system and reform efforts as irrelevant to mastery of academic content knowledge and problem solving. It will require envisioning teaching and learning as deeply determined by social and cultural processes tied to participation and development of students and their community agency in society and its institutions. It is also the case that it will very much require that teachers design instructional activities so that students are given the opportunity to analyze and master critical language skills expected of them.

Above all, given the dual-language circumstances of so many Latino students, the design of pedagogy will need to take on a more sophisticated view of what language competence and bi-literacy are about—one that acknowledges that languages are fundamentally socialized systems of conventions rather than rigid rule systems largely determined by genetic endowment (as is postulated in some models of language acquisition, such as those drawing from the early work of Chomsky). For a contemporary view of sociocultural perspectives in this regard, see http://ell.stanford.edu/, the website for the Understanding Language project. The new, emerging sociocultural views of language (see, e.g., Van Lier & Walqui, 2012) theorize and investigate *language as action*. This perspective is informed by both CHAT and long experience in supporting acquisition of English by Latino and other language learners. According to Van Lier (2007):

> In a classroom context, an action-based perspective means that ELs engage in meaningful activities (projects, presentations, investigations) that engage their interest and that encourage language growth through perception,

interaction, planning, research, discussion, and co-construction of academic products of various kinds. During such action-based work, language development occurs when it is carefully scaffolded by the teacher, as well as by the students working together. The goals and outcomes specify academic and linguistic criteria for success, and the road to success requires a range of focused cognitive and linguistic work, while at the same time allowing for individual and group choices and creativity. (p. 4)

How might such a perspective inform states' and schools' adoption and implementation of Common Core State Standards (CCSS) as the latest effort to realize educational reform, with special attention to the learning and schooling needs of Latino students?

The CCSS Movement

The current movement to adopt and implement Common Core Standards (National Governors Association Center for Best Practices & Council of Chief State School Officers, 2010) is the latest historical wave in the cycle to end the alleged U.S. education crisis. Will this movement attain its ends? If past history alone is an indicator, this movement will fail as have its predecessors. There is no simple answer to this dilemma. And arguably there is the possibility that the perceived "education crisis" is a "false crisis"; it can be perceived as a socially and politically induced crisis (see, e.g., Berliner & Biddle, 1995; P. R. Portes & Salas, Chapter 1, this volume) built on economic and social inequities systematically encountered by members from certain subgroups over a lengthy historical period that affects educational opportunity in classrooms in an enduring manner. The cumulative educational injustices endured by Latinos in U.S. education have been thoroughly characterized and documented (see, e.g., Murillo et al., 2010; Valencia, 2010; Valenzuela, 1999).

Skill Sets from a Standards Perspective: The Common Core English Language Arts (ELA) Example

It is hard for anyone concerned with improving the education of Latino and other students of color who underperform in classrooms to argue against the value of skills advocated by academic standards as desirable goals for student learning. Skills mentioned in statements of academic standards in language arts, mathematics, and science at grade level are undeniably important outcomes that underlie being able to function not only in classrooms, but also outside classrooms—though additional skills and knowledge, as well, are critically important as discussed in this chapter. Arguments for standards as classroom learning goals are made even more persuasive when policy makers and educators set out articulations of standards—statements that attempt to capture systematic development of key skills and knowledge across grades that eventuate in students being better prepared for college or the work-force upon completion of high school. Consider, for example, the CCSS stipulation of English Language Arts (ELA) and Literacy Standards.

We here elaborate on how the intention of the CCSS ELA standards can be attained by transforming our notion of classrooms as described in the previous section of this chapter. We start by stipulating what these standards are claimed to specify by their authors, and we then suggest how these claims could be attained under a more appropriate sociocultural framing of learning, consistent with findings from current learning sciences and CHAT perspectives cited previously.

The ELA Common Core Standards (see Common Core State Standards Initiative, 2012a) cover four areas: reading, writing, speaking and listening, and language skills at two grade ranges (K–5 and 6–12). In addition, a separate but complementary set of standards concerns additional "literacy" skills involving just reading and writing for grades 6–12, tied to ELA skills supporting learning and mastery of History/Social Studies, Science, and Technical Subject content. To reiterate, the ELA Common Core Standards separate the learning goals for the four areas of reading, writing, speaking and listening, and language across grades K–5 and 6–12 from the learning goals for ELA associated with using reading and writing to learn and communicate content in grades 6–12.

An additional noteworthy feature of the Common Core Standards ELA system is built around a set of umbrella College and Career Readiness Anchor Standards for each skill area that is shared across grades, but the implementation of which is sensitive to students' grade level. These Anchor Standards allegedly describe skill targets that are appropriate on the way to being ready for college or career. The idea behind Anchor Standards is that becoming ready for college and career is a developmental progression wherein students should be expected to begin acquiring advanced core skills via instructional activity and learning goals in the earliest grades, in a manner that progresses systematically in demands from grade to grade.

It is important to note that the Common Core ELA and related Common Core Literacy Standards place an emphasis, across grades, on students' developing the ability to comprehend and generate complex texts involving communication of information—and to do it in ways that involve high-level reasoning skills and linguistic skills, increasingly supporting academic content learning. Special attention is placed in delineating Common Core Reading Standards to setting higher and higher expectations across grades to students' capacity to independently understand linguistically complex informational texts. Nonetheless, it is fair to state that the model of reading and text complexity put forth by the Common Core Standards posits that text meaning is inherent in understanding the discrete linguistic statements making up a text and their grammatically signaled interrelationships. This perspective can be questioned if taken too simplistically. Words and sentences don't "mean" in isolation from humans as interpreters of language in authentic contexts and in the process of implementing language as action—a matter brought out by the researchers and practitioners cited earlier. To elaborate further, this point is also made by Bruner (1986). Language can only mean in the context of language users situating and interpreting the occurrence of written or spoken language and its perceived units of words, syntactic structure, and functions within the negotiation of self in relation to others in activity. Pertinent to Latinos, Gutiérrez (2008) describes findings where Latino immigrant and other students' processing of textual meaning in classrooms is linked strategically and deliberately to their negotiation of learning roles and perceptions of how roles are connected in a *third space*, wherein they negotiate and connect present experience with past experience and with the potential for future experience in classroom activity settings. She states:

> I use these examples to help us consider how the language practices and the grammatical accounts observed in a particular activity system, the surrounding discourse, and coordinated bodily practice create an interactional matrix that serves as a resource for constituting a social situation of development with particular types of activities, relations, and opportunities for movement across past, present, and future roles and practices (Ochs, Schegloff, & Thompson, 1996). Specifically, the language and embodied practices mediated the accomplishment of shared practices among the participants that functioned instrumentally to help students link the past and present to an imagined future and reorganize everyday concepts acquired through social interaction in joint activities into scientific or school-based concepts in ways that created a collective Third Space. (Gutiérrez, 2008, p. 158)

The concepts advanced by Gutiérrez and others adopting CHAT and other sociocultural perspectives have not yet been fully taken into consideration adequately by proponents of the Common Core Standards. The proponents do not include attention to ways that the design of pedagogy must connect issues of developing students' ability to deal with text complexity given the sociocultural and contextual demands of reading tasks and given student characteristics and social identities in classroom settings. The primary focus espoused obsessively by many proponents of the Common Core Standards is the preeminent need for students to process texts appropriately given their linguistic features including prominently vocabulary, sentence syntax, and intersentential discourse cohesion markers—the ways syntax glues together the meaning of different statements and the ideas they convey. The developers of the Common Core ELA Standards argue that in recent decades, instruction of U.S. students has not sufficiently emphasized having students process linguistically complex texts as part of their academic work. Rather, schools and instruction have increasingly placed heavy emphasis on instruction relying on texts whose linguistic reading demands are low relative to students' grade level. Proponents of the Common Core ELA Standards suggest that the solution to this problem is to require that ELA instruction should accordingly rely on linguistically more complex texts at a grade level for the completion of classroom assignments.

Interestingly, however, the developers of the Common Core Standards have been careful to separate the specification of the Common Core Standards from their implementation in instruction. Introducing the ELA, the website (www.corestandards.org/ELA-Literacy/introduction/key-design-consideration) explains:

> By emphasizing required achievements, the Standards leave room for teachers, curriculum developers, and states to determine how those goals should be reached and what additional topics should be addressed. Thus, the Standards do not mandate such things as a particular writing process or the full range of metacognitive strategies that students may need to monitor and direct their thinking and learning. Teachers are thus free to provide students with whatever tools and knowledge their professional judgment and experience identify as most helpful for meeting the goals set out in the Standards.

It seems clear that based on the foregoing sections of this chapter, the Common Core Standards in isolation—without concern for how they are actually incorporated in instruction—are misguided, given our research knowledge.

The standards isolated from a curriculum characterize learning as covering discrete bits of interconnected knowledge and skills defined by standards articulating the acquisition of ELA skills. Students are expected to achieve competence in ELA standards through exposure to unspecified lesson activities focused on specific skills and knowledge acquisition in a step-by-step manner, leading to mastery of a whole curriculum area. Evidence of student learning is then viewed in terms of standardized tests, structured to reflect discrete pieces of knowledge and skills represented by standards and an intended curriculum. Such approaches are bound to have limited value; they are misguided and distort what learning and mastery really are for students. They ignore deep attention to the socialization of learning opportunity and its foundation in students' sense of agency and identity as learners in a broader and more fundamental sense.

Yet the framers of the Common Core Standards dangle a hope that the field can seize on, if there is the will to draw on research of the sort mentioned in this chapter. Although stopping short of specifying a curriculum and pedagogy, the framers state:

> *Even many students on course for college and career readiness are likely to need scaffolding as they master higher levels of text complexity.* As they enter each new grade band, many students are likely to need at least some extra help as they work to comprehend texts at the high end of the range of difficulty appropriate to the band. For example, many students just entering grade 2 will

need some support as they read texts that are advanced for the grades 2–3 text complexity band. Although such support is educationally necessary and desirable, instruction must move generally toward *decreasing scaffolding* and *increasing independence,* with the goal of students reading independently and proficiently within a given grade band by the end of the band's final year (continuing the previous example, the end of grade 3. (Common Core State Standards Initiative, 2012b, p. 9)

How can educators, policy makers, and researchers take advantage of this opening for introducing transformative pedagogy and curricula addressing the learning needs of Latinos while responding in culturally appropriate way to the intent of standards bearers? Test results are unlikely to prove sufficient indicators of progress toward this end. What else remains to provide evidence of transformation? We need documentation of grounded examples of effective, culturally responsive instruction showing that Latino students can acquire skills relevant to mastery of standards and that students can communicate and act in ways manifesting standards as part of ongoing communities of learners making sense of their identities as learners and of the world around them. These documentations will be all the more powerful when they are communicated to policy makers and educational stakeholders through the voices of students, teachers, family members, and researchers working together. This is a possibility that needs to be pursued actively.

The chapter discussed how select theories and findings from sociocultural, critical pedagogy, and learning sciences research can create a different foundation for learning, instruction, and assessment, one that ought to be a more effective foundation for educational policies attempting to improve educational outcomes for underserved students. In particular, the chapter discussed how becoming an effective learner is coupled with participation in a local community of learners that introduces and reinforces social identities of learners as participants and transformers of the world around them.

References

Berliner, D. C., & Biddle, B. J. (1995). *The manufactured crisis: Myths, fraud, and the attack on America's public schools.* Reading, MA: Addison-Wesley.

Bransford, J., National Research Council Committee on Developments in the Science of Learning, & National Research Council Committee on Learning Research and Educational Practice. (2000). *How people learn: Brain, mind, experience, and school.* Washington, DC: National Academy Press.

Bruner, J. S. (1986). *Actual minds, possible worlds.* Cambridge, MA: Harvard University Press.

Cohen, E. G., & Lotan, R. A. (1997). *Working for equity in heterogeneous classrooms: Sociological theory in practice.* New York: Teachers College Press.

Cole, M. (1996). *Cultural psychology: A once and future discipline.* Cambridge, MA: Belknap Press of Harvard University Press.

Common Core State Standards Initiative. (2012a). Common core state standards initiative: Preparing America's students for college and careers. Retrieved from www.corestandards.org/ELA-Literacy.

Common Core State Standards Initiative. (2012b). *English Language Arts Appendix A Common core states standards*. Washington, DC: Author.

Daniels, H. (2001). *Vygotsky and pedagogy*. London: Routledge/Falmer.

Engeström, Y., Miettinen, R., & Punamäki, R.-L. (Eds.). (1999). *Perspectives on activity theory*. Cambridge, UK: Cambridge University Press.

Gutiérrez, K. (2008). Developing a sociocritical literacy in the third space. *Reading Research Quarterly, 43*(2), 148–164.

Gutiérrez, K., & Larson, J. (2007). Discussing expanded spaces for learning. *Language Arts, 85*(1), 69–77.

Hamilton, L., Stecher, B., & Yuan, K. (2008). *Standards-based reform in the United States: History, research, and future directions*. Santa Monica, CA: RAND.

Herrenkohl, L. R., & Mertl, V. (2010). *How students come to be and to know: A case for a broad view of learning*. New York: Cambridge University Press.

Hought, M., & Elliot, S. (Eds.). (2011). *Incentives and test-based accountability in education*. Washington, DC: The National Academies Press.

Jonassen, D. H., & Land, S. M. (2000). *Theoretical foundations of learning environments*. Mahwah, NJ: Lawrence Erlbaum.

Kafai, Y. B., Sandoval, W. A., Enyedy, N., Nixon, A. S., & Herrera, F. (Eds.). (2004). *ICLS 2004: Embracing diversity in the learning sciences: Proceedings: June 22–26, 2004*. Mahwah, NJ: Lawrence Erlbaum.

Lee, C. D. (2000). Signifying in the zone of proximal development. In C. D. Lee & P. Smagorinsky (Eds.), *Vygotskian perspectives on literacy research: Constructing meaning through collaborative inquiry* (pp. 191–225). New York: Cambridge University Press.

McDermott, K. (2011). *High-stakes reform: The politics of educational accountability*. Washington, DC: Georgetown University Press.

Moll, L. C., & Díaz, R. (1987). Teaching writing as communication: The use of ethnographic findings in classroom practice. In D. Bloome (Ed.), *Literacy and schooling* (pp. 193–231). Norwood, NJ: Ablex.

Murillo, E.G.J., Villenas, S. A., Galvan, R. T., Munoz, J. S., Martinez, C., & Machado-Casas, M. (Eds.). (2010). *Handbook of Latinos in education*. New York: Routledge.

National Governors Association Center for Best Practices & Council of Chief State School Officers. (2010). *Common core state standards*. Washington, DC: Author.

Ochs, E., Schegloff, E. A., & Thompson, S. A. (1996). *Interaction and grammar*. Cambridge, UK: Cambridge University Press.

Pacheco, M. (2012). Learning in/through everyday resistance: A cultural-historical perspective on community resources and curriculum. *Educational Researcher, 41*(4), 121–132.

Portes, P. R., & Salas, S. (Eds.). (2011). *Vygotsky in 21st century society: Advances in cultural historical theory and praxis with non-dominant communities*. New York: Peter Lang.

Rogoff, B. (2003). *The cultural nature of human development*. New York: Oxford University Press.

Sawyer, R. K. (2006). *The Cambridge handbook of the learning sciences*. Cambridge, UK: Cambridge University Press.

Scribner, S. (1979). Modes of thinking and ways of speaking, culture and logic reconsidered. In R. O. Freedle (Ed.), *New directions in discourse processing* (Vol. 2, pp. 223–243). Norwood, NJ: Ablex.

Shephard, L., Hannaway, J., & Baker, E. (2011). *Standards, assessments, and accountability* (Education Policy White Paper). Retrieved from http://files.eric.ed.gov/fulltext/ED531138.pdf

Solís, J., Kattan, S., & Baquedano-López, P. D. (2009). Locating time in science learning activity: Adaptation as a theory of learning and change. In K. Richardson Bruna & K. Gomez (Eds.), *Talking science, writing science: The work of language in multicultural classrooms* (pp. 139–166). New York: Routledge.

Valencia, R. R. (2010). *Dismantling contemporary deficit thinking: Educational thought and practice.* New York: Routledge.

Valenzuela, A. (1999). *Subtractive schooling: U.S.-Mexican youth and the politics of caring.* Albany, NY: State University of New York Press.

Van Lier, L. (2007). Action-based teaching, autonomy and identity. *Innovation in Language Learning and Teaching, 1*(1), 46–65.

Van Lier, L., & Walqui, A. (2012). *Language and common core state standards.* Retrieved from Understanding Language Stanford Graduate School of Education website: http://ell.stanford.edu/sites/default/files/pdf/academic-papers/04-Van%20Lier%20Walqui%20Language%20and%20CCSS%20FINAL.pdf

AFTERWORD

Eugene E. García

At the outset of this volume, P. R. Portes and Salas made very clear the discontent related to the present circumstances of Latino education and related policy. Other contributions in this volume attempt to address this discontent and begin to identify critical pieces of a puzzle that give form to important issues that must be addressed in putting together the policy/practice puzzle that can enhance Latino educational outcomes. Let me add yet one more piece to that puzzle, as an afterword, to the extensive and incisive contributions in this volume. Let me begin by expressing my deepest appreciation to the National Task Force on Early Childhood Education for Hispanics (2007) for their report on Latino education in the early years, along with elaborations of that report (L. S. Miller et. al. 2007). That report noted from an educational standpoint that Latinos are in a complex situation. They have made substantial educational progress over the past several decades. Yet, as a group, they are far from converging on the educational attainment and academic achievement patterns of Whites and Asian Americans in the United States or on the attainment and achievement norms of most industrialized nations (P. R. Portes, 2005).

As this volume has emphasized, the most formidable challenge in these circumstances is to build a much stronger education system for the Latino children of the very large number of adult Latino immigrants with little formal education and limited knowledge of the academic dimensions of the English language. Available evidence suggests that far too many of their children are struggling academically in the early years of school, not only in English literacy, but also in other key subjects including mathematics.

Moreover, as the underrepresentation of low socioeconomic status (SES) Latinos in preschool programs attests, many of these young children are not even gaining access to that key part of the early childhood education system. Beyond basic access to prekindergarten is the need for a much more time-intensive system at the pre-K,

K–3, 4–12, and beyond levels for many of these youngsters. In addition, it would be extremely helpful if that system's capacity to work with these youngsters in both English and Spanish were much more robust. That is the case because, as noted in this volume, many of these children are educationally at risk when viewed from either language—they lack, not as a fault of their own, rich language environments reflective of the academic discourses required to be successful in today's schooling venues.

Fortunately, there is a growing body of evidence that high-quality programs and K–3 education produce meaningfully higher levels of school readiness and academic achievement for Latino children from low SES and middle-class circumstances. Similarly, as is pointed to in this volume, promising programs at all levels are coming into existence as this population grows in all regions of the United States. Growing understanding of human development in cultural and transnational contexts and advances in theory and systemic thinking also provides a great deal of guidance regarding how programs might be strengthened from a school readiness and academic achievement standpoint. In an effort to more formally summarize, I leave you with what are my own concluding foundations from my research over the past 25 years.

Foster Academic Discourse Acquisition and the Development of Mature Literacy and Numeracy within Culturally Responsive Circumstances

Development and learning venues that build on the assets of children allow us to address Latinos within a development systems framework (García & García, 2012). Too often, policies and practices focus on eliminating or minimizing "risk factors" at the cost of ignoring the multiple assets and resources that Latino students, families, and communities bring to the formal learning enterprise. I have often characterized the misguided educational approach to Latinos as ignoring very substantive social, emotional, and learning *raíces*. I am not opposed to identifying needs, challenges, and risk factors, but not at the cost of ignoring linguistic and cultural assets that are part of the U.S. Latino and immigrant experiences. Programs that have emphasized native language abilities to develop literacy have been demonstrated to promote English literacy development (García & Náñez, 2011). These programs were more focused on mature development of educational discourses in Spanish than transitioning students quickly into English-language instruction. This approach paid off overall educationally and in English-language development at levels that allowed students to be successful in English instruction.

Protect and Extend Instructional Time

Put simply, Latino students need more opportunity to learn. Schools can offer after-school programs, supportive computer-based instruction, and voluntary Saturday schools and summer academies. These augmented learning venues can multiply in significant ways the opportunities for students to engage in academic learning. Regular teachers or trained tutors can be used to extend this learning time. Not surprisingly, a majority of students will take advantage of these voluntary extensions—these students and families have a high regard for "schooling" and are not afraid to work hard at it if given the opportunity. In addition, within the formal schooling context, care must be given to not erode the daily instructional time that is available—erosion often related to auxiliary responsibilities by teachers that take valuable time away from instruction.

Expand the Roles and Responsibilities of Teachers

In a development systems approach, the human capital available to build on the students' assets is critical. For Latino students at all levels, teachers participating in professional development activities designed to address their assets and teachers who are given much greater roles in curricular and instructional decision making are making a positive difference in academic outcomes (García & García, 2012). This decision making is much more collective in nature to ensure cross-grade articulation and coordination—the pre-K–3 connections are becoming more significant for Latino children. Teachers in these schools become full copartners utilizing high levels of language and content standards and devising responsible "authentic" assessments that inform instruction.

Address Students' Social and Emotional Needs

Many venues I have worked in are located in low-income neighborhoods serving poor families utilizing communities' existing strengths in networking, spiritual, and communal support. These communities are often seen as "risk generators." They are also "asset incubators and generators" as well. Therefore, a proactive stance with regard to issues in these communities must be adopted. The key ingredient is to engage the sources of these social and emotional support systems, formal and informal, in a community that may intersect with issues of alcohol and drug abuse, family violence, health care, and related social service needs.

Respect and Involve Families in Their Children's Learning. Family engagement programs have been critical as part of a more comprehensive development perspective focusing on assets. Family engagement is more than participation in school committees, school festivals and celebrations, student field trips, and other activities. It involves developing a partnership between the educator and family members—each taking appropriate responsibility for learning activities and learning outcomes. This is an important and evolving field of policy development that would establish opportunities for this type of family/educator partnerships.

The Four Rs—Las Cuatro Rs—and a T

This volume summons us to change educational policies and practices in the face of continued Latino student underachievement and the often "subtractive" paradigms that have driven high-stakes models of educational reform for children of nondominant communities (Valenzuela, 1999, 2002, 2004). I have often been called on to translate such calls in ways that might be helpful to educators and the general public at large. In so doing, I have often called on a set of recommendations that use a particular mnemonic, "remember the 4R's and the T" (García, 2001, 2005; García & García, 2012). In short, for me, educational programs, initiatives, strategies, and policies that assist Latino students are *respectful, responsive, responsible, resourceful,* and *theoretically* viable. I admit that I particularly like this focus on the *r* because in Spanish the pronunciation takes the form of a trilled *r;* phonetically, it is like placing multiple *r*'s together as in the roar of a motor "bah-r-r-room"—the term *Respeto* is pronounced "r-r-espeto."

Respectful. Everyone wants respect. Parents want to be respected and want their children respected. Over and over again, it is common to hear from Latino parents and their children that in schools they do not receive that respect. They are too often seen as the foreigner, the immigrant, the non-English speaker, or the disadvantaged—in short, someone who does not belong, who is "less than," and whom the schools want to change to belong.

Responsive. It is not enough just to have respect. Educational programs and those individuals who serve in them must be directly responsive to the assets of the students and families that they serve. This requires an active assessment of the learning tools that the student brings to the schooling process coupled with the utilization of those tools that optimize student learning. It means shifting the emphasis from "needs assessments" to "asset inventories." However, it is not enough just to know your students well, but to take that knowledge and make it come alive in organizing and implementing teaching and learning environments for those students. Borrowing from an unknown educational colleague whose name I can't recall, "The general can only be understood in its specifics." That is, we can come to know our Latino students in various intellectual ways, but until we can translate that knowledge into the very specific ways in which we teach them, the maximum benefits of the intellectual knowledge will go unrealized.

Responsible. In considering federal legislation related to the reauthorization of the Elementary and Secondary Education Act we were continually confronted with the unequal achievement outcomes for selected students in U.S. schools. It becomes evident that nationally we did not have a policy mechanism in place for holding educational institutions accountable for these disparate educational results. For Latinos, failures to make distinctions in this data for immigrants versus nonimmigrants, Spanish speakers versus English speakers, and those with a previous educational background versus those without one make interpreting this data confusing and unproductive. Most significantly, Latino limited-English-speaking students are often out of the bounds of accountability simply because they were not assessed at all. Confusion is added at this policy level with the failure to develop appropriate assessments as opposed to using inappropriate ones. These are clearly two different issues, each placing Latino students outside any system of accountability.

Resourceful. We often are encouraged, particularly in education, that less is more and that throwing money at a problem is not the solution. Jaime Escalante, as portrayed in the popular movie *Stand and Deliver,* takes low-achieving Latino students and, with little more than engendering *ganas* in these students, produces a cadre of mathematics success stories. For many Latinos, these adages sound hollow in the face of the challenges that they confront in everyday educational settings. *Ganas* is good, but a systematic effort to improve education on a variety of fronts is not enough.

My own research continues to highlight that the key resources for Latino children are the presence of high-quality staff and teachers that serve these children and their families. These resources are sometime hard to find, yet they are the most critical ingredient related to academic success for these children. We have also learned that taking good care of these teachers and staff members through ongoing professional development and in-classroom coaching can be a substantive investment in positive outcomes for children. Teachers, staff members, and institutional leaders who understand the cultural and linguistic assets that these children, families, and communities bring to the teaching/learning enterprise are critical. After-school programs, specifically targeted in-school reading programs, and community-based support programs are not free. They require public and private resourcefulness that is usually nonexistent. However, it doesn't always take a lot of resources.

Theoretically Viable. We all have theories. They guide our everyday activity, and often we do not realize how powerful they are. My mother had an important and common theory: When in need, pray to the Virgen de Guadalupe. If that does not resolve the problem, pray the rosary and do not hesitate to light a candle at the local church. Our fathers had another yet common theory: Work hard. If that does not resolve the problem, work harder, and even harder. We realize that Latinos have a high sense of spirituality and inclination to work hard—and we wonder where that comes from.

Educators have theories as well, and they guide our every action as we develop and implement practices that we trust will assist children develop and learn. For many educators, children who come to them are to be served by meeting a set of agreed on expectations (i.e., standards). I have realized that far too many individuals who serve Latino children are operating on a set of assumptions or theories that are too generic and do not take into consideration the complexities of this population—the language, cultural, and development diversity that these children bring. Moreover, these theories call on understanding risk factors and implementing interventions that minimize or "counteract" them (see also, P. R. Portes & Salas, 2010). I would offer a different developmental systems approach, a different theory—namely, focus on the assets that the children, families, and communities bring that can assist in our teaching and learning endeavors.

We find it in the work of my Arizona colleague, Luis C. Moll, and his theory of "Funds of Knowledge" (Moll, 2009) that we all need to understand the cultural, social, linguistic, and academic "funds" that these students bring to the schooling enterprise. That capital going unrecognized leads only to the faulty construction of developmental and early learning environments that are unresponsive and potentially deleterious to those whom they were specifically designed to assist. Following from this, I suggest adopting a conceptual framework, a new *theory,* with regard to Latinos: their *raíces* are a resource, not a problem.

References

García, E. E. (2001). *Hispanic education in the United Status: Raices y alas.* New York: Rowman & Littlefield.

García, E. E. (2005). *Teaching and learning in two languages: Bilingualism and schooling in the United States.* New York: Teachers College Press.

García, E. E., & García, E. H. (Eds.). (2012). Language development and the education of Hispanic children in the United States. In E. E. García (Ed.), *Teaching and learning in two languages: Bilingualism and schooling in the United States* (pp. 44–58). New York: Teachers College Press.

García, E. E., & Jensen, B. (2009). Early educational opportunities for children of Hispanic origins. *Social Policy Report, 23*(2), 1–20.

García, E. E., & Miller, L. S. (2008). Findings and recommendations of the National Task Force on Early Childhood Education for Hispanics. *Journal of Society for Research in Child Development, 2,* 53–58.

García, E. E., & Náñez, J. (2011). *Bilingualism and cognition: Joining cognitive psychology and education to enhance bilingual research, pedagogy and policy.* Washington, DC: American Psychological Association.

Miller, L.S., Andrews, A.S., Cuéllar, D & Jensen, B. (2007). *Para nuestros niños: Expanding and improving early childhood education for Hispanics—Executive report.* Tempe, Arizona: National Task Force on Early Childhood Education for Hispanics. Retrieved from www.newmexicoprek.org/Docs/expand_ExecReport.pdf

Moll, L. (2009). The civil rights of language minority students and their funds of knowledge. *Educational Researcher, 39*(4), 163–171.

National Task Force on Early Childhood Education for Hispanics. (2007). *Para nuestros niños: Expanding and improving early childhood education for Hispanics—Main report.* Tempe, AZ. Retrieved from www.ecehispanic.org/work/expand_MainReport.pdf

Portes, P. R. (2005). *Dismantling educational inequality: A cultural-historical approach to closing the achievement gap.* New York: Peter Lang.

Portes, P. R., & Salas, S. (2010). In the shadow of Stone Mountain: Identity development, structured inequality, and the education of Spanish-speaking children. *Journal of the National Association for Bilingual Education, 33*(2), 241–248.

Valenzuela, A. (1999). *Subtractive schooling: U.S.-Mexican youth and the politics of caring.* Albany, NY: State University of New York Press.

Valenzuela, A. (2002). Reflections on the subtractive underpinnings of education research and policy. *Journal of Teacher Education, 53*(3), 235–241.

Valenzuela, A. (2004). *Leaving children behind: Why Texas-style accountability fails Latino youth.* Albany, NY: State University of New York Press.

CONTRIBUTORS

Rebecca A. Alexander, DePauw University, USA

Patricia Baquedano-López, University of California, Berkeley, USA

Lidia Cabrera Perez, University of La Laguna, Tenerife, Canary Islands, Spain

Richard P. Durán, University of California, Santa Barbara, USA

Barbara Flores, California State University, San Bernardino, USA

Eugene E. García, Arizona State University, USA

Manuel S. Gonzalez Canché, University of Arizona, USA

Ruth Harman, University of Georgia, USA

Sera J. Hernandez, University of California, Berkeley, USA

Patricia D. López, University of Texas, Austin, USA

Ariana Mangual Figueroa, Rutgers University, USA

Paula J. Mellom, University of Georgia, USA

Noni Mendoza Reis, San Jose State University, USA

Luis C. Moll, University of Arizona, USA

Martha Montero-Sieburth, University of Amsterdam, The Netherlands

Sonia Nieto, University of Massachusetts, USA

Alejandro Portes, Princeton University and University of Miami, USA

Pedro R. Portes, University of Georgia, USA

Sergio Quesada Aldana, University of Georgia, USA

Cecilia Rios-Aguilar, Claremont Graduate University, USA

Spencer Salas, University of North Carolina at Charlotte, USA

Sandra L. Soto-Santiago, University of Arizona, USA

Angela Valenzuela, University of Texas, Austin, USA

INDEX

Page numbers in italics refer to topics in tables

1.5 generation xviii, 47, 99

Academic Yearly Progress (AYP) 3, 174, 189n1
ACCELA see Access to Critical Content and English Language Acquisition
Access to Critical Content and English Language Acquisition (ACCELA) 176–7, 178, 179, 182, 183, 187
achievement standards 197, 198, 204
Achievement via Individual Determination (AVID) 61, 62, 63
advocacy leadership 193, 194, 195–6
African Americans xi, 52 ; family 20; males 55; second-grade students 177, 179, 184
African American studies 42n2
Afro-Caribbean Blacks 103
agency 5, 24, 42, 204, 205, 211; community 38, 107, 207; historical 105–6; individual 86, 186
Aguado, T. 99
Aguamilpa Dam 116
Alabama 164
Alba, Richard 71, 101; The Children of Immigrants in Schools 109n1
Alexander, Rebecca A. 16–34
American Civil Liberties Union 163
American Community Survey 151
Americanization 19, 23, 60

Anderson, G. L. 195
Anderson, S. 196
Aranda, E. 126, 127
Arizona 6, 37, 100, 161, 220; S.B. 1070
Argentineans 96, 103
Article 27, 96
Asians 4, 48, 52, 53, 54, 55, 58, 59, 69, 77, 98, 105, 215; Southeast 49, 51, 53, 55
Athens, GA xv, 194, 199
AVID see Achievement via Individual Determination

Baquedano-López, Patricia xvii, 16–34, 30n5, 38, 161
Barrio Logan College Institute 63
Bartolome, L. I. 198, 199
Basaldúa, M. 119, 120
Batalova, Jeanne 93
Bella Vista del Rio 117, 120, 121, 122, 123, 124
Berry, J. 74, 86
Berry, J. W. xviii
Biden, Joe 35, 42
bilingualism 4, 75, 101; additive 10; education xiii, xvi, 5, 9–11, 13n1, 26, 53, 61, 63, 71, 75, 78, 79, 80, 81, 84, 87, 107, 108, 134, 138, 139, 144, 149, 160, 161, 173, 183; to English-only schooling 154–6; English proficiency 72–3; health clinic 151

Bolivians 96
Brazilians 96
Brooklyn 36

Cabrera Perez, Lidia xviii, 92–114
Cadereyta 119
Calderon, Felipe 123
California 37, 194; Affirmative Action
    Program 62; First Five 20; Home
    Teacher Act 19; immigrant youth 98;
    language policy 134–44, 173; Mexicans
    95; migrant workers 119, 133–44,
    140–1; migration 149; Northern 26;
    Proposition 187 161; Proposition 227
    133, 134, 138; second generations 55;
    Southern 53, 54; Specter bill 28; Treaty
    of Guadalupe-Hidalgo 100; see also
    Sacramento; San Diego 77; University
    of California
Callahan, R. M. 73–4, 194
Campbell-Jones, F. 195
Cambodians 53, 54, 55
Canary Islands 93, 96, 97, 100
Carbonell, J. 98
Castilian Spanish 101
Catalonia 98, 100, 109n1
Cazden, C. B. 175, 188
CBOs see community-based organizations
Center for Latino Achievement and
    Success. See CLASE
Chatel, Helen 174, 177, 178, 179–84,
    187–8
CHCI see Congressional Hispanic Caucus
    Institute
children of immigrants xviii, 9, 45–147,
    149, 150; achievement motivation 73;
    and the American school system 47–68,
    160, 161, 162, 164, 166; common
    trends in overcoming disadvantage in
    the American school system 59–65;
    divergent paths to school adaptation
    69–91; English proficiency and
    bilingualism 72–3; family SES 71; family
    ties/relationships 71–2; literature review
    70–4; multivariate findings on American
    school system 55–9; policy implications
    in the American school system 65–6,
    153; preliminary evidence on American
    school system 49–55; proposed model of
    school adaptation 75–6; school context
    73–4; theoretical framework 74–5;
    theoretical perspectives on the future
    of second generation 48–9; see also

1.5 generation; first generation; second
    generation; third generation
Children of Immigrants Longitudinal
    Study (CILS) 53, 55, 57, 59, 60, 61, 66,
    70, 76–7, 85
Chinese 49, 52, 53, 54, 55, 98
chi-square tests 78, 83
CILS see Children of Immigrants
    Longitudinal Study
Civilization Fund Act 19
civilizing function 17, 25
CLASE xvi, 194; follow-through coaching
    200; and the IC 199–200; individual
    coaching 199–200; Instructional
    Conversation Model 200; online NEA
    course 199; workshop-model training 199
classroom context 175, 207
classroom discourse strategies 173–89;
    context and methods 176–7
Cohen, E. G. 206
College and Career Readiness Anchor
    Standards 209
Colombians 54, 55, 96, 99, 137
Colorado 100, 173
Common Core Reading Standards 209
Common Core Standards 3, 7, 108, 208–12
Common Core State Standards (CCSS)
    165, 200, 208, 209
community-based organizations (CBOs)
    35, 36, 38, 39
community–school relation 16–34,
    37–9; decolonial turn and Latino parent
    involvement 16–19; Latina immigrant
    mothers 25–8; moving beyond the
    deficit narrative 22–5; parents-as-first-
    teachers trope 20–1; parents-as-learners
    trope 21; parents-as-partners trope 21–2;
    parents as problems and educational
    policy 19–22
Comparative Fit Index (CFI) 78, 83
compulsory education 96, 101
Condition of Education reports 4
Congressional Hispanic Caucus Institute
    (CHCI) 35
Connor, P. 102
counteraction 9–10, 11, 162, 163, 165, 166
critical race theory 30n7
Crul, Maurice 95; The Changing Face of
    World Cities 109n1
Cuban Americans 53, 55
Cubans 49, 51, 53, 55, 101
cultural capital 64–5, 66, 71, 94, 95, 104,
    108

cultural historical activity theory (CHAT) 23, 205, 207, 209, 210
cultural historical theory xvii, 5, 8
Current Population Survey (CPS) data 51
curriculum 7, 23, 36, 38, 41, 87, 97, 98, 144, 183, 188, 189n1, 192, 194, 204, 205, 211; common literacy 175; English-language 133; GYO 40; NLERAP 42; as praxis 39–40; "Smart" 108–9
curricular leadership 200

DACA see Deferred Action for Childhood Arrivals
Daza, S. L. 38–9
decolonial turn xvii, 16–30; and Latino parent involvement in schools 16–19
Deferred Action for Childhood Arrivals (DACA) 164, 165
deficit ideology 197, 198, 201
de Gortari, Salinas 116
Delgado-Gaitain, C. 24
deportation 153–4, 158, 159–60, 161, 164, 165, 167n4
Dialnet 93
Diaz, 175, 176, 183
Dominicans 95, 99; Black 104
Dornbusch, S. M. 72
Dream Act 163
dual-immersion bilingual education 9, 10
dual-language: children xvi, 207; curricula 10
Durán, Richard P. xix, 23, 204–14
Dyrness, A. 25

Ecuadorians 96, 99
Elementary and Secondary Education Act (ESEA) 20–1, 218
empowerment 3, 8, 10, 11, 12, 23, 24, 30n2, 38, 205; Latina immigrant mothers 25–8
engaged policy 36, 37, 41–2
English-as-a-second-language 9, 21, 73, 152, 173
English learners (ELs) xix, 173–4, 175, 176, 179, 181, 183, 188; achievement gap 194–5; changing the pedagogical culture of school 192–203; classroom discourse strategies that foster dynamic interactions 173–91; poverty 4
Escalante, Jaime 219
ESEA see Elementary and Secondary Education Act
ESL see English-as-a-second-language
ESOL 13n1

ethnogenesis 4
ethnographic research 19, 25, 27

family structure 50, 71
Fanon, F. 18, 30n1
Federal Commission of Electricity (CFE) 115, 117–19, 120, 121, 122
fertility rates 51, 52, 151
Fernández-Kelly, P. 104
Filipinos 49, 54, 55
First Five 20
first generation 25, 50, 53, 56, 58, 72, 93, 94, 95, 100
Fix, Michael 93
Flores, Barbara xix, 175, 176, 183, 192–203
Florida 55, 77, 149, 153; South 53, 54,
Florida International University 64
follow-through coaching 200
Ford Foundation 35
Foucault, M. 23
Fourteenth Amendment 164
Fox, Vicente 123
Freire, Paulo 18, 24, 27–8, 197
Fuentes, E. 25
funds of knowledge 23, 25, 37, 87, 107, 151, 197, 220

Gándara, P. 194
García, Eugene E. 215–20
García, Justa 25–6
Georgia 116, 164; see also Athens; University of Georgia
Gibbons, P. 176
Gibson, Margaret 98, 109n1
González, N. 21
González, Trujillo 98, 99
Gonzalez Canché, Manuel S. 69–91
Grande, S. 18
grant-science 38, 42
Gratius, S. 105
group-based inequality (GBI) xvi, 3, 4, 5, 7, 9, 10, 12, 13
"grow-your-own" (GYO) pipelines 36, 38; curriculum 40; students 42n1; teachers 39, 42
Guatemalans/Salvadorans 52, 55
Gutiérrez, K. 210

H1-B program 48
Haberman, M. 12
Haitians 49, 54, 55, 57
Hallinger, P. 196
Harman, Ruth xix, 173–91

Harvard University Press xvi
Head Start 20, 21, 158, 159, 160
Heck, R. H. 196
Hernández, Ramona 28–9
Hernandez, Sera J. 16–34
Herrenkohl, L. R. 206
Hidalgo 117
Holland, D. C. 8
Holman, Angela 174, 177, 178, 179,
    183–8
Homeland Security 166
Home Teacher Act 19–20
Hong, S. 24–5
Hornig, E. L. 192
human capital 4, 12, 48, 49, 53, 56, 59, 71,
    72, 95, 217

ICE see Immigration and Customs
    Enforcement; imputation by chained
    equations
ideological clarity 192, 193, 193, 197–9,
    200, 201
IFI see Incremental Fit Index
illegal aliens 28, 61, 63, 64, 120, 166,
    167n1
immigration 4, 93, 98, 100, 101, 105,
    116, 123, 126, 143; and the American
    school system 47–68, 160, 161, 162, 164,
    166; common trends in overcoming
    disadvantage in the American school
    system 59–65; laws xix, 127, 164, 165;
    multivariate findings on American
    school system 55–9; policy implications
    in the American school system 65–6,
    153; preliminary evidence on American
    school system 49–55; reform 66, 167n1;
    theoretical perspectives on the future of
    second generation 48–9
Immigration and Customs Enforcement
    (ICE) 152
imputation by chained equations (ICE)
    77
incarceration rates 51, 52, 53, 54, 55
Incremental Fit Index (IFI) 78, 83
India 48, 52
Indiana 164
individual coaching 199–200, 201
initiation-response-evaluation (IRE) 175–6,
    179–86
Instituto Nacional Indigenista (INI) 117
instructional time 194, 216–17
instructional leadership xix, 192, 193,
    193–4, 196–7, 200
International Monetary Fund 116

Johnson, Lyndon: Great Society 6; War on
    Poverty 6, 20, 21
Jones, R.: Matthew and Tilly 183

Kalogrides, D. 192
Kellogg Foundation 35
Kennedy, John F. 35
Kleyman, K. 78
know-how 65
Komaie, G. 66
Koreans 52

labor markets 49, 74, 93, 97, 188, 192
labor unions 18, 25
Lacayo, Martin 63–4, 65
La Clase Mágica 106
Laotians/Cambodians 53, 55
LatCrit conference 30n5
Latina/o Academy of Arts and Sciences
    28–30, 30nn6–7
Latin Americans 92–114
Latinas Unidas 63
Latino diaspora xix, 150, 151, 161
leadership, advocacy see advocacy
    leadership
leadership, curricular see curricular
    leadership
leadership, instructional see instructional
    leadership
leadership, reculturing instructional see
    reculturing instructional leadership
Leithwood, K. 196
Ley Orgánica 96
Ley Orgánica de Educación 96
Ley Orgánica de Ordenación General del
    Sistema Educativo 96
LGBTQ students 23–4
Lindo, F. 106–7
Lindsey, R. 195
Loeb, S. 192
López, M. H. 95
López, Patricia D. xvii, 35–44
Louis, Seashore 196

MacLeod, D. 71
McVean, A. 78
Maldonado-Torres, Nelson 17, 30nn5–6
Mangual Figueroa, Ariana xix, 149–72
Mariel exodus 53
Massachusetts xix, 37, 173, 182, 187; see
    also River Town
Massachusetts Comprehensive Assessment
    System (MCAS) 173–4
Massey, D. S. 102

Maxwell-Jolly, J. 194
Mendoza Reis, Noni xix, 192–203
Mertl, V. 206
Mexican-American War 100
Mexicans 19, 49, 51, 53, 55, 58, 95, 100,
  102, 103, 118, 127, 137, 151
Mexico 48, 77, 100, 115, 116, 118, 119,
  120, 121, 127; immigration 123, 153–4,
  160; landless peasants, 122; women 123;
  see also Cadereyta; Federal Commission
  of Electricity; Hidalgo; Mexico City;
  Querétaro; Salinas, Carlos; Zimapán
  Hydroelectric Project
Mexico City 63, 119, 123
migrants: population 47, 69, 73; workers
  48, 119, 120
Migration Policy Institute xvi
Millvalley, PA: bilingual to English-
  only schooling 154–6; demographic
  changes in schools 156–8; establishing
  and dismantling social networks
  158–60; mixed-status families 150,
  151–61; parental participation 160–1;
  undocumented migrant drivers 167n4
Millvalley Public School District (MPSD)
  152, 156
mixed-status families xix, 149–72; diversity
  150–1; Millvalley, PA 150, 151–61;
  parental participation 160–1; policy
  considerations on a national level 162–7
mode of incorporation 49, 50, 51
Moll, Luis C. xix, 21, 23, 126–46, 220
Mollenkopf, John 95; The Changing Face
  of World Cities 109n1
Montero-Sieburth, Martha xviii, 92–114
Moran, Rachel 30n5
Morroccans 96, 98, 88, 104, 109n1
Moya, Paula 30n5
Moynihan, P. 20
multicultural education 6, 7, 103, 174,
  176
Myrdal, Gunnar: An American Dilemma 94

NACARA law 64
NAEP scores 4, 6
Napolitano, Janet 166
National Latina/o Education Research and
  Policy Project/National Latino Education
  Research Agenda Project (NLERAP) xvi,
  xvii, 35–7, 38, 107, 109; California State
  University, Sacramento 42n1; curriculum
  39, 42; engaged policy 41–2
National Science Foundation 38

National Task Force on Early Childhood
  Education for Hispanics 215
Native Americans 18, 19, 177
NEAE—Policy for Specific Educational
  Support 97
Netherlands 93, 99
Nevada 100
New Mexico 100
New York, NY xi, xii
New York 37; Dominicans 95; migration
  149; see also Brooklyn
Nicaraguans 53, 54, 63, 64
Nieto, Sonia xi–xiv
NLERAP see National Latina/o Education
  Research and Policy Project/National
  Latino Education Research Agenda
  Project
NNFI see Non-Normed Fit Index
No Child Left Behind (NCLB) xvi, 7, 11,
  173–4, 188; post– 93–5
Non-Normed Fit Index (NNFI) 78, 83
North American Free Trade Agreement
  xviii, 117

Obama, Barak 35, 163, 164, 165; Winning
  the Future 188
Orange Grove, FL 153, 154, 157
Ortiz, V. 57, 58, 59

Pamies, Jordi 99
Papademetriou, D. G. 94
PAR see participatory action research
parents: empowered 27; exclusion 25,
  30; -as-first-teachers trope 20–1;
  involvement 16–19; Latina immigrant
  mothers 25–8; -as-learners trope 21;
  moving beyond the deficit narrative
  22–5; -as-partners trope 21–2; as
  problems and educational policy 19–22
Parent-Teachers Association 19–20
Parsimony Normed Fit Index (PNFI)
  78, 83
participatory action research (PAR) 36,
  42, 42n1; community-based 37; critical
  methodologies 40–1
Pash, D. 186
Pedraza, Pedro 35
Pennsylvania 167n4 see also Millvalley
Peruvians 96, 99, 103
Pew Research Center xvi, 95
Philippines 48, 77
Plyler v. Doe 161–2, 163, 164
PNFI see Parsimony Normed Fit Index

poor children 3, 6, 11; non-White 95
population: U.S. xii, 47, 188
Portes, Alejandro xviii, 47–68, 71, 72, 73, 86, 95
Portes, Pedro R. xvii, 3–14, 69–91, 215
positive cultural identities (CID+) 9, 10, 12
Presidential Advisory Commissions on Educational Excellence for Hispanic Americans xvi
PREUSS Program 63
professional development 3, 8, 87, 188, 194, 200–1, 219
Programme for International Student Assessment 108
Proposition 187 161
Proposition 227 133, 134, 138
Puerto Ricans xi, 101, 185; challenge of return migration 138–9; learning English while making friends 136–7; language support through sports 137; reducing English to help friends 139–40; teacher who made a difference 137–8; transnational mobility xix, 126–46
Puerto Rico: influence of circular migration on academic perceptions 140–2; political relations with United States 127–9; teachers 140; transnational mobility between United States xix, 126–46; using English at home 135–6
Purkey, S. C. 196

Querétaro 116, 117, 118, 119, 123, 124; Bella Vista del Rio 117, 120, 121, 122, 123, 124; see also San Juan del Rio
Quesada Aldana, Sergio xviii, 115–25, 128
Quijano, A. 29–30
Quintana, A. 98

Race to the Top xvi, 7, 188
racialization 58, 94, 100
reculturing instructional leadership xix, 193, 194
reductionism 29, 105
refugees 47, 51, 53; middle-class 65; Nicaraguan 64; Southeast Asian 55
remedial education 10, 17, 18, 29
repositioning: knowledge systems 17–18; parents 24; students xix, 126

Ridge Elementary School 152, 156, 160
Rios-Aguilar, Cecilia xviii, 69–91
Rios Rojas, A. 98
Rivera, Melissa 35
River Town, MA 174, 176, 177, 178
RMR see Root Mean Square Residual
RMSEA see Root Mean Square Error of Approximation
Roberts, L. 195
Rogers, J. 25
Romanians 98
Root Mean Square Error of Approximation (RMSEA) 78, 83
Root Mean Square Residual (RMR) 78, 83
Rubin, C. L. 24
Rumbaut, R. 51–2, 72, 75, 99
Rumberger, R. 194
Rust Belt xix, 150, 151
Rymes, B. 176, 186

Sacramento, CA 36
Salas, Spencer xvii, 3–15, 215
Salinas, Carlos 121
Salvadorans 52, 55
San Diego, CA 77
Sandoval, C. 17
Sandoval, W. A. 205
San Juan del Rio 119, 123
Schmid, C. L. 71
School-Family Compacts 22
school adaptation model 75–87, 75, 132; data 76–7; data analyses 78; dependent variables 78, 80; descriptive statistics 79–81; discussion and implications 84–7; findings 79–81; independent variables 78, 80; limitations 78; method 76–7; missing data 77; policy recommendations 87; sample 77; SEM analyses 81–4; standardized coefficients 82; structural equation model fit indices 83; variables 78–9; 79, 80
Scribner, S.: "Modes of Thinking and Ways of Speaking, Culture and Logic Reconsidered" 207
second generation 47, 50, 51, 53, 55, 56, 57, 58, 59, 65, 69, 70, 71, 72, 75, 76, 77, 78, 79, 81, 84, 85, 86, 87, 93–4, 95, 98, 99, 100, 101, 104, 109n1; adaptation outcomes in early childhood 54; theoretical perspectives on the future of 48–9

segmented assimilation xviii, 48, 49, 51, 55, 59, 65, 74, 99
segregation 7, 12, 94, 95, 100, 104, 194
selective acculturation 50, 60–4, 66, 74, 75, 76, 85, 86
SES see socioeconomic status
Simó, N. 98
single-parent families 49, 57, 59
Smith, M. S. 196
social class 8, 64, 95, 100, 104
sociocultural perspectives 150, 174–5, 196, 207, 210; classroom context and student identity 175
sociocultural theory (SCT) 174–5, 176, 196
socioeconomic status (SES) 87, 215, 216; family 57, 59, 71, 75, 78, 79, 80, 81, 82, 84, 85; parental, 70, 71, 73; school 70, 75, 78, 79, 80, 81, 82, 84, 85
Somerville, W. 94
Soto-Santiago, Sandra L. xix, 126–46
South Carolina 164
South Korea 48
Spain xviii; rapid assimilation approach 96–100; recommendations from a comparative analysis of educational policies 92–114; Puerto Rico 127
Spanish Ministry of Education 98, 100, 102
special education 11, 96, 133
Specter bill 28
Stand and Deliver 219
STEM 3, 5, 11, 13
Stiglitz, Joseph: The Price of Inequality 94–5
structural equation modeling (SEM) 70, 78, 83; analyses 81–4 , 85, 86
student identity 104, 175, 206
Suárez-Orozco, C. 69
subtractive schooling 23, 195
Sumption, M. 94
Supreme Court 5, 161, 163, 164

Taiwan 48
teachers 217; cultivating critically conscious 35–44; community and family engagement 37–9; curriculum as praxis 39–40; engaged policy 41–2; PAR and critical methodologies 40–1; preparation xvii, 36–7, 38, 39, 40, 41–2
Teachers College Press xvi

Telles, E. 57, 58, 59
Terriquez, V. 25
testing xiii, xvi, 7, 12, 17, 41, 102, 165, 179; language learners 26
third generation 50, 95, 101
Tienda, M. 72
Tieran, Ned 152
Title I 21–2; Parent Compacts 20
Title III 189n1
Tomás Rivera Institute xvi
Torres, Raquel 61–2, 66
Tort, A. 98
transnational mobility xix, 126–46
Treaty of Guadalupe-Hidalgo 100
Trost, Christine 30n5
Trueba, Henry 109
Turks 95

UCSD see University of California, San Diego
unauthorized immigration 47, 65, 167n1
Undergraduate Students Association 166
Understanding Language project 207
undocumented persons xix, 25, 66, 97, 102, 149, 152, 153, 160, 161, 162, 163, 164–6, 167n1, 167n4
Universidad Autónoma de Querétaro (UAQ) 115, 117
Universidad Nacional Autónoma de México 117
University of California, Berkeley 28, 30n5
University of California, Los Angeles 166
University of California, San Diego 62
University of Georgia 165, 199
University of Texas, Austin 37
USAID 116
Utah 100
Uy, P. S. 24

Valenzuela, Angela xvii, xx, 35–44
Valsiner, J. 8
Van Lier, L. 207–8
Velasco, G. 95
Vietnamese 54, 55
Villenas, S. 24
vivencias, 9, 10, 85, 126
Vygotsky, L. S. 7–8, 174, 182, 196, 198

Wahlstrom, K. 196
Warren, M. R. 24

West Indians 54, 55, 57
Willett, J. 175
Workforce Investment Act 21
World Bank 115, 116–17, 118, 122
Wyoming 100

Yebala, 99

Zavete, María 26–7
Zedillo, Ernesto 123
Zhou, M. 86
Zimapán Hydroelectric Project 115–25;
    aftermath of relocation 121–3; culture
    of migration 119–21; escaping violence
    123; policy and its consequences 123–4